Residential Conveyancing Practice

SECOND EDITION

Other titles available from Law Society Publishing:

Compliance and Ethics in Law Firms: A Guide for Legal Support Staff (2nd edition)
Tracey Calvert

Conveyancing Checklists (4th edition, forthcoming)
Frances Silverman and Russell Hewitson

Conveyancing Handbook (27th edition)
General editor: Frances Silverman, Consultant Editors: Russell Hewitson and Anne Rodell

Titles from Law Society Publishing can be ordered from all good bookshops or direct (telephone 0370 850 1422 or visit our online shop at **www.lawsociety.org.uk/bookshop**).

RESIDENTIAL CONVEYANCING PRACTICE

A Guide for Support Staff and Paralegals

Second edition

Russell Hewitson

Crown copyright material is reproduced with the permission of the Controller of Her Majesty's Stationery Office

ISBN-13: 978-1-78446-151-5

First edition published in 2017

This second edition published in 2021 by the Law Society
113 Chancery Lane, London WC2A 1PL

Typeset by Columns Design XML Ltd, Reading
Printed by TJ Books Ltd, Padstow, Cornwall

FSC
www.fsc.org
MIX
Paper from
responsible sources
FSC® C013056

The paper used for the text pages of this book is FSC® certified. FSC (the Forest Stewardship Council®) is an international network to promote responsible management of the world's forests.

Contents

Preface

As with the first edition, the aim of this new edition is to provide unqualified conveyancers with an introduction to residential conveyancing of registered land so that they can develop their understanding of the conveyancing process and the skills which they will need when carrying out residential conveyancing on a daily basis. In addition, it is hoped it will provide conveyancing firms with a resource to help them develop and train their unqualified conveyancers.

No offence is intended by reference in the text to 'he', for which please read 'he or she' as appropriate. I have also referred throughout the text to 'solicitor' for convenience.

In between preparing this new edition and its publication there have been temporary changes to HM Land Registry practice, as well as temporary reductions in stamp duty land tax as a result of the coronavirus pandemic. As these are intended to be temporary measures, I have not included them in the text.

I have also not included the Town and Country Planning (Use Classes) (Amendment) (England) Regulations 2020, SI 2020/757, which were made on 20 July 2020 and came into force on 1 September 2020, as at the time of writing there is an outstanding legal challenge to the validity of these changes. These Regulations significantly amend the Town and Country Planning (Use Classes) Order 1987 (see **6.1**). The main changes are to:

- revoke Parts A and D of the Schedule to the 1987 Order in relation to England (subject to transitional and savings provisions); Part A contains use classes A1 to A5 (this includes uses commonly found on the high street including shops, cafes and takeaways) and Part D contains use classes D1 (Non-residential institutions) and D2 (Assembly and leisure);
- insert a new Schedule 2 which provides for new Class E (Commercial, business and service), Class F.1 (Learning and non-residential institutions) and Class F.2 (Local community);
- introduce new *sui generis* uses.

I would like to thank the staff at the Law Society, in particular Christa Biervliet and Sarah Kent.

Finally, my thanks go to Andrea, Dominique and Moyra without whose constant help, support and encouragement this new edition would not have seen the light of day.

The law is stated as at 1 October 2020.

R. Hewitson
Cleadon Village
October 2020

Table of cases

Table of statutes

Table of statutory instruments

Abbreviations

ATED	annual tax on enveloped dwellings
BID	business improvement district
BSA	Building Societies Association
CGT	capital gains tax
CIL	Community Infrastructure Levy
CLC	Council for Licensed Conveyancers
CQS	Conveyancing Quality Scheme
ED	electronic discharge
EPC	Energy Performance Certificate
FENSA	Fenestration Self-Assessment
HMO	house in multiple occupation
HMRC	HM Revenue and Customs
ISA	Individual Savings Account
Lenders' Handbook	UK Finance Mortgage Lenders' Handbook
LTT	land transaction tax
NCA	National Crime Agency
NHBC	National House Building Council
NI	National Insurance
NLIS	National Land Information Service
NPV	net present value
RICS	Royal Institution of Chartered Surveyors
SC	standard condition
SDLT	stamp duty land tax
SRA	Solicitors Regulation Authority
SuDS	sustainable urban drainage systems
VAT	value added tax

CHAPTER 1

Introduction to conveyancing

1.1 WHAT IS CONVEYANCING?

Conveyancing is the term given to the law and practice whereby the ownership of land or of an interest in land is transferred from one person to another. It is about how to transfer ownership in land, about the rights of the parties at different stages in real property transactions, and about their respective positions if things should go wrong in the course of the transaction.

1.2 AIM OF THIS BOOK

This book is intended to provide an introduction to residential conveyancing of registered land in practice so that the reader can develop their understanding of the conveyancing process and the skills which they will need when carrying out conveyancing. In addition, it is hoped that this book will continue to be of use to them on a daily basis as they carry out conveyancing transactions.

1.3 PRACTITIONERS' BOOKS

These are particularly useful in conveyancing. You can usefully look at the precedents which they contain and the notes explaining the reason for the inclusion of particular clauses and variations in precedents.

Particularly useful to look through are vols 35 to 38 (inclusive) of the *Encyclopaedia of Forms and Precedents* (LexisNexis) which deal with the sale of land; *Practical Conveyancing Precedents* (Sweet & Maxwell); *Practical Lease Precedents* (Sweet & Maxwell); and the *Conveyancing Handbook* (Law Society, 27th edition, 2020). Nor should you shrink from other professional texts such as *Emmet & Farrand on Title* (Sweet & Maxwell) and *Ruoff and Roper: Registered Conveyancing* (Sweet & Maxwell).

There are many references throughout the book to forms used by conveyancers, and countless more forms are found in practice. Land Registration forms can be obtained from HM Land Registry's website at **www.gov.uk/government/**

1

organisations/land-registry. HM Land Registry also publishes a very helpful set of practice guides which can be consulted on the various issues raised by registered land conveyancing. Again these can be viewed at HM Land Registry's website.

1.4 THE TWO SYSTEMS OF CONVEYANCING

In England and Wales the method of conveyancing to be used in any particular case depends on whether or not the title to the land has been registered at HM Land Registry.

Where the land has not been registered, it is subject to the older system of unregistered conveyancing. Under this system a seller's title is traced through the title deeds disposing of the property.

If the land has been registered, it is subject to the system of registered conveyancing. Under this modern system, title to land is proved by entry of the seller's name on the official register of title which is kept at HM Land Registry. Perusal of the title deeds is therefore dispensed with. In addition, the title is guaranteed by HM Land Registry.

In this book we will be dealing with land where the title is registered.

1.5 FREEHOLD AND LEASEHOLD CONVEYANCING

Many of the procedures involved in conveying a leasehold title are the same as for a freehold title. Consequently, we will not be considering the procedures involved in conveying a leasehold title separately, although, where appropriate, we will draw attention to any specific points relevant to leaseholds. We will, however, look at the grant of a lease.

1.6 AN OUTLINE OF A TYPICAL TRANSACTION

The table below sets out the main steps in a basic conveyancing transaction in chronological order.

Seller's solicitor	Buyer's solicitor
Take instructions	Take instructions
Prepare the pre-contract package	
	Carry out pre-contract searches and enquiries
	Investigate title
	Approve draft contract

Exchange of contracts	
	Draft the transfer deed
Approve the transfer deed	
	Make pre-completion searches
Prepare for completion	Prepare for completion
Completion	
Post-completion matters	Post-completion matters

A conveyancing transaction can be divided into the following parts:

(a)   Pre-contract.
(b)   Exchange of contracts.
(c)   Pre-completion.
(d)   Completion.
(e)   Post-completion.

1.6.1   Pre-contract

A firm regulated by the Solicitors Regulation Authority (SRA) must comply with the SRA Transparency Rules. These require the firm to publish price and service information for certain areas of law on its website, or on request if the firm does not have a website. One of the areas to which this applies is residential conveyancing, specifically freehold or leasehold residential sales or purchases, mortgages and remortgages. The information to be provided includes the total cost of the service (or the average cost or range of costs), the basis for the charges, including any hourly rates or fixed fees, a description of, and the cost of, any likely disbursements (or the average cost or range of costs) and whether any fees or disbursements attract value added tax (VAT). The purpose behind the SRA Transparency Rules is to give individual and business clients the information they need to make an informed choice of solicitor.

A solicitor must always take instructions from the client at the start of the transaction, and these should normally be confirmed in writing together with information relating to costs. The solicitor will also need to obtain proof of the client's identity to comply with the Money Laundering, Terrorist Financing and Transfer of Funds (Information on the Payer) Regulations 2017, SI 2017/692. It may also be necessary to check the client's identity to satisfy HM Land Registry and/or a lender's requirements.

The seller's solicitor will then prepare a draft contract. Before he can do this he will need to obtain evidence of the seller's title to the property. Once he has this he should investigate the seller's title and then prepare the draft contract.

The contract contains:

(a)   a description of the property;
(b)   a statement of whether the title is freehold or leasehold;

(c)   details of anything affecting or benefiting the property, e.g. easements or covenants;

(d)   the conditions on which the property is to be sold.

Two copies of the draft contract are forwarded to the buyer's solicitor for approval together with evidence of the seller's legal title.

The buyer's approval of the contract will be dependent on the results of his searches and enquiries. The seller has only a limited duty to disclose defects in title and the buyer must discover for himself everything which he may need to know about before he exchanges contracts.

The buyer's solicitor must make sure that the buyer is able financially to purchase the property. This includes having funds not only for the balance due on completion but also for the deposit payable on exchange. If the buyer is obtaining a mortgage, his solicitor must be satisfied that the mortgage arrangements are in order.

Once the buyer's solicitor has approved the draft contract he will return one copy. Each party then signs their respective part of the contract in readiness for exchange.

1.6.2   Exchange of contracts

Once contracts have been exchanged, a binding contract is created between the parties and neither of them can then withdraw without being liable to the other for breach of contract. Until exchange, either party is free to change their mind and withdraw from the transaction.

The usual method of exchange is physically to exchange two identical signed contracts. Modern practice is for exchange to take place by telephone.

At the time of exchange the buyer usually pays a deposit of 10 per cent of the purchase price. If he later fails to complete the purchase the seller may be able to keep this deposit.

A date for completion of the transaction will also be agreed at exchange.

1.6.3   Pre-completion

The buyer's solicitor will raise requisitions on the seller's title. These mainly consist of procedural queries, as the modern practice is for the buyer's solicitor to investigate the title and raise any requisitions on it before exchange of contracts.

The buyer's solicitor will also make his pre-completion searches. Where the title is registered, the buyer's solicitor will carry out an official search of the register at HM Land Registry in order to make sure that nothing has changed since the official copies were issued.

At the same time, the buyer's solicitor will also prepare and submit to the seller's solicitor a draft transfer deed in duplicate for approval. This must reflect the terms of the contract and, accordingly, the seller's solicitor will check to make sure that it does. Once it has been approved, an original is prepared for execution by the parties. This must always be signed by the seller otherwise the legal estate will not pass.

If the buyer is obtaining a mortgage and his solicitor is acting for the lender his solicitor will also have to:

(a)   prepare the mortgage deed;
(b)   advise the lender that the legal title is in order; and
(c)   carry out a bankruptcy search against the buyer's name.

The buyer's solicitor must make sure that the buyer has sufficient money to complete the purchase.

If the seller has a mortgage, then the seller's solicitor must obtain details of the exact amount required to pay this off on completion.

1.6.4   Completion

Completion traditionally took place at the seller's solicitor's office when the balance of the purchase price was handed over by the buyer's solicitor in return for the deeds. Today it is more common to complete through the post and there are guidelines published by the Law Society which can be used so that both solicitors know what is required of each of them on completion. In effect, a postal completion means that the seller's solicitor is temporarily appointed to be the agent for the buyer's solicitor, and while acting as such must carry out all the steps which the buyer's solicitor instructs him to do.

On the day of completion, the buyer's solicitor will transmit to the seller's solicitor the money required to complete. This is normally done by way of what is commonly referred to as a telegraphic transfer but is now an electronic transmission of the completion money from the buyer's solicitor's bank account to the seller's solicitor's bank account. On receipt of funds, the seller's solicitor will notify the buyer's solicitor and completion will take place. The deeds are then sent by post from the seller's solicitor to the buyer's solicitor and the clients informed.

1.6.5   Post-completion

The seller's solicitor must redeem the seller's mortgage and confirm to the buyer's solicitor that this has been done by sending him the lender's form of discharge. He must also account to the seller for the sale proceeds, which should be done on the day of completion or as soon as is possible. Once these matters have been dealt with, the seller's solicitor may close his file.

The buyer's solicitor must deal with stamp duty land tax (SDLT) formalities. A land transaction return (SDLT1) giving details of the transaction must be delivered to HM Revenue and Customs (HMRC) within 14 days of completion and where the purchase price exceeds the appropriate threshold SDLT must also be paid within 14 days of completion otherwise a penalty will be charged. A certificate is then issued by HMRC as proof that these requirements have been complied with. Without this certificate the buyer's solicitor will not be able to register the transaction at HM Land Registry. Where the property is in Wales, the buyer's solicitor must deal instead with land transaction tax (LTT) formalities. Details of LTT can be found at **https://gov.wales/land-transaction-tax-guide**.

The title must then be registered at HM Land Registry. Once the title has been registered HM Land Registry will issue a Title Information Document which comprises a copy of the register and, where the application has resulted in the preparation of a new or amended title plan, a copy of that title plan. This is not a document of title and is issued for information only. When he has checked that the details contained in the Title Information Document are correct, the buyer's solicitor should forward it, together with any other relevant documents, to the lender or, if the property is not subject to a loan, to the buyer, for safe-keeping. After he has received an acknowledgement from the lender or buyer and all other outstanding matters have been satisfactorily dealt with, the buyer's solicitor may close his file.

1.7 THE LAW SOCIETY CONVEYANCING PROTOCOL AND THE CONVEYANCING QUALITY SCHEME

The National Conveyancing Protocol was first introduced in March 1990 by the Law Society with the aim of streamlining domestic conveyancing procedures. The current version – the Law Society Conveyancing Protocol – came into effect on 19 August 2019 and is set out in **Appendix B** (also available at **www.lawsociety. org.uk**). The Protocol sets out a framework of some of the work undertaken in a conveyancing transaction. The procedures laid down by the Protocol are intended to regulate the relationship between the seller's and buyer's solicitors, and do not affect dealings with third parties such as estate agents or lenders.

The Law Society has also established the Conveyancing Quality Scheme (CQS) which provides a recognised quality standard for residential conveyancing practices. All firms that undertake residential conveyancing and want to be members of the CQS are required to sign up to comply with the Law Society Conveyancing Protocol, a Client Service Charter, and mandatory training and enforcement procedures. Membership of the CQS is essential for any firm wanting to be on the panels of solicitors approved by the residential mortgage lenders to act for lenders where the buyer is taking out a residential mortgage. Many mortgage lenders have made CQS accreditation a prerequisite for a firm wishing to join their panel, in addition to their own criteria and panel management procedures. Further information about the CQS can be found at **www.lawsociety.org.uk**.

1.8 E-CONVEYANCING

Traditionally, conveyancing was based on written documents. The Land Registration Act 2002 created a framework in which registered conveyancing could be carried out electronically. However, this is now on hold. Certain Land Registry services are available electronically through either the HM Land Registry portal or

Business Gateway. The portal allows solicitors with a network access agreement to have direct access to the register via the internet. The Business Gateway is a way in which a solicitor's case management systems can interact with Land Registry systems to access electronic services, other than directly through the portal. In addition the National Land Information Service (NLIS) enables searches and enquiries, such as local searches and coal mining searches to be made using the internet (**www.nlis.org.uk**) and aims to speed up the supply of the results of such searches.

1.9 ENERGY PERFORMANCE CERTIFICATES

An Energy Performance Certificate (EPC) must be made available to prospective buyers and tenants whenever a building is constructed, sold or rented.

An EPC is broadly similar to the labels provided with domestic appliances such as refrigerators and washing machines. Its purpose is to record how energy efficient a property is as a building. The certificate will provide a rating of the energy efficiency and carbon emissions of a building from A to G, where A is very efficient and G is very inefficient. An EPC will be accompanied by a recommendation report that lists cost-effective and other measures (such as low and zero carbon generating systems) to improve the energy rating of the building together with information about the rating that could be achieved if all the recommendations were imple-mented. As from 1 April 2018 there has been a requirement for any properties rented out in the private rented sector to normally have a minimum energy performance rating of E on an EPC.

When a property is to be sold or let, the seller or landlord must provide any prospective buyer or tenant with a valid EPC, free of charge, at the earliest opportunity.

There is an obligation to commission an EPC before the property is marketed and to use all reasonable efforts to ensure that an EPC is obtained within seven days of marketing the property. There is also a further 21-day period during which the EPC can be obtained, if it has not been obtained within the initial seven-day period. An EPC must be provided with the sale particulars.

An EPC will be prepared by an energy assessor, who must be a member of a government accredited scheme. Once prepared, an EPC must be entered on the EPC register. Once registered, an EPC cannot be altered and must be stored on the register for at least 20 years. A registered EPC is allocated a reference number, which must be quoted before a copy of the EPC will be provided. This measure is intended to limit public access to the register and protect the privacy of building owners and occupiers. It is a criminal offence to unlawfully disclose an EPC, punishable by a fine of up to £5,000.

The local Trading Standards Officers are responsible for enforcing the EPC requirements. Enforcement will normally be carried out by issuing penalty charge notices to those who fail to comply. The penalty when selling or renting out a dwelling is £200.

An EPC will also disclose to the buyer the existence of a Green Deal plan. The Green Deal is a government initiative that was launched in January 2013 which enables property owners and tenants to carry out a range of energy efficiency measures with no upfront cost. The finance is provided by Green Deal providers (private companies, charities and local authorities) and the repayments are spread over a period of up to 25 years through a separate charge added to the property owner's electricity bill. The charge should not be more than the estimated energy bill savings and is payable by the occupier from time to time, so when the property is sold it will transfer to the buyer. The seller is therefore obliged to provide prospective buyers with an EPC containing the required Green Deal plan information and ensure that the contract for sale includes an acknowledgement by the buyer that the bill payer at the property is obliged to make payments under the Green Deal plan.

If the seller fails to disclose the existence of a Green Deal plan or obtain the necessary acknowledgement from the buyer, the Secretary of State may cancel the liability of the buyer to make payments under the Green Deal plan and may require the seller to pay compensation (which in most cases would equate to the amount outstanding on the Green Deal plan less a discount for early settlement). The seller's solicitor should therefore ensure that the EPC is checked before the contract is drafted, so that any required acknowledgement can be included in the contract. The buyer's solicitor should also check the EPC, as when deciding whether to cancel liability the Secretary of State will consider what knowledge of the Green Deal the buyer had. If the information is contained on a disclosed EPC (even if it has not been acknowledged by the buyer in the contract), there is a risk that the Secretary of State may decline to cancel the obligation to pay the charge.

1.10 SUMMARY

- There are two systems of conveyancing – unregistered and registered.
- It is possible for some dealings with registered land to be made electronically.
- A typical conveyancing transaction can be broken down into the following stages – pre-contract; exchange of contracts; pre-completion; completion; and post-completion.
- The Law Society Conveyancing Protocol standardises the residential conveyancing procedure and must be used by members of the Conveyancing Quality Scheme.
- An EPC must be made available to prospective buyers and tenants whenever a building is constructed, sold or rented.

CHAPTER 2

Land registration

2.1 INTRODUCTION

As we will be looking at registered land throughout this book, in this chapter we will consider the principles of registration of title.

2.2 HM LAND REGISTRY

HM Land Registry was established in 1862. Its existence was expressly continued by the Land Registration Act 2002, s.99(1) which provides that it 'is to deal with the business of registration under this Act'. Its more detailed rules are found in the Land Registration Rules 2003, SI 2003/1417.

HM Land Registry now offers a variety of services electronically, including the facility to lodge certain types of application. All of HM Land Registry's e-services are accessed through two online channels, the HM Land Registry portal and Business Gateway. Business Gateway is an alternative way in which a solicitor's case management systems can interact with Land Registry systems to access e-services.

2.3 ESTATES CAPABLE OF REGISTRATION

The estates and interests which can be registered are:

(a)   a freehold;
(b)   a lease that has more than seven years left to run;
(c)   leases of any length where the right to possession is discontinuous (e.g. a time share);
(d)   leases of any length granted to take effect in possession more than three months after the date of grant;
(e)   a rentcharge that is either perpetual or for a term of which more than seven years are unexpired;

(f)   a *profit à prendre* in gross (e.g. a fishing right) that is either perpetual or for a term of which more than seven years are unexpired;

(g)   a franchise (e.g. a right to hold a market) that is either perpetual or for a term of which more than seven years are unexpired.

2.4   FIRST REGISTRATION

One of the objectives of the Land Registration Act 2002 is to encourage and compel more landowners to register their land at HM Land Registry.

2.4.1   Voluntary first registration

Voluntary first registration is possible at any time, and as an incentive a reduced fee is payable.

2.4.2   Compulsory first registration

The events which trigger compulsory registration are:

(a)   a transfer of a qualifying estate for valuable or other consideration, by way of gift, in pursuance of a court order, by means of an assent or vesting assent or giving effect to a partition of land subject to a trust of land;

(b)   the transfer of a qualifying estate by a deed that appoints, or by virtue of the Charities Act 2011, s.334 has effect as if it appointed, a new trustee or is made in consequence of the appointment of a new trustee, or by a vesting order under the Trustee Act 1925, s.44 that is consequential on the appointment of a new trustee;

(c)   the grant of a lease for a term of more than seven years;

(d)   the grant of a reversionary lease taking effect in possession more than three months after the date of the grant;

(e)   the grant of a first legal mortgage of a qualifying estate; and

(f)   certain 'right to buy' leases.

A 'qualifying estate' is defined as either a legal freehold estate in land or a legal lease which has more than seven years to run.

An application for compulsory first registration must be made within two months from the date of the disposition. HM Land Registry may extend this period if it is satisfied that there is good reason. The effect of late registration is to vest the legal estate in the new proprietor at the actual date it is registered in the same way as any other registration.

2.4.3 Failure to apply for first registration

If a disposition transferring the legal title is not registered within two months, the transfer becomes void and the transferor will hold the legal estate on a bare trust for the transferee.

If the disposition is one granting a lease or creating a protected mortgage, it similarly becomes void so far as passing the legal estate is concerned at the end of the two-month period. From that time the disposition takes effect as a contract for valuable consideration to grant or create the lease or mortgage.

This means that a buyer who has failed to apply for first registration will not have a good title to pass on to a subsequent buyer.

2.5 CLASSES OF TITLE

On first registration, HM Land Registry will decide which class of title should be granted to the estate which is being registered.

2.5.1 Absolute title

Most titles are registered with absolute title. An absolute title may be approved if HM Land Registry considers that title to the estate is such that a willing buyer could properly be advised by a competent professional adviser to accept. HM Land Registry may disregard a defect in the title if it is of the opinion that the defect will not cause the holding under the title to be disturbed. Where the title is leasehold, absolute title is granted where HM Land Registry also approves the landlord's title to grant the lease.

2.5.2 Possessory title

Possessory title may be granted where HM Land Registry considers that the applicant is in possession of the land, or in receipt of rents and profits, and there is no other class of title with which he may be registered. In practice, a possessory title will be granted where the applicant's title is based on adverse possession or where title cannot be proved satisfactorily because the title deeds have been lost or destroyed. Possessory title can be given to either a freehold or leasehold estate in the land.

2.5.3 Qualified title

A person may be registered with qualified title if HM Land Registry is of the opinion that title has been established only for a limited period, or subject to certain reservations which cannot be disregarded. A qualified title is very rare in practice. Qualified title can be given to either a freehold or a leasehold estate in the land.

2.5.4 Good leasehold title

Registration with good leasehold title will be granted where HM Land Registry is satisfied only as to the title to the leasehold estate. Such a title will therefore generally only result where the title to the freehold reversion is unregistered and where the applicant for registration of the leasehold interest does not submit evidence of title to the freehold reversion when making his application. A good leasehold title is regarded by some mortgagees as being unsatisfactory, and for this reason is sometimes difficult to sell or mortgage.

2.5.5 Effect of first registration – freehold estates

On first registration with absolute title, the legal estate is vested in the proprietor together with all interests subsisting for the benefit of the estate, such as appurtenant implied or prescriptive easements. The registered estate is subject only to the following interests affecting the estate at the time of registration:

(a)   interests which are entered in the register;

(b)   overriding interests falling within the Land Registration Act 2002, Sched.1; and

(c)   interests acquired under the Limitation Act 1980 of which the proprietor has notice.

Where the proprietor is a trustee, the estate is vested in him subject to the rights of the beneficiaries under the trust of which he has notice.

Registration with qualified title has the same effect as registration with absolute title except that it does not affect the enforcement of any estate, right or interest appearing from the register to be excepted from the effect of registration.

Registration with possessory title has the same effect as registration with absolute title, except that it does not affect the enforcement of any estate, right or interest, adverse to, or in derogation of, the title subsisting at the time of registration.

2.5.6 Effect of first registration – leasehold estates

In general terms, the registration of a proprietor with absolute, qualified or possessory title to a leasehold estate has the same effect as registration with the corresponding title to a freehold estate. The difference is that a leaseholder is also subject to implied and express covenants, obligations and liabilities incident to the leasehold estate.

Registration with good leasehold title has the same effect as registration with absolute leasehold title except that it does not affect the enforcement of any estate, right or interest affecting, or in derogation of, the title of the landlord to grant the lease.

2.6 CONVERSION OF TITLE

HM Land Registry has power to upgrade a title in the following circumstances:

(a) from possessory or qualified freehold title to absolute freehold title if it is satisfied as to the title to the freehold estate;

(b) from good leasehold title to absolute leasehold title if it is satisfied as to the superior title;

(c) from possessory or qualified leasehold title:

    (i) to good leasehold title, if it is satisfied as to the title to the leasehold estate; and

    (ii) to absolute leasehold title if it is satisfied both as to the title to the leasehold estate and as to the superior title;

(d) from possessory freehold title to absolute freehold title or from possessory leasehold title to good leasehold title if the title has been registered for at least 12 years and it is satisfied that the proprietor is in possession of the land.

HM Land Registry cannot upgrade a title if there is any outstanding adverse claim under any estate, right or interest whose enforceability is preserved by the existing class of title. Any adverse claim must be resolved before the title can be upgraded.

For more information, see HM Land Registry Practice Guide 42 (Upgrading the Class of Title).

2.7 THE REGISTER OF TITLE

The register for each title is now kept in electronic form by HM Land Registry and consists of three parts:

(a) the property register;

(b) the proprietorship register; and

(c) the charges register.

2.7.1 The property register

This contains the following.

2.7.1.1 Description of the land

The register contains a description of the land in the title together with a reference to the title plan which is an integral part of the description. It also describes the estate for which the land is held (i.e. freehold or leasehold).

2.7.1.2 Interests and benefits

The register also contains details of:

(a) any easements, rights, privileges, conditions and covenants of which the land has the benefit;

(b) all exceptions arising on enfranchisement of formerly copyhold land; and

(c) any other matter required to be entered in any other part of the register which HM Land Registry considers may more conveniently be entered in the property register.

Thus, for example, the description could state that the registered land has the benefit of a specified right of way. If HM Land Registry is not satisfied that such a right is demonstrated sufficiently clearly to be guaranteed by HM Land Registry, then it will be referred to in a qualified way, e.g. 'the conveyance to AB of 6 July 1979 states that the land has the benefit of a right of way therein mentioned'.

2.7.1.3 Mines and minerals rights

The register may also contain a note of who owns any mines and minerals under the land. If no mention is made of these then their ownership by the registered proprietor is not guaranteed.

2.7.1.4 Leasehold titles

In the case of a leasehold title, the property register must also contain sufficient particulars of the registered lease to enable it to be identified – for example, its date, the parties, the term and the rent.

2.7.2 The proprietorship register

This contains the following information.

2.7.2.1 Type of title

The proprietorship register first of all states the type of registered title owned by the registered proprietor, for example the land may be registered with 'Title Absolute'. If the title is not stated to be leasehold, then it will be freehold.

2.7.2.2 Name and address

There will then be set out the full name and address of the registered proprietor or proprietors. The address is important, as it is to this address that HM Land Registry will send any notices affecting the land. A proprietor may have up to three addresses entered, including an email address.

2.7.2.3 Other entries

The register must contain any entries intended to protect third-party interests or restrict dealings with the registered land. These will be either restrictions or notices.

Other matters which must be contained in the register include positive covenants by a transferor or transferee and indemnity covenants by a transferee.

2.7.2.4 Price paid

Since 1 April 2000 HM Land Registry has noted the price paid for a property on the register where it is practicable to do so. The entry will be made whenever an application for registration is lodged.

2.7.3 The charges register

This contains the encumbrances affecting the registered property as follows:

(a) *All encumbrances subsisting at the date of first registration.* Where these are lengthy, they are referred to briefly in the register and then set out at length in a schedule or by referring to an annexed copy of the relevant document. It may be that the deed containing the encumbrances is not available at the time of first registration as it is lost but it is referred to in later deeds, and in such a situation the following entry would be made:

> A conveyance of 26 November 1896 between AB and CD contained restrictive covenants, but neither the original nor an abstract was produced on the application for first registration.

(b) *All subsequent charges or encumbrances.* A typical example of one of these would be a registered mortgage made by the registered proprietor.

2.8 ALTERATION AND INDEMNITY

The system of land registration provides a guarantee that once a person is registered as proprietor the legal estate is vested in him. The strength of the system is in the reliance that can be placed on the indefeasibility of this title once registration is obtained. Nevertheless, there must be provision to correct the register in the cases of mistakes or fraud. The Act provides for 'alteration' of the register. 'Rectification' is defined as an alteration which involves the correction of a mistake and which prejudicially affects the title of a registered proprietor. Where the register is corrected, compensation ('indemnity') may be payable. For more information see HM Land Registry Practice Guides 39 (Rectification and Indemnity) and 77 (Altering the Register by Removing Land from a Title Plan).

15

2.8.1 Mistakes in an application

HM Land Registry has power to make alterations of the register in order to correct a mistake in any application or accompanying document, e.g. clerical errors.

2.8.2 Alteration by the court

The court may order alteration of the register:

(a) to correct a mistake;
(b) to bring the register up to date; and
(c) to give effect to any estate, right or interest excepted from the effect of registration.

This does not apply to an alteration that amounts to rectification. The court is not obliged to make an order if there are exceptional circumstances that justify not doing so.

2.8.3 Proprietor in possession

An order for the alteration of the register that amounts to rectification cannot be made without the registered proprietor's consent where he is in possession, except where:

(a) the proprietor has by fraud or lack of proper care caused or substantially contributed to the mistake; or
(b) it would for any other reason be unjust for the alteration not to be made.

A proprietor will be in possession where:

(a) the land is physically in his possession;
(b) the land is physically in possession of a person who is entitled to be registered as proprietor;
(c) the registered proprietor is the landlord and the person in possession is the tenant;
(d) the registered proprietor is a mortgagor and the person in possession is the mortgagee;
(e) the registered proprietor is a licensor and the person in possession is the licensee; or
(f) the registered proprietor is a trustee and the person in possession is a beneficiary under the trust.

Where the court can order rectification and the land is not in the proprietor's possession, the court must make an order unless it considers there are exceptional circumstances which justify it not doing so.

2.8.4 Alteration by HM Land Registry

HM Land Registry also has powers to alter the register in the following cases:

(a)   to correct a mistake;
(b)   to bring the register up to date;
(c)   to give effect to any estate, right or interest excepted from the effect of registration; and
(d)   to remove a superfluous entry.

2.8.5 Costs in non-rectification cases

If the register is altered in a case that does not involve rectification, HM Land Registry may pay such amount as it thinks fit in respect of any costs or expenses reasonably incurred by a person in connection with the alteration and which have been incurred with the consent of HM Land Registry. If HM Land Registry has not given consent, it may still pay costs and expenses where it appears to it that they had to be incurred urgently and it was not reasonably practicable to apply for consent in advance. HM Land Registry may also subsequently approve the incurring of them.

2.8.6 Indemnity

2.8.6.1 Right to an indemnity

The right to indemnity is available to someone who suffers loss by reason of:

(a)   rectification of the register;
(b)   a mistake whose correction would involve rectification of the register;
(c)   a mistake in an official search;
(d)   a mistake in an official copy;
(e)   a mistake in a document kept by HM Land Registry which is not an original and is referred to in the register;
(f)   the loss or destruction of a document lodged at HM Land Registry for inspection or safe custody;
(g)   a mistake in the cautions register; or
(h)   failure by HM Land Registry to perform its duty under the Land Registration Act 2002, s.50 (this is the duty to notify a prior chargee when HM Land Registry registers a statutory charge which has priority over a prior charge on the register).

2.8.6.2 No right to an indemnity

The right to an indemnity is excluded in the following cases:

17

(a) where the claimant has suffered loss wholly or partly as a result of his own fraud;

(b) where the claimant has suffered loss wholly as a result of his own lack of proper care;

(c) in respect of any mineral rights unless such are specifically included in the register of title; or

(d) in respect of costs incurred in taking or defending proceedings without the consent of HM Land Registry, unless they had to be incurred urgently and it was not reasonably practicable to apply for consent in advance.

In respect of (a) and (b), any fraud or lack of care on the part of a person from whom the claimant derives title is treated as if it were fraud or lack of care on the part of the claimant, unless the claimant claims through a disposition for valuable consideration which is registered or protected on the register.

2.8.6.3 Amount of indemnity

If rectification is not ordered, the amount of indemnity will not exceed the value of the claimed estate, charge or interest at the time of the making of the error or omission. If rectification is ordered, the amount of indemnity will not exceed the value of the claimed estate, charge or interest at the time just before rectification took place.

2.9 THIRD-PARTY RIGHTS IN REGISTERED LAND

Third-party interests in registered land can be protected in the following ways:

(a) as registered charges;

(b) as overriding interests;

(c) by entry of a notice or a restriction on the register.

2.9.1 Registered charges

A mortgage of registered land will be protected by a registered charge in the charges register.

2.9.2 Overriding interests

Overriding interests are interests to which a registered title is subject, even though they do not appear on the register. They are binding not only on the registered proprietor but also on anyone who acquires an interest in the property. The Land Registration Act 2002 distinguishes between interests that override first registration and those that override subsequent dispositions.

2.9.2.1 Unregistered interests which override first registration

Schedule 1 to the Land Registration Act 2002 contains a list of unregistered interests which will bind the owner of the legal estate on first registration. These include:

(a) a leasehold estate granted for a term not exceeding seven years from the date of grant;
(b) an interest belonging to a person in actual occupation;
(c) a legal easement or *profit à prendre*; and
(d) a local land charge.

2.9.2.2 Unregistered interests which override registered dispositions

A registered disposition for valuable consideration of a registered estate or a registered charge will take subject to those overriding interests affecting the estate or charge that are listed in Schedule 3 to the Land Registration Act 2002. These include:

(a) a leasehold estate in land granted for a term not exceeding seven years from the date of the grant;
(b) an interest belonging at the time of the disposition to a person in actual occupation, so far as relating to land of which he is in actual occupation, except for:

　(i) an interest under a settlement under the Settled Land Act 1925;
　(ii) an interest of a person of whom inquiry was made before the disposition and who failed to disclose the right when he could reasonably have been expected to do so;
　(iii) an interest:

　　• which belongs to a person whose occupation would not have been obvious on a reasonably careful inspection of the land at the time of the disposition, and
　　• of which the person to whom the disposition is made does not have actual knowledge at that time;

　(iv) a leasehold estate in land granted to take effect in possession after the end of the period of three months beginning with the date of the grant and which has not taken effect in possession at the time of the disposition;

(c) certain legal easements and profits; and
(d) a local land charge.

2.9.2.3 Disclosing overriding interests

On either an application for first registration or an application to register a disposition of a registered title, the applicant must disclose any overriding interests within his actual knowledge. This will enable these interests to be noted on the register and they will, as a result, lose their overriding status.

The obligation to disclose does not extend to, for example:

(a)   an interest under a trust of land;
(b)   a lease granted for a term of three years or less, unless it is of a kind that has to be registered;
(c)   a local land charge;
(d)   a public right; or
(e)   any interest apparent from the deeds and documents accompanying an application for first registration.

2.9.3 Notices

A notice is an entry in the charges register in respect of the burden of an interest affecting a registered estate or charge. The effect of registration of a notice is that it operates by way of notice only and so dispositions of the land concerned take effect subject to the notice and are thus bound by the estate, interest or claim to the extent that it is valid. Registration does not validate an otherwise invalid claim against the land.

Notices are used to protect interests such as:

(a)   restrictive covenants;
(b)   estate contracts;
(c)   an unpaid seller's lien; and
(d)   a statutory right of occupation under the Family Law Act 1996 of a spouse or civil partner who does not own the legal estate.

Apart from notices entered by HM Land Registry, a notice will be either a unilateral notice or an agreed notice. Unilateral notices are entered without the consent of the registered proprietor, while the proprietor's consent is normally required for an application for an agreed notice. The entry of a unilateral notice is subject to notice to the registered proprietor and anyone else provided for in the Land Registration Rules 2003. A specific person will be shown as the beneficiary of a unilateral notice and the entry can be updated where the protected interest is passed to someone else.

An application for an agreed notice (other than for a home rights notice under the Family Law Act 1996) must be made on Form AN1. The applicant must also lodge the order or instrument giving rise to the interest, if there is one. Otherwise, the applicant must provide sufficient details of the interest to satisfy HM Land Registry as to the nature of the applicant's claim. HM Land Registry can only approve an application for an agreed notice in three situations:

(a)   the applicant is the proprietor or entitled to be registered as such;

(b)   the consent of the proprietor or the person entitled to be registered has been provided; or

(c)   HM Land Registry is otherwise satisfied of the validity of the applicant's claim.

There are some special cases (for example, a home rights notice and an inheritance tax notice) which can be protected only by agreed notice. Exceptionally, an application for registration of a home rights notice is made in Form HR1.

An application for a unilateral notice must be in Form UN1. The applicant does not need to lodge any consents or documentary evidence of the interest claimed. Instead the entry is made simply on the basis of the applicant's statutory declaration, or a conveyancer's certificate, as contained in the form. However, the applicant is under a statutory duty to act reasonably in exercising the right to apply for entry of a notice on the register, and this duty is owed to anyone suffering damage in consequence of a breach of the duty.

2.9.4   Restrictions

A restriction is an entry on the proprietorship register which operates to prevent a disposition being registered which does not conform to the terms of the restriction. The prohibition can be indefinitely, for a limited time or until the occurrence of a specified event (for example, the giving of notice, the obtaining of consent, and the making of an order by the court or HM Land Registry). Although the Act places no particular limitation on the events that may be specified in a restriction, HM Land Registry is only empowered to accept an application for a restriction that is not in one of the forms prescribed in the Land Registration Rules 2003 if it appears that its terms are reasonable and that applying the restriction will be straightforward and will not place an unreasonable burden on HM Land Registry.

An application for a restriction can be made by:

(a)   the registered proprietor or someone entitled to be registered as such;

(b)   someone who has the consent of the registered proprietor or someone entitled to be registered as such; or

(c)   someone who otherwise has a sufficient interest in making the entry (see rule 93 of the Land Registration Rules 2003 for a list of the categories of interests capable of protection by a restriction and the persons who can apply).

Where an application is made without the consent of the registered proprietor (or someone entitled to be registered as such), HM Land Registry must serve notice of the application on the proprietor in order to give him the opportunity to object.

Where someone claims to have a beneficial interest in registered land under a trust of land or a settlement, the only way of protecting the interest on the register is by way of restriction.

Where it is possible to enter a notice, a restriction cannot be used instead to protect the priority of the interest claimed. However, both a notice and a restriction may be used – for example, where the seller has entered into a contract to sell the land to the buyer and completion is some time after exchange, the buyer could enter a notice to protect the contract and a restriction to prevent dispositions by the seller.

There are standard forms of restriction set out in Schedule 4 to the Land Registration Rules 2003 in order to achieve a streamlined form of protection, operable with the minimum of Land Registry involvement and delay. If an applicant uses a standard form of restriction, it will automatically be deemed acceptable in format. A non-standard restriction will be approved only if it appears reasonable and applying it would be straightforward and place no unreasonable burden on HM Land Registry.

Provided the restriction is in one of the prescribed standard forms, it may be applied for in the additional provisions panel of any of the prescribed forms of transfer or assent, in panel 8 of Form CH1 (prescribed form of charge, if used), in an electronic legal charge, in any charge the form of which has been previously approved by HM Land Registry, or in a prescribed clauses lease. In any other case the applicant must apply using Form RX1.

HM Land Registry also has the power to enter a restriction without an application having been made – for example, to prevent unlawfulness or invalidity, or to ensure that beneficial interests are overreached by specifying the number of trustees who must give a receipt. Someone who claims an interest that cannot be protected by a notice may apply for a restriction without obtaining the consent of the registered proprietor. In such a situation, HM Land Registry must notify the proprietor and anyone else specified in the Land Registration Rules 2003, giving them an opportunity to object to the restriction.

2.9.5 Cautions against first registration

Anyone claiming an interest in unregistered land which would allow him to object to a disposition of it may enter a caution against first registration. This ensures that HM Land Registry will notify the cautioner of any application for registration of the land. The cautioner then has an opportunity to show cause why the registration should not proceed by making an objection within a specified period. An application for a caution against first registration to be entered must be made on Form CT1 accompanied by a statutory declaration setting out briefly the basis of the claim. Form CT1 combines both the application form and a supporting statutory declaration.

2.9.6 The possibility of a constructive trust

Even if a new registered proprietor purchased the land for valuable consideration, he may be subject to an equitable interest not amounting to an overriding interest or protected on a register but imposed on him by a constructive trust: thus, in *Peffer* v.

Rigg [1977] 1 WLR 285, it was suggested that a registered proprietor could be subject to an equitable interest subject to which the seller to him had held the land where it would be unconscionable for him to take free from the interest; and in *Lyus* v. *Prowsa Developments Ltd* [1982] 2 All ER 953, it was similarly suggested that a registered proprietor could take subject to an unregistered estate contract entered into by a previous proprietor if it was unconscionable for him to take free therefrom.

2.10   EXEMPT DOCUMENTS AND THE OPEN REGISTER

The register and the documents registered in respect of each title are open to the public. Copies of documents held by HM Land Registry can be obtained by applying on form OC2. Further information can be found in HM Land Registry Practice Guide 11 (Inspection and Application for Official Copies).

There may be documents which the registered proprietor does not wish to be made available to the public. The Land Registration Rules 2003 make allowance for such documents to be exempted from the open register. An application for exemption must be made on forms EX1 and EX1A. This procedure will usually be used where the document contains commercially prejudicial information which the registered proprietor does not wish to disclose. Further information can be found in HM Land Registry Practice Guide 57 (Exempting Documents from the General Right to Inspect and Copy).

2.11   ENTRIES ON THE REGISTER MADE UNDER THE LAND REGISTRATION ACT 1925

From time to time you will come across entries made under the pre-Land Registration Act 2002 law. These may be inhibitions which were entered to prevent any dealings with land under a title and which are now dealt with by restrictions. There may also be cautions which were entries used to protect third-party claims against registered land. Under the Land Registration Act 2002 the work of cautions is carried out by notices. The Land Registration Act 2002 contains transitional provisions to deal with such cases.

2.12   SUMMARY

- Events which trigger compulsory first registration include a transfer, first legal mortgage and the grant of a lease for a term of more than seven years and failure to register within two months of completion renders the disposition void.
- An estate will be registered with one of four classes of title – absolute, qualified, possessory or good leasehold.

- There are three parts to the register – the property register, the proprietorship register and the charges register.
- Third-party rights can be protected by an entry on the register or may be overriding.
- Unless it is overriding, an interest must be on the register in order to be binding.
- An applicant for registration must disclose any overriding interests that he knows about.
- Entries made under the pre-Land Registration Act 2002 legislation may still be encountered.

CHAPTER 3

Preliminary matters

3.1 TAKING INSTRUCTIONS

You should take full instructions at the outset of the transaction so that you will be able to give full and proper advice to the client and have sufficient information to carry out the transaction.

The client's name and address and the identity of the other party to the transaction should be requested from the client in order to check for an actual or potential conflict of interest before you take instructions.

Ideally, you should take instructions from the client in person. Instructions may also be taken over the telephone. In each case, you should consider whether the Consumer Contracts (Information, Cancellation and Additional Charges) Regulations 2013, SI 2013/3134 apply to the contract for conveyancing services and, if they do, comply with the requirements of these regulations (see the Law Society's Consumer Contracts Regulations 2013 Practice Note (22 November 2019), available at **www.lawsociety.org.uk** when you sign in using 'My LS').

Instructions may be received via a third party, such as an estate agent or a mortgage broker, and these instructions must be confirmed with the client to avoid misunderstandings. A solicitor may accept instructions which have been received through a referral from such a third party, provided paragraph 5.1 of the SRA Code of Conduct for Solicitors, RELs and RFLs is complied with (this also applies to firms regulated by the SRA by virtue of paragraph 7.1 of the SRA Code of Conduct for Firms). If a referral fee is paid to an introducer, the client must be told about it.

Where a solicitor receives instructions from one of two or more persons who are either selling, or buying, or both selling and buying together, the solicitor must obtain confirmation of his instructions from everyone who is to be his client (*Penn* v. *Bristol & West Building Society* [1997] 3 All ER 470).

A checklist should be used when taking instructions to ensure that nothing is overlooked. Using a checklist will focus your mind on the relevant information, minimise preparation time and ultimately save you time in the interview itself, but remember that it should be used sympathetically so that the client does not feel he is being processed in an impersonal way.

3.2   IDENTITY OF THE CLIENT

A solicitor must check the client's identity as a precaution against mortgage fraud and money laundering. This will establish that the client is the person who he says he is, thus ensuring that the solicitor has the client's authority to act in the transaction. A solicitor should therefore check the identity of a client whom he does not know or for whom he has not previously acted. The Money Laundering, Terrorist Financing and Transfer of Funds (Information on the Payer) Regulations 2017, SI 2017/692 require you to obtain satisfactory evidence of the client's identity when you establish a business relationship with the client. The Legal Sector Affinity Group, which includes the Law Society and all the legal sector supervisors named in the anti-money laundering regulations, has published guidance on anti-money laundering. The guidance can be downloaded at **www.lawsociety.org.uk**. A court is required to consider this guidance in assessing whether a solicitor committed an offence or took all reasonable steps and exercised all due diligence to avoid committing an offence. In addition, where a solicitor is acting for both borrower and lender, the identity of the borrower must be verified in accordance with paragraph 3.1.5 of the UK Finance Mortgage Lenders' Handbook ('Lenders' Handbook') and paragraph B.13 of the Building Societies Association (BSA) Mortgage Instructions.

You must also consider whether HM Land Registry's confirmation of identity requirements will apply, and if so, what will be required to satisfy them. Land Registry forms AP1, DS2 and FR1 require the applicant to give details of the conveyancers acting for each party and, where a party is not represented, to provide appropriate evidence of that party's identity. Full details are set out in HM Land Registry Practice Guide 67 (Evidence of Identity: Conveyancers).

3.3   ACTING FOR THE SELLER

3.3.1   Information required

When taking initial instructions from the seller the information which a solicitor will require will usually consist of the following:

(a)   Full names and addresses (including postcodes) of the parties, the buyer's solicitor and any estate agents involved; and contact telephone numbers and email addresses for the seller (both home and business), buyer's solicitor and estate agent.

(b)   Particulars of the property, including the full address and postcode, and whether it is freehold or leasehold.

(c)   The price.

(d)   Whether any preliminary deposit has been paid and, if so, to whom. The buyer may have paid a small deposit to the estate agent and this must be taken into account later in the transaction.

(e)   Details of any mortgage on the property, including the name and address of the lender, the account number and the outstanding balance. This information is required as the mortgage will usually need to be discharged on completion and such documents as are held by the lender will need to be obtained. The seller should also be asked whether there are any second or subsequent mortgages, and if there are then similar information will be needed in respect of these as well. You should obtain written authority from the seller to deal with the lender. You should examine the mortgage or other loans and consider obtaining a redemption statement to ascertain redemption penalties or negative equity. If it is apparent that there is a negative equity or for some other reason the seller will not be able to discharge the registered charges from the proceeds of sale, you should discuss what actions need to be taken.

(f)   Whether any chattels are to be included in the sale and, if they are, whether any extra money is being paid for them. In addition, the seller should also be asked if he wishes to remove any fixtures. The contract will, if nothing is said, include all the fixtures and so if the seller wishes to remove any they must be specifically referred to in the contract.

(g)   Whether the seller is buying another property. If he is, then the purchase may be dependent on the sale of the seller's existing property, which means that the two transactions must be synchronised. If the seller requires a mortgage offer in connection with any related purchase, check whether he has made an application and whether a mortgage offer has been made.

(h)   Any anticipated completion date which the seller may have in mind.

(i)   If the sale is of part of the seller's property, then a plan will be needed and instructions must be taken as to the covenants which the seller may wish to impose and the easements which will need to be granted and reserved. In addition, if the property is mortgaged, arrangements may have already been made for the release of the part being sold from the mortgage, and these arrangements may need to be clarified.

(j)   The identity of anyone aged 17 or over other than the seller living in the property, and whether they have made any financial contribution towards its purchase or subsequent improvement. Consider whether their consent to the sale is required and whether they need to take independent advice.

(k)   Where there is no related purchase, instructions must be taken over the proceeds of sale. The seller may want these sending to his bank and so the name and address of the client's bank and account number will be required.

(l)   The present use of the property. This should be checked against the authorised planning use and any restrictive covenants affecting the use of the property.

You should request payment on account in relation to disbursements.

You should also consider which, if any, documents may need to be signed by an attorney and check whether powers of attorney are available. You should prepare any power that may be necessary.

3.3.2 Advice

Matters on which the seller should be advised include:

(a) finance;
(b) legal costs and expenses, including VAT and disbursements; and
(c) taxation.

Where there is more than one seller, you may need to give advice on whether the sellers are joint tenants or tenants in common. You should look at the proprietorship register to see whether there is a restriction preventing the registration of a disposition by a sole proprietor under which capital money arises unless authorised by a court order. Such a restriction means that the registered proprietors are tenants in common. If there is no restriction, they are joint tenants.

3.3.3 Law Society Conveyancing Protocol

Under the Law Society Conveyancing Protocol (2019), the seller's solicitor must obtain his client's answers to the questions contained in the TA6 Property Information Form, obtain from his client any relevant documents relating to such matters as planning permissions, building regulations consents, plans, completion certificates and guarantees, and ask his client to complete the TA10 Fittings and Contents Form showing which items are to remain at the property after the sale and which are to be removed. The solicitor must explain the nature of the questions in these forms and warn the seller that the forms may require later re-verification.

3.4 ACTING FOR THE BUYER

3.4.1 Information required

If acting for the buyer, much of the information which should be obtained at the initial interview will be the same as above:

(a) Full names and addresses (including postcodes) of the parties, the seller's solicitor and any estate agents; and contact telephone numbers and email addresses for the buyer (both home and business), seller's solicitor and estate agent. Sometimes instructions are received from someone who is married or who intends to live in the property with someone else, e.g. a cohabitee. In this situation, it will usually be the case that the property should be purchased in their joint names. If a mortgage is being taken out to purchase the property, the lender will insist on it being in joint names.
(b) The buyer's National Insurance (NI) number and date of birth. These will be required later when completing the land transaction return (SDLT1) for SDLT purposes.

(c)   Particulars of the property, including the address and postcode, and whether it is freehold or leasehold.

(d)   The price.

(e)   Whether any preliminary deposit has been paid and, if so, to whom.

(f)   Availability, amount and source of deposit funds and purchase monies.

(g)   Whether any financial contribution is to be made by a third party and, if so, whether they require independent advice. Consider the advice to be given to the lender about such contributions.

(h)   Buildings insurance: suggest the buyer obtains quotations and advise that the terms of any policy taken out must be compliant with the lender's requirements (where applicable).

(i)   If there is more than one buyer, whether the property is to be bought as joint tenants or as tenants in common.

(j)   Details of any chattels, e.g. carpets and curtains, included in the sale, and of any fixtures to be removed by the seller.

(k)   Whether the buyer has had a survey carried out. Suggest the buyer consults an independent surveyor for advice on valuation and survey.

(l)   Whether a mortgage is being obtained. If so, from whom and for how much? Has a mortgage offer been made or an 'in principle' offer received? Also check which firm the lender will be instructing if you will not be instructed by the lender.

(m) Whether the buyer is selling a property and if so, is the purchase dependent on this sale?

(n)   Whether the buyer is in rented accommodation and the termination date or arrangements needed to give notice to terminate.

(o)   Anticipated completion date.

It is usual for a solicitor to request a payment on account from a buyer to cover the fees for any searches which will need to be carried out before exchange of contracts.

   You should also consider which, if any, documents may need to be signed by an attorney and check whether powers of attorney are available. You should prepare any power that may be necessary.

3.4.2   Advice

When acting for a buyer you may need to give advice on the following:

(a)   finance, including mortgage advice;

(b)   possible future liability to capital gains tax (CGT);

(c)   legal costs and expenses, including VAT and disbursements;

(d)   surveys;

(e)   implications of buying property in joint names;

(f)   SDLT.

In certain circumstances, consideration should be given as to whether to apportion the purchase price between the amount being paid for the land and any sum being paid for chattels included in the sale, as this may result in a saving of SDLT. Where the purchase price is just over one of the SDLT thresholds, the SDLT payable could be reduced or even avoided if it is possible to apportion the price between the land and any chattels so as to reduce the price for the land to below the appropriate threshold. However, the price which is apportioned for the chattels must be realistic and not merely one to avoid or reduce SDLT. If the price for the chattels is an over-valuation, it may amount to a fraud on HMRC by both the solicitor and his client, and could also render the contract unenforceable (*Saunders* v. *Edwards* [1987] 1 WLR 1116). In addition, if the buyer is obtaining a mortgage to assist with the purchase, the buyer's solicitor must report any reduction in the purchase price to the lender.

Items which HMRC will regard as chattels include: carpets, curtains, light shades, pot plants, free-standing kitchen white goods and portable electric or gas fires. The following are regarded as fixtures, and apportionment is not available: fitted bathroom sanitary ware, central heating systems, plants growing in the soil and gas fires connected to a piped gas supply.

Any apportionment must also be reported to the buyer's lender.

3.4.3 Joint buyers

If there is more than one buyer, instructions must be taken as to co-ownership, and it will be necessary to give advice to the clients as to the nature and effect of the different types of co-ownership in such a way that the clients clearly understand.

3.4.3.1 Legal estate

Co-owners must always hold the legal estate on a joint tenancy. Thus, if a property is to be purchased by a married couple or civil partners they will always hold the legal title as joint tenants whatever their beneficial interest.

3.4.3.2 Equitable interest

The equitable interest can be held by co-owners either as joint tenants or as tenants in common. Thus a married couple or civil partners will hold the legal estate as joint tenants on trust for themselves either as joint tenants or tenants in common in equity.

If the equitable interest is held on a joint tenancy, then each joint tenant will own the whole of the equitable interest, and on the death of a joint tenant the right of survivorship will apply to vest the interest in the survivor. As a result, a joint tenancy cannot be left by will although it can be severed. This type of tenancy will usually be used by married couples and civil partners.

Under a tenancy in common, each tenant owns a specific share of the equitable interest which can be left by will or can pass under the intestacy rules. The right of survivorship does not apply. This type of tenancy should be considered by people who are not married or in a civil partnership, and should also be used for property being bought by people in partnership. Tenants in common should also be advised to consider making a will.

The purchase deed must record which type of ownership is applicable (*Hunting-ford* v. *Hobbs* [1992] EGCS 38). Where there is a tenancy in common, it is important that the shares of each owner are agreed and set out either in the purchase deed or more usually in a separate deed of trust. In the absence of such a deed, the court has a discretion to assess the respective shares of the parties having regard to their conduct and contributions (*Oxley* v. *Hiscock* [2004] EWCA Civ 546). A purchase of residential property in joint names of the cohabitants will establish a *prima facie* case of joint and equal beneficial interests unless the contrary is proved (*Stack* v. *Dowden* [2007] UKHL 17).

The cases of *Stack* v. *Dowden* [2007] UKHL 17 and *Jones* v. *Kernott* [2011] UKSC 53 have highlighted the problems that can occur when joint owners of a property fail to declare how they hold their beneficial interests at the outset. The Law Society's Joint Ownership Practice Note (10 June 2020) gives guidance on joint ownership and the methods of making a joint declaration of trust. The practice note advises solicitors that they should make their clients aware of the potential consequences of not making a declaration of trust at the time of the purchase, i.e. that a dispute might arise, necessitating expensive litigation, with the court eventually dividing the property in a way that is different from what the parties intended.

Once advice has been given to the clients and they have decided how they want to hold their beneficial interests, their decision can be recorded in:

(a) HM Land Registry transfer form (see panel 10 of Form TR1);
(b) Land Registry Form JO; or
(c) a separate declaration of trust.

A separate declaration of trust should be used where the buyers want the details of their interests in the property to be private.

HM Land Registry will automatically enter a Form A restriction in the register whenever two or more people apply to be registered as joint proprietors of an estate in land, unless it is clear that they will be holding the property for themselves alone as joint tenants.

3.5 PROFESSIONAL CONDUCT ISSUES

A solicitor's conduct is governed by the SRA Code of Conduct for Solicitors, RELs and RFLs which sets out the standards expected of individual solicitors, registered European lawyers and registered foreign lawyers. A firm's conduct is governed by the SRA Code of Conduct for Firms. Both Codes form part of the SRA Standards and Regulations, which also include the SRA Principles which comprise the fundamental tenets of ethical behaviour that the SRA expects all those which it regulates to uphold. The SRA Standards and Regulations can be found at **www.sra.org.uk/solicitors/standards-regulations**.

3.5.1 Acting for seller and buyer

Subject to certain exceptions, a solicitor cannot act if there is a conflict of interest, or a significant risk of a conflict of interest, between two or more clients (SRA Code of Conduct for Solicitors, RELs and RFLs, para.6.2; SRA Code of Conduct for Firms, para.6.2). A 'conflict of interest' is defined in the SRA Glossary as 'a situation where your separate duties to act in the best interests of two or more clients in relation to the same or a related matter conflict'.

Paragraph 6.2 (in both Codes) supports SRA Principle 7 which requires a solicitor to act in the best interests of each client. A solicitor should have effective systems and controls to help identify and assess conflicts of interest. So, the decision as to whether to act for both seller and buyer rests with the solicitor. A solicitor should consider such factors as whether:

(a)   the clients' interests are different;
(b)   the solicitor's ability to give independent advice to the clients may be fettered;
(c)   there is a need to negotiate between the clients;
(d)   there is an imbalance in bargaining power between the clients; and
(e)   any client is vulnerable.

Acting for seller and buyer is an area which carries a high risk of conflicts of interest and the decision rests with the solicitor and the firm as to whether there is a conflict of interest or a significant risk of one in the circumstances, taking into account whether or not the seller and buyer are, for example, persons related by blood or marriage, the sale is at an undervalue or a gift, or the seller and the buyer are both established clients of the firm.

Paragraph 6.2 provides that a solicitor can act for more than one party even if there is a client conflict where the clients have a substantially common interest in relation to a matter or a particular aspect of it. The SRA Glossary defines a 'substantially common interest' as 'a situation where there is a clear common purpose between the clients and a strong consensus on how it is to be achieved'. The decision as to whether the clients have a substantially common interest is one for the solicitor and the firm.

So, a solicitor or firm may only act for a buyer and a seller where they are satisfied that there is no existing conflict of interest and no significant risk of a conflict arising in future, or there is a conflict of interest but the parties share a substantially common interest. Where the land or interest in land is being transferred for value, this will be difficult to establish. It might be possible to act where the land is being gifted, or transferred between related parties (i.e. in the context of private individuals, where the parties are related by blood, adoption, marriage, civil partnership or living together). However, if a conflict were to arise during the course of the transaction, the solicitor would have to stop acting for at least one of the clients and could only continue acting for the other client if the duty of confidentiality to the former client is not at risk.

If a solicitor is satisfied there is no conflict of interests, he should also satisfy himself that if he were to act, there is no other risk of non-compliance with the SRA Principles. In particular, the decision to act for a buyer and seller should be of benefit to both clients, rather than in the solicitor's own commercial interests. As the solicitor may be asked to demonstrate compliance with the SRA Principles, a record of the decision to act for both clients should be kept.

If a decision is made to act under the 'substantially common interest' exception, the conditions in paragraph 6.2(b)(i)–(iii) (in both Codes) must be complied with. These require:

(a)   the parties to have given 'informed consent' (in writing or evidenced in writing) to the solicitor or firm acting for both of them, meaning that the parties must appreciate the issues and risks of the solicitor or firm acting for both of them;

(b)   the firm (where appropriate) to put in place effective safeguards to protect the parties' confidential information; and

(c)   the solicitor to be satisfied that it is reasonable to act for both parties, meaning that the solicitor should consider whether one client will be prejudiced (e.g. due to vulnerability or unequal bargaining power) if not separately represented.

The other key principles to consider where a solicitor is considering acting for seller and buyer are that a solicitor must act:

(a)   with independence (SRA Principle 3); and

(b)   with integrity (SRA Principle 5).

Also, the duties of confidentiality and disclosure may become relevant (SRA Code of Conduct for Solicitors, RELs and RFLs, paras.6.3–6.5; SRA Code of Conduct for Firms, paras.6.3–6.5). There may be a situation where a buyer wants his solicitor to keep information confidential, but this information may be material to the seller. In this situation, the solicitor's duty of confidentiality will prevail and the solicitor will usually have to cease acting for the seller. In addition, confidentiality issues may arise in relation to former clients. The duty to maintain confidentiality about the affairs of a client is ongoing, and as a general rule, a solicitor must not disclose information about any client, present or former, without their consent.

3.5.2   Acting for joint buyers

A solicitor can usually act for joint buyers if there is no conflict of interests. Where the buyers of residential property are neither married to each other nor in a civil partnership, separate advice about their rights in the property may be necessary.

3.5.3 Acting for both lender and borrower

Where a buyer is obtaining a mortgage to assist with the purchase of a property, the lender may instruct the buyer's solicitor to act on its behalf in connection with the completion of the mortgage. Acting for both borrower and lender is possible unless there is a conflict of interest or a significant risk of a conflict of interest (SRA Code of Conduct for Solicitors, RELs and RFLs, para.6.2; SRA Code of Conduct for Firms, para.6.2). Where there is a conflict of interest, it might be possible to act under paragraph 6.2 if the clients have a substantially common interest and:

(a)　the parties have given 'informed consent' (in writing or evidenced in writing) to the solicitor or firm acting for both of them, meaning that the parties must appreciate the issues and risks of the solicitor or firm acting for both of them;

(b)　the firm (where appropriate) has put in place effective safeguards to protect the parties' confidential information; and

(c)　the solicitor is satisfied that it is reasonable to act for both parties, meaning that the solicitor should consider whether one client will be prejudiced (for example due to vulnerability or unequal bargaining power) if not separately represented.

The substantially common interest in this situation is that both borrower and lender will want to make sure that the borrower will have good title to the property and that the property does not suffer from any problems that would adversely affect its value.

In residential transactions, the borrower will usually be obtaining a mortgage from a bank or building society where the mortgage is offered on standard terms and conditions and a standard form of mortgage deed is used. The SRA Code of Conduct 2011 did indicate that it may be acceptable to act for both borrower and lender where the mortgage was on standard terms. However, the 2011 Code also indicated that in order to act for both borrower and lender, a significant part of the lender's activities must consist of lending, the mortgaged property must be the borrower's private residence and the certificate of title required by the lender must be in the form approved by the Law Society and UK Finance. While the current SRA Codes of Conduct do not give such an indication as to the SRA's view on acting for both borrower and lender, it is likely that solicitors will continue to act for both in such circumstances.

If a solicitor is acting for a borrower and a lender and a client conflict occurs during the transaction, the solicitor must cease acting for both parties unless he can, with the consent of one party, continue to act for the other. Examples of where a conflict may arise include:

(a)　where facts about the borrower's financial position or arrangements are disclosed to the solicitor which if known by the lender would affect its decision to lend and the borrower refuses to allow these facts to be disclosed to the lender;

(b)　where the terms of the mortgage offer are unfair to the borrower; and

(c)　where the borrower is misrepresenting the purchase price to the lender.

When a solicitor acts for both lender and borrower, a duty is owed to both clients. Following *Mortgage Express Ltd* v. *Bowerman & Partners* [1996] 2 All ER 836 a solicitor who acts for both lender and borrower may be in breach of his duty to the lender if he fails to disclose any material information which he has received from the borrower, even though the borrower did not consent to the disclosure.

In residential conveyancing transactions most lenders use standard mortgage instructions, either the Lenders' Handbook produced by UK Finance, or the Mortgage Instructions produced by the BSA. Each of these provides a full set of conveyancing instructions for conveyancers acting on behalf of the lender.

The Lenders' Handbook is divided into three parts:

(a)   Part 1 sets out the main instructions and guidance which must be followed by conveyancers.

(b)   Part 2 details each lender's specific requirements which arise from the instructions in Part 1. A lender which adopts the Lenders' Handbook will send its own Part 2 to conveyancers direct. A lender may change its Part 2 requirements from time to time.

(c)   Part 3 sets out the standard instructions in the event that a conveyancer is representing the lender separately from the borrower in a residential convey-ancing transaction.

The Lenders' Handbook is available at **https://lendershandbook.ukfinance. org.uk**.

The BSA Mortgage Instructions are also divided into two parts:

(a)   A core set of mortgage instructions.

(b)   Specific requirements setting out individual lenders' policies.

The BSA Mortgage Instructions are available via the BSA website, at **www.bsa. org.uk**.

3.5.4   Acting for two or more joint borrowers

A solicitor may act for joint borrowers provided that there is no conflict of interest. A common situation where a problem can arise is where a spouse, usually the husband, needs to borrow money for his business and the lender requires security over the matrimonial home which is in joint names with the spouse. The wife agrees to a mortgage over the house for the benefit of her husband's business, but the husband defaults. The bank then seeks to enforce its security and the wife then claims that the mortgage is not valid as her signature was obtained only because of the undue influence of her husband.

In *Royal Bank of Scotland* v. *Etridge* [2001] UKHL 44, the House of Lords laid down detailed guidance for solicitors acting in such a loan situation.

The burden of proof that a mortgage was entered into because of undue influence rests on the person claiming undue influence. Where there is a special relationship – e.g. parent and child or solicitor and client – there is a rebuttable presumption of undue influence. In the case of a husband and wife, there is no presumption of undue influence, but where a wife proposes to mortgage the matrimonial home as security for a bank loan to her husband, or to a company through which he operates his business, the lender is put on enquiry. This is because, *prima facie*, such transaction is not to the wife's advantage and there is a substantial risk of undue influence.

Where the lender is put on enquiry, it should take reasonable steps to make sure that the practical implications of the proposed transaction have been explained to the wife in a 'meaningful way', so that she understands the basics of the transaction. In practice, a lender will rely on confirmation from a solicitor acting for the wife that he has advised her appropriately.

The solicitor should:

(a)   explain to the wife the purpose for which he has become involved;

(b)   explain that, if it becomes necessary, the lender will rely on the solicitor's involvement to counter any suggestion that the wife has been unduly influenced or has not fully understood the nature of the transaction; and

(c)   obtain confirmation from the wife that she wishes the solicitor to act for her in the transaction and to advise her on the legal and practical implications of the transaction.

The nature and extent of the advice given will depend on the facts of the case, but must include an explanation as to the nature of the documents and the practical consequences to the wife of her signing them, and a warning as to the seriousness of the risks involved. The solicitor must explain to the wife that she has a choice as to whether or not to go ahead with the transaction and check whether she wishes to proceed. She should be asked whether she wants the solicitor to write to the lender confirming that matters have been explained to her. The solicitor should meet face-to-face with the wife in the absence of the husband, and his advice should be given in non-technical language.

The lender should, with the consent of the husband, supply the solicitor with the following financial information:

(a)   the purpose for which the loan is being made available;

(b)   the current amount of the husband's indebtedness;

(c)   the amount of the current overdraft facility;

(d)   the amount and terms of the new loan;

(e)   a copy of any written application made by the husband for the loan.

If the husband does not consent to the release of this information, the transaction cannot proceed.

3.5.5   Acting for seller and lender

It is usual for the solicitor acting for the seller to be instructed by the seller's lender in connection with the discharge of the seller's mortgage. There is normally no problem with this.

3.5.6   Contract races

Where the seller is anxious to secure a quick sale he may instruct his solicitor to forward draft contracts to solicitors acting for different prospective buyers. These will be forwarded on the basis that the seller will sell to the first buyer to return a signed contract and a deposit, though there will not necessarily be an obligation on the seller to sell to the first buyer who complies with this requirement.

A solicitor and the firm must not abuse their position by taking unfair advantage of clients or others (SRA Code of Conduct for Solicitors, RELs and RFLs, para.1.2; SRA Code of Conduct for Firms, para.1.2). In addition, a solicitor and the firm must not mislead or attempt to mislead their clients, the court or others, either by their own acts or omissions or by allowing or being complicit in the acts or omissions of others (including their client) (SRA Code of Conduct for Solicitors, RELs and RFLs, para.1.4; SRA Code of Conduct for Firms, para.1.4). The solicitor should therefore immediately inform all buyers of the seller's intention to deal with more than one buyer. Should the seller refuse to authorise the disclosure then the solicitor must immediately cease to act.

The seller's solicitor must explain to his client that he is required to comply with paragraph 1.4. The seller should also be warned of the danger of losing the buyers if he goes ahead with a contract race as once a buyer is aware that there is a contract race, he may decide to withdraw because of the wasted time and expense he may incur. If the seller still wishes to proceed with the contract race, the seller's solicitor must immediately disclose the seller's decision to conduct a contract race and this disclosure should be made direct to the solicitor acting for each prospective buyer, or, where no solicitor is acting, to the prospective buyer(s) in person. He should make clear to each of them the precise terms of the race. If the seller refuses to allow the solicitor to notify all the buyers of the contract race, the solicitor cannot disclose the contract race to the buyers as he has a duty of confidentiality to his client under paragraph 6.3 (both Codes) and he must decline to act for the seller.

A solicitor must not accept instructions to act for both seller and any of the buyers in a contract race as there will be a conflict of interest between the clients and paragraph 6.2 (both Codes) will apply. There will also be a conflict of interest if the solicitor acts for more than one prospective buyer in a contract race.

It is sometimes the case that a contract is submitted to a buyer's solicitor but nothing is heard from him for some time. If the seller decides to proceed with another buyer, his solicitor must give written notice to the original buyer's solicitor that the contract is withdrawn. Only one buyer will then be in possession of a draft contract, and there will not be a contract race.

3.5.7   Undertakings

At certain stages during a conveyancing transaction a solicitor may be required to give an undertaking, which is a promise by that solicitor to do or not to do something. For example, undertakings may be given:

(a)   when obtaining the title deeds from a building society or bank;

(b)   to repay a bridging loan; and

(c)   to discharge a mortgage on completion.

Once an undertaking has been given, the solicitor who has given it is personally bound to carry out that undertaking. Should the undertaking not be honoured, the solicitor will also be guilty of professional misconduct. In addition, the court can also enforce an undertaking as it has an inherent jurisdiction over its officers, which includes solicitors. Consequently, a solicitor must take great care when giving an undertaking and should only undertake to do what is within his control, otherwise the undertaking must be qualified by words such as 'to use best endeavours'. Before giving an undertaking in respect of bridging finance, a solicitor must obtain the client's express and irrevocable authority.

An undertaking should always be given in writing; where it is given orally (as is sometimes the case) it should be confirmed in writing.

When drafting an undertaking a solicitor should:

(a)   see what is to be undertaken and then identify whether this can be undertaken and whether the undertaking should be limited by reference to a timescale;

(b)   consider obtaining the client's express and irrevocable authority; and

(c)   consider whether all stages of the undertaking are within his control, or whether the undertaking needs to be qualified.

An undertaking must be performed within the agreed timescale or, in the absence of an agreed timescale, within a 'reasonable amount of time' (SRA Code of Conduct for Solicitors, RELs and RFLs, para.1.3; SRA Code of Conduct for Firms, para.1.3).

3.5.8   Dealing with persons other than solicitors

It may be that one of the parties to a transaction is not represented by a solicitor. The following situations could arise.

3.5.8.1   Party represented by a licensed conveyancer

The Council for Licensed Conveyancers (CLC) has made rules covering licensed conveyancers. As these rules are similar to those affecting solicitors it is safe to deal with a licensed conveyancer. However, care must be taken to ensure that the particular person in question is in fact a licensed conveyancer, and this can be done by contacting the CLC.

3.5.8.2   Unqualified persons

The Legal Services Act 2007 provides that it is an offence for a person to carry on reserved legal activity if they are not entitled to do so. This includes certain conveyancing services such as preparing a contract for the sale of land or a transfer or charge for the purposes of the Land Registration Act 2002. The Law Society has published guidance for solicitors who are asked to deal with unqualified conveyancers. As soon as it becomes clear that a solicitor is dealing with an unqualified person, he should write to that person drawing attention to the Law Society's guidelines and asking for confirmation that no offence will be committed. The solicitor should also inform his client of the matter.

An undertaking cannot be enforced against an unqualified person and so should never be accepted from one.

3.5.8.3 Unrepresented party

A solicitor is under a duty in conduct to act in the best interests of his client (SRA Principle 7), but also to act with integrity (SRA Principle 5) and not to abuse his position by taking unfair advantage of third parties (SRA Code of Conduct for Solicitors, RELs and RFLs, para.1.2; SRA Code of Conduct for Firms, para.1.2). A solicitor should not take unfair advantage of an opponent's lack of legal knowledge where they have not instructed a lawyer. Thus a solicitor should not draw up a contract which he knows will be placed before a party for signature without that party having had an opportunity to obtain legal advice. In the case of a solicitor acting for a seller, the solicitor must write to the buyer advising him to take legal advice before signing the contract.

Where a transaction is over £6,000 in value and one of the parties is unrepresented, HM Land Registry requires a solicitor making certain applications (including applications to register a transfer or discharge a mortgage) to provide certified details and evidence of the unrepresented party's identity (see HM Land Registry Practice Guide 67 (Evidence of Identity: Conveyancers)).

3.5.9 Client confidentiality

Paragraph 6.3 of the SRA Code of Conduct for Solicitors, RELs and RFLs and paragraph 6.3 of the SRA Code of Conduct for Firms provide that a solicitor must keep the affairs of clients and former clients confidential except where disclosure is required or permitted by law or by the client or former client.

3.5.10 Money laundering

Money laundering is the process by which the proceeds of crime, and the true ownership of those proceeds, are changed so that the proceeds appear to come from a legitimate source. Solicitors involved in conveyancing transactions are at risk of being involved in money laundering because property transactions can involve any stage of the money laundering process. The law relating to money laundering is found in the Proceeds of Crime Act 2002, the Terrorism Act 2000 and the Money

Laundering, Terrorist Financing and Transfer of Funds (Information on the Payer) Regulations 2017, SI 2017/692.

The Proceeds of Crime Act 2002 establishes a number of money laundering offences including:

(a) the principal money laundering offences;
(b) offences of failing to report suspected money laundering; and
(c) offences of tipping off about a money laundering disclosure, tipping off about a money laundering investigation and prejudicing a money laundering investigation.

The Terrorism Act 2000, as amended, contains offences relating to engaging in or facilitating terrorism, as well as raising or possessing funds for terrorist purposes. There are also tipping off offences.

The Money Laundering, Terrorist Financing and Transfer of Funds (Information on the Payer) Regulations 2017 apply to all legal professionals acting in any real property transaction and set out the requirements for the anti-money laundering regime and outline the scope of customer due diligence.

Customer due diligence will be carried out at the start of the retainer and involves identifying the client and then verifying that identity using documents, data or information from a reliable and independent source, e.g. a client's passport. While a solicitor cannot avoid conducting customer due diligence, a risk-based approach can be taken to determine the extent and quality of information required and the steps to be taken to meet the requirements. A solicitor is required to keep copies of the verification documents for five years after the relationship with the client has ended.

The regulations also require a firm of solicitors to appoint a member of the firm as its nominated officer. Any suspicions of money laundering must be reported to the nominated officer. The nominated officer must then consider the report and, where necessary, disclose it by submitting a suspicious activity report to the National Crime Agency (NCA). Within seven days, the NCA must advise the nominated officer whether the firm is allowed to continue with the transaction or not. Further information can be found on the NCA website (see **www.nationalcrimeagency. gov.uk**).

The Legal Sector Affinity Group, which includes the Law Society and all the legal sector supervisors named in the anti-money laundering regulations, has published guidance on anti-money laundering. The guidance can be downloaded at **www.lawsociety.org.uk**. A court is required to consider this guidance in assessing whether a solicitor committed an offence or took all reasonable steps and exercised all due diligence to avoid committing an offence.

Particular signs to watch out for include:

(a) unusual instructions, in particular from people who live far away and who could use a solicitor nearer to them;

(b)   a client who asks you to hold a large amount of cash in your firm's client account;

(c)   a client who asks you to hold a large sum of cash and then asks you for a cheque from your firm; and

(d)   a secretive client who is reluctant to provide details of his identity.

The Money Laundering and Terrorist Financing (Amendment) Regulations 2019, SI 2019/1511 came into force on 10 January 2020. These regulations have amended the Money Laundering, Terrorist Financing and Transfer of Funds (Information on the Payer) Regulations 2017, SI 2017/692. These include changes to customer due diligence and enhanced due diligence. The Legal Sector Affinity Group is expected to update its guidance on anti-money laundering in the light of these changes.

3.5.11   Mortgage fraud

Mortgage fraud occurs where a person defrauds a lender through the mortgage process. All solicitors who do conveyancing involving a mortgage must be alert to mortgage fraud. A solicitor can find himself criminally liable if his client commits mortgage fraud. The definition of fraud in the Fraud Act 2006 covers fraud by false representation and fraud by failure to disclose information where there is a legal duty to disclose. Additionally, a mortgage obtained through fraud will be the proceeds of a crime and so a solicitor can be liable under the anti-money laundering regime if he acquires, uses, has possession of, enters into an arrangement with respect to, or transfers this criminal property.

The Law Society's Mortgage Fraud Practice Note (13 January 2020) highlights the warning signs of mortgage fraud and outlines how a solicitor can protect himself from being used to commit mortgage fraud.

3.5.12   Property and title fraud

The Law Society's Property and Registration Fraud Practice Note (26 June 2020) highlights the threat of fraudsters targeting property. The practice note has been produced jointly with HM Land Registry. It contains examples of fraud threats for property transactions, such as the impersonation of conveyancers, conveyancing firms and property owners. The practice note also contains suggested steps to mitigate the risk of property fraud.

In *P&P Property Ltd* v. *Owen White & Catlin LLP* and *Dreamvar (UK) Ltd* v. *Mishcon de Reya* [2018] EWCA Civ 1082, fraudulent sellers had purported to sell a high value property to innocent buyers. The fact that the fraudsters did not own the properties was not discovered until after the purchase monies had been handed over. The Court of Appeal held that, although there was no negligence on the part of the buyers' solicitors, they were liable for the losses suffered by their buyer clients. This was on the basis that the buyers' solicitors had received the money from their clients on trust to use for a genuine completion. As there had, in fact, not been a genuine completion, the buyers' solicitors were in breach of trust. This was despite the fact that in the *Mishcon de Reya* case, the seller's solicitor had not carried out adequate identity checks on its own client. The court held that the seller's solicitor was not liable in tort to the buyer or its solicitor, as it had no general duty of care to them. However, the buyer's solicitor could claim a contribution from the seller's solicitor towards the buyer's losses, as the previous edition of the Law Society's Code for Completion by Post, which the parties had adopted, required the seller's solicitor to use the purchase money for a genuine completion.

The Law Society, after considering the implications of the case, published a new edition of its Code for Completion by Post in 2019. The Code expressly provides that the seller's solicitor holds the purchase money on trust for the buyer and is under a fiduciary duty not to deal with that money other than in accordance with the terms of the Code. The seller's solicitor also undertakes that he has authority from the true owner of the property to receive the money and that the person named as the owner in the contract is entitled to transfer the property to the buyer. The Law Society has also suggested that buyers' solicitors consider asking sellers' solicitors questions, for example, about whether they have carried out their anti-money laundering investigations. Additional questions of sellers' solicitors should also be raised by buyers' solicitors where there are indicators of potential fraud of the type highlighted in the Law Society's Property and Registration Fraud Practice Note (26 June 2020).

3.6   FINANCIAL MATTERS

Advice must always be given to clients regarding their general financial situation.

3.6.1   Acting for a seller

A client who is only selling will want to know how much the net sale proceeds will be after any mortgage and all expenses, for example the estate agent's fees and the legal costs, have been paid.

3.6.2   Acting for a buyer

The questions here are whether the buyers will have sufficient funds to complete the purchase once legal fees and other disbursements have been taken into account, and whether they have sufficient funds available to pay the deposit on exchange of contracts.

3.6.3   Acting for a client both selling and buying

Where a client has a dependent sale and purchase, the financial situation can become quite complex. There are two main concerns:

(a) *Payment of a deposit on exchange of contracts.* The client has to pay a 10 per cent deposit on exchange of contracts in respect of the property which is being bought. It is possible that the client can use the deposit which is paid in respect of the property being sold as the deposit on the purchase, but if the property being purchased is more expensive than the one being sold this deposit will not cover the whole amount of the deposit payable on the purchase. It may be possible that the seller will accept a reduced deposit, but if this is not acceptable alternative sources of funding will need to be considered, such as:

   (i)   bridging finance, whereby the client borrows the money from a bank;
   (ii)   borrowing the money from an alternative source; or
   (iii)   a deposit guarantee scheme.

(b) *Does the client have sufficient money to complete?* A calculation will need to be made to ensure that the net sale proceeds are sufficient to cover the balance required to complete the purchase. It is important to take into account fees and disbursements when making this calculation. If there is a shortfall, then this must be discussed with the client and instructions taken as to how the shortfall is to be made up, for example by borrowing more money from the lender.

3.7 MORTGAGE ADVICE

A solicitor may sometimes be called upon to give advice on the different types of mortgages which are available. A client will usually have arranged a mortgage before instructing a solicitor, so the solicitor will just need to check that the client has taken all items of expenditure into account.

3.7.1 Financial services

When giving mortgage advice to a client it is important that a solicitor does not fall foul of the Financial Services and Markets Act 2000. This provides that in order to carry out 'regulated activities', a person must either be regulated by the Financial Conduct Authority or be covered by an exemption under the Financial Services and Markets Act 2000. The Financial Services and Markets Act 2000 (Regulated Activities) Order 2001, SI 2001/544 defines regulated activities and these will include arranging and/or advising a client about obtaining a regulated mortgage contract, or an insurance contract (e.g. endowment, mortgage protection, defective title, household contents or building policies).

   A regulated mortgage contract is a contract where:

(a)   the borrower is an individual or a trustee;
(b)   the lender takes a first legal charge over property in the UK; and
(c)   at least 40 per cent of the property is occupied by the borrower or a member of his immediate family, or is intended for their occupation.

Purely commercial mortgages, buy-to-let mortgages (unless the tenant is a member of the borrower's immediate family, or the borrower intends to occupy the property at some stage), second charges on residential property, or mortgages on overseas property are unregulated.

A solicitor carrying out a regulated activity in relation to a regulated mortgage contract, who is not authorised, will need to rely on the 'professional firms exemption'. This allows a solicitor to arrange or advise on a regulated mortgage contract, subject to certain conditions, even though the solicitor is not authorised by the Financial Conduct Authority. The ability to 'advise' under the professional firms exemption does not include recommending a client to enter into a regulated mortgage contract, except where that advice consists of an endorsement of a recommendation given to the client by an authorised person. A solicitor does not need to be authorised in order to introduce a client to an authorised or exempt person for independent advice. General advice about what type of mortgage a client should take out will not be a regulated activity.

3.7.2 Sources of mortgages

The most usual lenders are building societies and banks, but mortgages may sometimes be obtained from less usual sources such as insurance companies, finance companies, local authorities and the buyer's employer.

3.7.3 Types of mortgages

Common types of mortgage include:

(a) *Repayment mortgages* where the loan is repayable over a set period (usually 25 years) by monthly repayments consisting of both interest and capital.

(b) *Endowment mortgages* where the monthly repayments are made up of interest only. As well as mortgaging the property, the borrower also takes out a life assurance policy on his life. This policy may be assigned or mortgaged by a separate deed to the lender, although the more usual modern practice is to merely deposit it with the title deeds. When the policy matures, either on the death of the borrower or at the end of the term, it is expected to produce enough money to repay the mortgage capital.

(c) *Interest-only mortgages* where the monthly repayments are made up of interest only but there is no life assurance policy. The borrower must be advised that he will need to have some other way of paying off the mortgage at the end of the term.

(d) *Pension mortgages* where the loan is linked to a personal pension policy and the monthly repayments are made up of interest only. The proceeds of the pension on maturity are then used to repay the mortgage capital.

(e) *Sharia compliant mortgages.* Islamic law forbids the payment of interest and so there are a number of lenders which offer sharia compliant alternatives, for example the *Murabaha* under which the lender buys the property and immediately transfers it to the buyer at a profit. The price paid by the buyer to the lender is then repaid over a deferred period and consists of the price paid by the lender, less any deposit paid by the buyer, and an element of profit for allowing repayment over time.

3.8 TAXATION

3.8.1 Capital gains tax

Where appropriate, a seller should be advised at the initial interview about any possible liability to CGT as a result of the sale. A buyer may require advice about any possible liability he may face should he later sell the property. Capital gains tax is *prima facie* payable on the disposal of an interest in land. In practice it is rarely payable on the sale of a residential property because of the private residence exemption. Further details of CGT are available at **www.gov.uk/capital-gains-tax**.

3.8.1.1 *Private residence exemption*

Under the Taxation of Chargeable Gains Act 1992, s.222 CGT is payable on any gain made on the disposal of a chargeable asset. This includes freehold and leasehold property. Some transactions which are incidental to the sale of land also give rise to a charge to CGT, for example where a separate payment is made for the release or modification of an easement or covenant. Gifts also fall within the meaning of 'disposal' for the purpose of CGT. However, where the sale is of an individual's principal private dwelling house together with grounds of up to half a hectare (approximately one and a quarter acres) any gain is exempt from CGT.

This exemption will only apply if the dwelling house has been the seller's only or main residence throughout his period of ownership. In deciding this, the following periods of ownership during which the seller is absent may be disregarded:

(a)   the last 18 months of ownership (extended to 36 months if the seller is disabled or in long-term residential care);

(b)   the first 12 months of ownership if the house was being built, renovated or the owner could not sell his old house;

(c)   any temporary periods of absence not exceeding three years in total during the period of ownership;

(d)   any periods during which the seller was working outside the UK as an employee; and

(e)   any periods not exceeding four years in total during which the seller was prevented from living in the dwelling house because of his conditions of employment.

45

If the taxpayer is absent for longer periods, the proportion of the gain attributable to periods in excess of those mentioned above loses the benefit of the exemption and will therefore be chargeable to CGT.

Where a property is let during the period of ownership, it will cease to be the individual's only or main residence (unless the absence can be disregarded as above). Letting relief may be available.

If the grounds of the property exceed half a hectare, then CGT will be payable on the additional land unless the seller can show that such additional land is necessary for the reasonable enjoyment of the dwelling house.

A sale of part of the grounds will also be exempt provided that the part sold does not exceed half a hectare and it is sold before the dwelling house is sold.

If any part of the dwelling house is or has been used exclusively for business purposes, only part of the gain will be exempt. An example of this would be where a dentist uses part of the ground floor of his house as his surgery.

Where a person owns more than one dwelling house, an election needs to be made as to which one the exemption is to apply to. Such an election can be made within two years of acquiring a second property. Only one exemption is available to a married couple or civil partners who are living together. So, if they own more than one house they have to decide which house is to have the exemption. However, once made, the decision is revocable and can be changed.

3.8.1.2   Calculation of the gain

The gain is calculated by taking the sale price of the property and deducting from it the following:

(a)   the price which the seller paid for the property (or its base value in 1982 if purchased earlier than this);
(b)   incidental acquisition costs, including legal fees and disbursements;
(c)   costs of any improvements; and
(d)   incidental disposal costs.

Any gain may be reduced by carrying forward any losses from previous years and setting these off against the gain. A person's annual exemption can also be set against the final figure. Higher or additional rate taxpayers pay 28 per cent on their gains from residential property. Basic rate taxpayers pay 18 per cent on the gain where the total of their taxable income and the gain is within the basic income tax band, and 28 per cent on any amount above this.

3.8.2   Stamp duty land tax

SDLT is charged on land and property transactions. The tax rate and payment threshold can vary according to whether the property is in residential or non-residential use, and whether it is freehold or leasehold. SDLT relief is available for certain kinds of property or transaction. Further details of SDLT are available at **www.gov.uk/stamp-duty-land-tax**.

Acquisitions of land in Wales are subject to land transaction tax (see **www.gov.wales/land-transaction-tax-guide**).

3.8.2.1   SDLT rates for residential property

For those who are not first-time buyers, the table below applies for all freehold residential purchases and transfers and the premium paid for a new lease or the assignment of an existing lease. If the transaction involves the purchase of a new lease with a substantial rent, there may be an additional SDLT charge to that shown below, based on the rent.

Purchase price/lease premium or transfer value	SDLT rate
Up to £125,000	Zero
The next £125,000 (the portion from £125,001 to £250,000)	2%
The next £675,000 (the portion from £250,001 to £925,000)	5%
The next £575,000 (the portion from £925,001 to £1.5 million)	10%
The remaining amount (the portion above £1.5 million)	12%

Example If a house is purchased for £275,000, the SDLT the buyer owes is calculated as follows:

- 0% on the first £125,000 = £0
- 2% on the next £125,000 = £2,500
- 5% on the final £25,000 = £1,250
- Total SDLT = £3,750

A buyer will usually have to pay three per cent on top of the normal SDLT rates if buying a new residential property means that they will own more than one. A buyer will not pay the extra three per cent SDLT if the property they are buying is replacing their main residence and that has already been sold. If there is a delay selling their main residence and it has not been sold on the day of completion of the new purchase, the buyer will have to pay higher rates because they own two properties, but they may be able to get a refund if they sell their previous main home within 36 months.

There are different SDLT rules and rate calculations for:

- corporate bodies – a rate of 15 per cent applies to residential purchases of over £500,000 by certain corporate bodies and 'non-natural persons';
- people buying six or more residential properties in one transaction;
- shared ownership properties;
- multiple purchases or transfers between the same buyer and seller ('linked purchases');

- purchases that mean the buyer owns more than one property;
- companies and trusts buying residential property.

Certain transactions may be entitled to relief from SDLT. First-time buyers purchasing for £500,000 or less can claim relief so that no SDLT is payable on the first £300,000, and thereafter SDLT is payable at five per cent on the portion from £300,001 to £500,000. Relief is also available on transfers between group companies and purchases by charities. Certain transactions, such as where property is left in a will or is transferred following divorce or dissolution of a civil partnership, are exempt from SDLT.

3.8.2.2   SDLT on rent – new residential leasehold purchase

When a new residential lease has a substantial annual rent, SDLT is payable on both of the following, which are calculated separately and then added together:

(a)   the lease premium (purchase price); and
(b)   the 'net present value' (NPV) of the rent payable.

The NPV is based on the value of the total rent over the life of the lease and can be worked out using HMRC's online calculator at **www.tax.service.gov.uk/calculate-stamp-duty-land-tax/#/intro**.

In practice, SDLT only becomes payable on a fairly high rent – starting at around £4,500 a year for a 99-year lease, for example; however, the exact amount depends on the length of the lease.

NPV of rent – residential	SDLT rate (includes first-time buyers)
Up to £125,000	Zero
Over £125,000	1% of the value that exceeds £125,000

3.8.3   Annual tax on enveloped dwellings

The annual tax on enveloped dwellings (ATED) is an annual tax payable by companies, collective investment vehicles (e.g. a unit trust) and partnerships with company members, that own UK residential property valued at more than £500,000.

The property is said to be 'enveloped' because the ownership sits within a corporate 'wrapper' or 'envelope'. The amount of ATED is worked out using a banding system based on the value of the property. Its primary purpose is to discourage the use of corporate wrapper schemes as a method of avoiding SDLT. There are a number of reliefs from ATED designed to exempt genuine commercial activity. See **www.gov.uk/guidance/annual-tax-on-enveloped-dwellings-the-basics**.

3.9 ACTION AFTER THE INTERVIEW

3.9.1 Acting for the seller

The following action should be taken after the initial interview:

(a)   write up an attendance note setting out details of the instructions received from the client, the advice given and the time spent in the interview;

(b)   write to the seller confirming the instructions received and any advice given;

(c)   contact the estate agent and the buyer's solicitor either by letter or by telephone to confirm that you are instructed, and in the case of the estate agent to obtain a copy of the sale particulars if not already supplied;

(d)   obtain any title deeds;

(e)   apply for official copies of the register and the title plan;

(f)   send a TA6 Property Information Form and a TA10 Fittings and Contents Form to the seller (with a warning that these documents may require later re-verification). Explain to the seller the nature of the questions in the forms and ask the seller for documentation such as planning permissions, building regulations consents, plans, completion certificates and any guarantees.

If the property is leasehold, you should also:

(a)   obtain the lease or an official copy of the lease;

(b)   send a TA7 Leasehold Information Form (in addition to the TA6 Property Information Form) to the seller and obtain any documents that will be required, including a receipt for ground rent, service charge accounts and insurance details;

(c)   obtain from the seller the contact details for the landlord and/or managing agent and establish whether a standard form of landlord/management company replies to enquiries can be obtained and, if so, the cost;

(d)   consider submission of a questionnaire to the landlord/managing agent;

(e)   consider whether any third parties will need to consent to the sale (e.g. landlord or management company). If so, establish the costs of obtaining such consent. It should generally be accepted that the seller will discharge this liability.

3.9.2 Acting for the buyer

The following action should be taken after the initial interview:

(a)   write up an attendance note setting out details of the instructions received from the client, the advice given and the time spent in the interview;

(b)   write to the buyer confirming the instructions received and any advice given;

(c)   contact the estate agent and the seller's solicitor; again this can be either by letter or by telephone, and in the case of the estate agent a copy of the sale particulars should be requested if these have not already been supplied.

3.10 SUMMARY

- Full instructions should be taken at the outset of the transaction.
- Advice should be given on the costs of the transaction.
- When acting for the seller, you should check that there will be sufficient funds to discharge all outstanding mortgages.
- When acting for the buyer, you should check that there will be sufficient funds to complete the purchase.
- Advice should be given about any tax implications of the transaction.
- A buyer should be advised about the need for a mortgage, survey and insurance.
- Where a client is both selling and buying, instructions must be taken about synchronising the transactions.
- You must advise co-owners about the ways in which they can own the property.
- If co-owners hold as joint tenants, survivorship applies on the death of one co-owner and his share will pass automatically to the survivor.
- If co-owners hold as tenants in common, the shares should be recorded and on the death of a tenant in common his share will pass under his will or the intestacy rules.
- A joint tenancy is suitable for co-owners in a permanent relationship, such as a married couple or civil partners.
- You cannot act for more than one party if there is a client conflict or a significant risk of such a conflict.
- There will be a risk of a conflict if you act for both the seller and the buyer in the same transaction.
- It is usually possible to act for both the buyer and lender if the mortgage is on standard terms.
- You must keep your client's affairs confidential.
- Customer due diligence requirements are imposed on you by the Money Laundering, Terrorist Financing and Transfer of Funds (Information on the Payer) Regulations 2017.
- Watch out for signs of money laundering and mortgage fraud.
- A mortgage may be obtained from a bank, building society, employer or relative.
- A buyer will usually obtain a repayment mortgage or an interest-only mortgage.
- Advising on a residential mortgage is a regulated activity under the Financial Services and Markets Act 2000.
- A CGT liability may arise on the disposal of land.
- There is an exemption from CGT for gains made on the disposal of a principal private dwelling house.
- SDLT is charged on freehold and leasehold property transactions at rates depending on the type of property, the price and, if the property is leasehold, the rent.
- Acquisitions of land in Wales are subject to land transaction tax.

CHAPTER 4

Drafting the contract

The contract is prepared by the seller's solicitor, whose aim is to ensure that it deals with all the property which the seller wishes, and is able, to sell. The contract also contains the terms on which the property is sold. In this chapter we will look at how the contract should be drafted and the terms which it should include.

4.1 PRELIMINARY MATTERS

4.1.1 Obtain the title deeds

Before you can draft the contract, you first need to obtain the title deeds, if any, and apply for official copies of the register and the title plan.

Even though the Land Registration Act 2002 abolished land and charge certificates, they will still exist for titles registered prior to 13 October 2003. While they are no longer required for registration purposes, it is still necessary to request the certificate from either the seller or the seller's lender as there may be other documents with the certificate which will be required for the sale, e.g. copies of planning permissions, guarantees, etc.

If there is no mortgage on the property, the seller may have the title deeds or they may be with the seller's solicitor or the seller's bank. If there is a mortgage on the property, the title deeds will be held by the seller's lender. The deeds will usually only be released to the seller's solicitor if that particular solicitor is on the lender's panel of solicitors and, in addition, if the solicitor gives an undertaking to hold the title deeds to the lender's order, to return them on demand, and not to release them to a third party unless the mortgage is redeemed. When writing to the lender requesting the title deeds, the solicitor should include the mortgage account number in the letter.

Should the seller be using a solicitor who is not on the lender's panel, the lender will instruct its own solicitor and will supply the seller's solicitor with the title number so that the seller's solicitor can apply for official copies.

Where a mortgage is with a clearing bank, the seller's solicitor will normally have to give an undertaking in one of the forms which the Law Society has agreed with the banks. The solicitor must obtain the seller's written irrevocable authority before giving this undertaking.

4.1.2 Obtain official copies

Once you have the title number, you should apply on form OC1 to HM Land Registry for official copies of the register and the title plan. You can apply either by post or electronically. Form OC1 must be used when lodging a paper application. Paper official copies will normally only be issued in response to paper-based applications. If you apply through Business e-services, Business Gateway or NLIS you will receive electronic official copies where HM Land Registry has electronic versions of the documents requested. A fee is payable whichever method is used.

You can apply for an official copy of any documents referred to in the register of title and which are kept at HM Land Registry, such as conveyances imposing restrictive covenants, leases and mortgages. If you apply in writing you must use form OC2. If you apply through Business e-services, Business Gateway or NLIS you can also apply for an electronic official copy of a document referred to in the register, where HM Land Registry holds the original in electronic format. A fee is payable whichever method is used.

An official copy of the register shows the state of the register on the date on which the official copy is issued. As the register is updated on the day that an application for registration is received, and more than once in a day if necessary, an official copy is marked with both the date and time of issue so that it is clear that it is a true record of the entries on the register at that specific time. An official copy of a title plan is similarly dated and timed. The time will be important as it may be the case that different versions of the register exist on the same day. Official copies are also marked with the 'search from date' which the buyer's solicitor will use later in the transaction when carrying out his pre-completion search of the register.

At this initial stage you will use the official copy to check the current state of the register before you draft the contract. It is important that you check the official copy to ensure that there are no entries which you do not know about. If there are any, you must contact the seller and take immediate instructions.

4.1.3 Investigation of title

When acting for the seller, you should always investigate the title before you draft the contract to make sure that the seller is able to sell the property and that the title is in order. The methods of investigating title are set out in **Chapter 7**.

4.2 THE PARTS OF THE CONTRACT

A contract for the sale of land comprises:

(a) the particulars of sale, which describe the property; and
(b) the conditions of sale, which state the terms on which the property is being sold.

4.2.1 Open contract

A contract which expressly provides for nothing beyond describing the parties, the property and the price is called an 'open' contract. A contract may be totally open or partially open; the latter will occur where a particular point is not dealt with by the contract.

Where the contract is an open one, the rights and duties of the parties will be dealt with by a combination of statutory and common law. For example, under an open contract:

(a) the seller will sell the fee simple free from encumbrances;
(b) the seller will show a good title;
(c) vacant possession will be given on completion;
(d) completion will be within a reasonable time; and
(e) time is not 'of the essence of the contract'.

4.2.2 Standard Conditions of Sale

As it is clearly unsatisfactory to rely on the open contract rules, most contracts will adopt standard conditions of sale to deal with procedural matters. The conditions most commonly used by solicitors are the Standard Conditions of Sale (fifth edition – 2018 revision) and a standard form of contract incorporating these Conditions is usually used (see **Appendix A**).

The Law Society Conveyancing Protocol (2019) discourages the addition of further clauses to the standard contract. Further clauses should not be included unless they are necessary to accord with current law, or specific and informed instructions have been given by the seller that inclusion of such clauses is necessary and they are required for the purposes of the particular transaction.

4.2.3 Special conditions

In order to deal with any matters which are specific to an individual property, individual parties or an individual transaction, solicitors use special conditions. On the standard form of contract these are found on the back page. These can be used to deal with matters which are not adequately covered by the Standard Conditions of Sale. Standard condition (SC) 1.1.4 provides that where there is a conflict between a special condition and a standard condition, the special condition will prevail.

A special condition must be used to make amendments to the standard conditions rather than making an alteration to the relevant standard condition on the inner pages of the standard form of contract.

4.3 THE PARTICULARS OF SALE

The particulars of sale contain a physical description of the land being sold and also a description of the estate which is being sold, i.e. whether it is freehold or leasehold.

4.3.1 Physical description

You should take care to describe the property accurately. In practice, where the property can be clearly identified by its postal address and has clear boundaries, then it will usually be described by means of its postal address and the title number. Where the property cannot be clearly identified, e.g. on a sale of part, a more detailed description will be required together with a plan. In such cases, the description of the land in the property register or in the title deeds will be used as the basis for the description.

A substantial difference between the area of the property as stated in the contract and what it actually is can give the buyer the right to rescind the contract (see **4.3.3**). Lesser inaccuracies may lead to the seller being obliged to accept a reduction in the purchase price. If measurements are part of the description, these must be accurate.

A plan may be attached to the contract as part of the description. Where the sale involves only part of the seller's property a plan is essential so that both the parties understand exactly what is the subject matter of the sale (see **4.5.1**). Care must be taken to ensure that the plan accurately identifies the extent of the property to be sold and its boundaries. It is advisable to have the plan prepared by an architect or surveyor to a scale of at least 1:1250. However, the scale of the plan must be appropriate to the transaction and the use of small-scale ordnance survey plans when selling plots of land or where a house is being split into flats will be inadequate (see *Scarfe* v. *Adams* [1981] 1 All ER 843). All measurements on the plan must be metric.

The land being sold should be edged red. On the sale of part of the seller's land, the land being retained by the seller should be edged blue. A right of way should be shown by a broken line of a different colour. Ownership of boundaries should be indicated by inward facing 'T' marks.

A plan may be incorporated into the property description by using one of the following two phrases:

(a) *'For identification purposes only'*. In this case the verbal description will be paramount and the plan only illustrative. In the event of a dispute the verbal description will prevail.

(b) *'More particularly delineated'*. In this case the plan will prevail in the event of a dispute. It is therefore vital that if these words are used the plan is to scale.

These two phrases are mutually exclusive and should not be combined (*Neilson* v. *Poole* (1969) 20 P & CR 909).

4.3.2 Legal description

The legal description consists of:

(a) *The estate or interest.* The description of the property will include a description of the estate or interest which is being sold. In the standard form of contract the description of the legal estate or interest is dealt with by simply deleting the reference to either freehold or leasehold on the first page.

(b) *Benefits passing with the property.* Rights, such as easements and restrictive covenants which are for the benefit of the property, should be expressly referred to in the particulars of sale. When the property is conveyed to the buyer the Law of Property Act 1925, s.62, will come into operation so that, subject to any contrary intention expressed in the conveyance, all privileges, rights, easements and advantages appertaining or reputed to appertain to the property will pass to the buyer. It should be noted that s.62 does not apply to the contract, only to the transfer.

(c) *Burdens affecting the property.* The seller is bound to disclose all latent defects known to him which affect the title, including any encumbrances affecting the property, such as restrictive covenants, easements and leases. These may be disclosed either in the particulars or in the special conditions. It is sometimes found that existing liabilities are referred to in the particulars and new liabilities in the special conditions – this is a matter of practice only. In the standard form of contract the existing burdens are set out under the reference to 'Specified incumbrances' on the first page.

4.3.3 Misdescription

4.3.3.1 Definition

An error in the particulars of sale will amount to a misdescription. Such errors can include:

(a) describing the estate incorrectly, e.g. describing leasehold land as freehold land;

(b) wrongly describing the extent of the land being sold.

4.3.3.2 Remedies where the misdescription is substantial or material

If the misdescription is substantial or material, the buyer is entitled to rescind the contract.

To be material the misdescription must affect the subject matter of the contract so that it may be reasonably supposed that, but for the misdescription, the buyer might never have entered into the contract at all. Whether or not the misdescription is material is a question of fact to be decided in the light of the individual circumstances of each case.

The above comments apply equally where the misdescription is an inaccurately drawn plan or map.

Instead of rescinding the contract, the buyer may elect to proceed with the transaction subject to a price reduction for the inaccuracy. However, this right to a reduction may be barred if the buyer does not claim before completion. In addition, the right will be lost if the misdescription cannot be quantified in monetary terms.

4.3.3.3 Remedies where the misdescription is not substantial or is immaterial

Where the misdescription is not substantial or is immaterial (and assuming that it is not also a misrepresentation), the buyer has no right to rescind the contract.

In the absence of fraud, the buyer must complete subject to a price abatement if the misdescription affects the value of the property. This procedure is justified on the basis that where the misdescription is immaterial the buyer is getting substantially what he expected.

The buyer should claim the price abatement before completion takes place, because once a conveyance is taken by the buyer without making this claim it is deemed to have been waived unless the buyer could not have discovered the truth before completion.

4.3.3.4 Implied title guarantee

If the misdescription is embodied in the purchase deed, the buyer may have an action against the seller for breach of the implied title guarantee.

4.3.3.5 Does the seller have any remedies?

The seller has no right to rescind the contract where the misdescription is in the buyer's favour, such as where the contract gives the buyer a greater area of land than the buyer bargained for. Nor can the seller compel the buyer to pay an increased purchase price.

4.3.3.6 Conditions of sale and misdescription

A clause in a contract which purports to deprive the buyer of his right to rescind the contract or to claim compensation because of the misdescription will not prevent the buyer from resisting an application for specific performance by the seller where the misdescription is material. However, if the buyer wishes to complete the purchase, such a clause will deny him a price reduction. In a situation where the seller seeks to compel the completion of the contract against the wishes of the buyer, such a condition will not prevent the court ordering a reduction in the purchase price.

In *Walker* v. *Boyle* [1982] 1 All ER 634, the court considered the effect of one particular condition from a former set of general conditions. The buyer was entitled to rescind the contract because of the seller's innocent misrepresentation when the true facts were within the seller's knowledge and the buyer could reasonably have refused to exchange contracts if he had known these. The seller was not entitled to rely on the relevant condition and, even if he could, the condition did not satisfy the test of reasonableness contained in the Unfair Contract Terms Act 1977, s.11, which applied as the condition was an exclusion clause within the Misrepresentation Act 1967, s.3.

Standard condition 7.1 will cover misdescription as well as misrepresentation.

4.3.4   The seller's duty of disclosure

Before we look at the conditions of sale, we must first consider the seller's duty of disclosure.

4.3.4.1   Open contract rule

As the seller is selling the fee simple free from encumbrances, he must disclose latent encumbrances and defects in his title of which he is aware.

(a)   *Latent defects.* Latent defects are matters affecting the seller's title which would not be discoverable on a reasonable inspection of the property by the buyer, e.g. restrictive covenants. However, latent defects which have ceased to be enforceable do not have to be disclosed. In *Hepworth* v. *Pickles* [1900] 1 Ch 108, a restrictive covenant had been breached for the past 20 years and it was held to have been waived or released as the breach had been quite open, and no disclosure was necessary.

(b)   *Patent defects.* Other defects are patent and the buyer is deemed to have knowledge of these. Patent defects are apparent on inspection, and so a buyer should therefore always arrange for the property to be inspected otherwise he will be deemed to have constructive notice if a reasonably careful inspection would have disclosed them.

(c)   *Physical defects.* A seller is not required to disclose physical defects in the land, whether these are latent or patent.

(d)   *Local land charges.* If the seller is aware of a local land charge it must be disclosed (see *Rignall Developments Ltd* v. *Halil* [1987] 3 All ER 170). In the case of non-disclosure, a buyer will be entitled to insist that the seller removes a removable land charge, e.g. a financial charge. In the case of an irremovable charge, the buyer may be able to rescind or claim damages.

4.3.4.2 Standard condition 3

Where the contract is governed by the Standard Conditions of Sale, SC 3 deals with the seller's duty of disclosure.

Under SC 3.1.1, the seller is selling the property free from encumbrances other than those listed in SC 3.1.2.

The encumbrances listed in SC 3.1.2 are:

(a) *Those specified in the contract.* By disclosing encumbrances in the agreement, the seller will perform his duty of disclosure under SC 3.1.1. Thus, if the seller knows of any encumbrance it must be clearly identified in the contract. This will be done by a special condition identifying the encumbrance and stating that the property is sold subject to it.

(b) *Those discoverable by inspection of the property before the date of the contract.* In practice it is usual for the seller to disclose all encumbrances, whether or not they could be discovered on an inspection of the property.

(c) *Those the seller does not and could not reasonably know about.* This benefits the seller as it puts the risk of any hidden encumbrances on to the buyer. However, there is no definition of knowledge and this may well include imputed and constructive knowledge as well as actual knowledge.

(d) *Those, other than mortgages, which the buyer knows about.* It is not considered fair for a buyer to be able to take action against a seller in respect of a matter which he knew about, but which was not expressly a matter subject to which the property was sold. It means that the property is sold subject to any encumbrance the buyer knows about, other than mortgages as these are usually paid off before or immediately after completion.

(e) *Entries made before the date of the contract in any public register, except those maintained by the Land Registry or its Land Charges Department or by Companies House.* As a result of this the buyer must inspect other registers, e.g. the local land charges register, as he will take the property subject to any entries on those registers.

(f) *Public requirements.* A public requirement is defined in SC 1.1.1(j) as 'any notice, order or proposal given or made (whether before or after the date of the contract) by a body acting on statutory authority'. Examples include an enforcement notice issued by the local planning authority, and an obligation to pay the cost of road works.

Standard condition 3.1.3 continues the seller's duty of disclosure by providing that after the contract is made the seller has a duty to give the buyer without delay written details of:

(a) any new public requirement; and

(b) anything in writing which he learns about concerning a matter covered by SC 3.1.2.

4.3.4.3 Disclosure in the contract of defects in title

The seller must disclose in the contract any defects in the title, e.g. restrictive covenants. Under the open contract rule the seller cannot force a defective title on a buyer unless he makes a full disclosure of the defect in a way which can be understood by a reasonable person and the buyer then agrees to accept the title offered.

If the seller is in doubt as to whether a matter should be disclosed as a latent defect or not, the safest course is to disclose the matter in the contract and provide that the buyer cannot raise any requisitions after exchange of contracts in respect of the defect. In the standard form of contract, SC 4.2.1 provides that the buyer cannot raise any requisitions after exchange of contracts on any title shown by the seller before the contract was made or in relation to the matters covered by SC 3.1.2.

By clearly disclosing the defect, the seller gives the buyer an opportunity to make further enquiries before exchange of contracts. If the buyer is not then prepared to accept the risk involved, he can refuse to proceed to exchange. Sometimes the buyer will proceed after obtaining defective title indemnity insurance.

Examples of how to deal with defects are as follows:

(a) A property is subject to a restrictive covenant which requires consent by a third party to any alterations to the property. The property has been altered and there is no evidence of the consent with the deeds. The consent cannot now be obtained. The seller will deal with this in a special condition in which, first, the restrictive covenant will be disclosed and which, secondly, will provide that 'the buyer shall assume, although there is no evidence that consent was obtained and consent cannot now be obtained, that the appropriate consent was obtained for the alteration'.

(b) A property is subject to a restrictive covenant but details of it are not available as the conveyance containing the covenant has been lost. In a special condition the seller will provide that 'the buyer shall raise no requisition or objection in relation to the restrictive covenant contained in a conveyance dated .... and made between .... and .... details of which the seller is unable to produce'.

4.3.4.4 Effect of non-disclosure

If the effect of the non-disclosure is substantial the buyer may rescind the contract. If it is not substantial, then the buyer must complete with a price abatement.

4.3.4.5 Green Deal

If there is a Green Deal plan (see **1.9**), the seller's solicitor must ensure that the contract includes an acknowledgement by the buyer that the bill payer at the property is liable to make payments under the Green Deal plan and that certain terms of that plan are binding on the bill payer.

4.4 CONDITIONS OF SALE

4.4.1 Title guarantee

The contract will specify which of the implied covenants for title under the Law of Property (Miscellaneous Provisions) Act 1994 the seller will give the buyer when the property is transferred. If the seller sells with full title guarantee, the buyer will be given the benefit of the full range of covenants implied by the 1994 Act. A more limited set of covenants is implied if the seller sells with limited title guarantee. It is also possible for the seller to state that he is giving no title guarantee.

4.4.1.1 Full title guarantee

A full title guarantee will usually be given where the seller has a good title and knowledge of the encumbrances affecting the property.

Where a full title guarantee is given, the following covenants are implied:

(a)   That the seller has the right to dispose of the property.
(b)   That the seller will at his own cost do all that he reasonably can to transfer the title.
(c)   That the property is disposed of free from encumbrances, other than any charges, encumbrances or rights which the seller does not and could not reasonably be expected to know about.

If the property is leasehold, then in addition to the above implied covenants, a further covenant is implied that the lease is subsisting at the time of the disposal and that there is no breach of covenant which would give rise to forfeiture.

4.4.1.2 Limited title guarantee

A limited title guarantee will usually be given by a personal representative, or a trustee who holds the property on trust for persons other than himself.

Where a limited title guarantee is given, the implied covenants set out in (a) and (b) in 4.4.1.1 are also implied. However, the implied covenant set out in (c) in 4.4.1.1 is limited so that the seller covenants that he has not encumbered the property and that he is not aware that anyone else has done so since the last disposition for value.

If the property is leasehold, then in addition a covenant is also implied that the lease is subsisting at the time of the disposal and that there is no breach of covenant which would give rise to forfeiture.

4.4.1.3 No title guarantee

A seller who has little or no knowledge of the property will not usually give any title guarantee. Other situations where no title guarantee will be given include gifts or where the title is possessory. When a lender sells under a power of sale, it is common for no title guarantee to be given.

4.4.1.4 Standard Conditions of Sale

The standard form of contract provides a space on the front for the seller's solicitor to state whether the seller is giving a full title guarantee or a limited title guarantee. Special condition 2 provides that the seller will transfer the property with either full title guarantee or a limited title guarantee as specified on the front page of the agreement. Standard condition 4.6.2, which provides that if the agreement is silent as to the title guarantee the seller will transfer with full title guarantee, will apply. Accordingly, if no title guarantee is to be given, then the Standard Conditions of Sale require amendment by writing in the appropriate space on the front: 'No title guarantee is given'.

4.4.1.5 Lender requirements

Paragraph 5.18.1 of the Lenders' Handbook provides that while a borrower should try to obtain a full title guarantee from the seller, the lender does not insist on this. The lender will, however, require the borrower to give a full title guarantee in the mortgage deed. Paragraph D.6 of the BSA Mortgage Instructions provides that the lender requires the borrower to give a full title guarantee in the mortgage deed. These provisions mean that if either a limited title guarantee or no title guarantee is given by the seller, the borrower must still give a full title guarantee in the mortgage.

4.4.2 Vacant possession

4.4.2.1 Open contract

Under an open contract it will be an implied term of the contract that the property is sold with vacant possession.

4.4.2.2 Standard Conditions of Sale

In the standard form of contract, the position is covered by special condition 4 which provides that either the property is sold with vacant possession on completion, or it is sold subject to those leases or tenancies set out in the contract. The seller's solicitor will delete whichever alternative does not apply. If vacant possession is not being given, then full details of any lease or tenancy must be set out in the contract.

4.4.2.3 Leases affecting the property

Standard condition 3.3 contains provisions which apply where any part of the property is sold subject to a lease.

4.4.2.4 Non-owning spouse or civil partner

The Family Law Act 1996, Sched.4, para.3, implies into a contract for the sale of a dwelling house which has been the matrimonial or civil partnership home of the seller and his spouse or civil partner and which is not held by them as co-trustees, a term that if the property is sold with vacant possession the seller will, before completion, have discharged any notice registered by the spouse or civil partner to protect his rights of occupation.

This provision applies even though:

(a) the seller did not know that such a charge had been registered; or

(b) the charge is registered after the contract has been made.

The entry on the register is cancelled by using Form HR4. The application must be supported by evidence that will satisfy HM Land Registry that the registration should be cancelled. This evidence should be one of the following:

(a) a death certificate;

(b) an office copy of the decree absolute or nullity;

(c) an office copy of the final dissolution or nullity or presumption of death order, or of the separation order, relating to the civil partnership;

(d) an office copy of a court order ending the home rights; or

(e) a release of the home rights signed by the spouse or civil partner and either made by letter or using form HR4.

A spouse or civil partner may also have an equitable interest in the property and so should give written confirmation that he consents to the sale and be made a party to the contract.

Special Condition 7 contains appropriate wording for such circumstances. In other cases, a suggested form of wording for a release both of a statutory right of occupation and of an equitable interest is:

> I [name of spouse or civil partner] of [address of spouse or civil partner] agree to the sale of [address of property] and agree that I will vacate the property by the completion date. I hereby release my rights of occupation under the Family Law Act 1996 Part IV in the property. I also agree to release any equitable interest which I may have in the property, such release to be effective from the date of completion of the sale of the property. I agree to remove any registrations made by me in relation to these rights before the date of completion.

It is important to ensure that the spouse or civil partner giving this release takes independent legal advice.

4.4.2.5   Other occupiers

If there is anyone else occupying the property, e.g. a cohabitee, enquiry should be made to see whether they have an equitable interest in the property. If they have then they must either release their interest in writing or, preferably, join in the contract to release their interest.

4.4.3   Title to be shown

Standard condition 4.1.2 provides that the buyer must be supplied with official copies of the register, the title plan and any document referred to in the register of title and kept by HM Land Registry. A buyer should insist on official copies and should not accept photocopies of the register in lieu of these as he will not then have a 'search from date' which he will need later (see **10.5.1**) and which can only be obtained from official copies issued by HM Land Registry.

There is space on the front page of the standard form of contract to include the title number. In addition, if the title is not absolute the class of title should be stated.

4.4.4   Completion

4.4.4.1   Open contract

Under an open contract, completion will take place within a reasonable time.

4.4.4.2   Standard Conditions of Sale

Standard condition 6.1.1 provides that the completion date is 20 working days after the date of the contract.

Standard condition 6.1.2 provides that if the money due on completion is received after 2.00 pm, completion will be treated as taking place on the next working day for the purposes of calculating apportionments and compensation for late completion. This is not a time limit on completion, and if a time for completion is required it must be dealt with by way of a special condition. There is also an obligation on the seller under SC 6.1.3 to vacate the property by 2.00 pm otherwise SC 6.1.2 will not apply.

Standard condition 6.7 provides that the buyer is to pay the money due on completion by a direct transfer of cleared funds from an account held in the name of a conveyancer at a clearing bank and, if appropriate, an unconditional release of a deposit held by a stakeholder. Standard condition 1.1.1(b) defines a 'clearing bank' as a bank admitted by the Bank of England as a direct participant in its CHAPS system.

4.4.4.3 Time of the essence

In a routine transaction it would not be normal to make time of the essence in relation to completion as delay is common. 'Time of the essence' means that the actual date for completion is a condition of the contract for which rescission may be available for non-compliance. Under SC 6.1.1, time will not be of the essence unless a notice to complete has been served. Occasionally it will be implied, e.g. where the contract deals with a wasting asset such as a short lease or the sale of a business as a going concern. Time may be made of the essence by a special condition in the contract.

4.4.4.4 Special condition

It is usual to provide a specific date for completion by way of special condition. This date will be agreed between the parties and should be added just before exchange of contracts rather than when the contract is drafted. There is a space on the front page of the standard form of contract in which to add the completion date. Although time for completion on this date will not usually be of the essence, important consequences will follow from late completion.

If the client is both selling and buying, it is important that the completion dates for both transactions are the same.

Consideration should also be given as to whether the 2.00 pm time limit in SC 6.1.2 should be varied. This can be done using special condition 5. If the seller has a related purchase, the sale proceeds will usually be needed to complete the purchase. Obviously if both contracts provide for a 2.00 pm time limit, difficulties can arise if the money on the sale is received very close to 2.00 pm, and the seller may then have little or no time in which to complete the purchase before the deadline and he may then be liable to pay compensation to his seller for late completion. The solution would be for the seller's solicitor to amend the time for completion in the sale contract by way of special condition so that it is earlier than 2.00 pm, say 12.00 noon or 1.00 pm. This will then give the seller time to complete the related transaction before the 2.00 pm deadline in that contract.

4.4.5 Deposit

4.4.5.1 Open contract

Under an open contract no deposit is payable. However, a seller will invariably require a deposit to be paid on exchange as it acts as a part payment and also as a guarantee that the buyer will complete. There must therefore be specific provision in the contract for a deposit to be paid.

4.4.5.2 Capacities in which a deposit can be held

A deposit can be held by the seller's solicitor either as agent for the seller or as stakeholder.

If it is held as agent for the seller it belongs to the seller and his instructions as to its use must be followed. Thus, it can be paid over to the seller or used towards the deposit on a property which the seller may be purchasing.

However, if it is held as stakeholder the money belongs to neither the buyer nor the seller and it may not be paid to either party without the other's consent, except that on completion it must be paid to the seller.

There are dangers for the buyer where the seller's solicitor holds the deposit as agent for the seller, as if the buyer becomes entitled to have the deposit returned to him he may find that the seller's solicitor no longer has it. In this case the buyer will have a right of action against the seller but the seller may be bankrupt or otherwise be unable to pay. The buyer will also have a lien over the property in respect of his deposit and he may protect this by way of a notice.

If the contract is silent about the capacity in which the seller's solicitor will hold the deposit, then he will hold it as agent for the seller.

4.4.5.3 Standard Conditions of Sale

Under SC 2.2.1, the buyer is to pay a deposit of 10 per cent of the purchase price no later than the date of the contract. Under SC 2.2.4 the deposit is to be paid except in the case of an auction:

(a) by electronic means from an account held in the name of a conveyancer at a clearing bank to an account in the name of the seller's conveyancer or (in a case where SC 2.2.5 applies) a conveyancer nominated by him and maintained at a clearing bank; or

(b) to the seller's conveyancer or (in a case where SC 2.2.5 applies) a conveyancer nominated by him by cheque drawn on a solicitor's or licensed conveyancer's client account.

There is space on the front page of the standard form of contract to include the amount of the deposit.

In many transactions the seller will accept a deposit of less than 10 per cent. In this situation a special condition to this effect must be included in the contract. The seller's solicitor must explain to the seller that there are risks involved in accepting a reduced deposit, and following *Morris* v. *Duke-Cohan & Co.* (1975) 119 Sol Jo 826, the seller's express authority to accept a reduced deposit should be obtained, otherwise the solicitor may be negligent in accepting such a deposit.

Where a reduced deposit has been paid and the seller becomes entitled to forfeit the deposit, SC 6.8.3 provides that if the seller serves a notice to complete on the buyer, the buyer must forthwith pay a further deposit equal to the balance of a 10 per cent deposit.

Standard condition 2.2.5 allows the seller to use all or any part of the deposit received on his sale as a deposit on a related purchase of a residence in England and Wales provided that it is held on similar terms. The effect of this is that the deposit used in this way is held by the seller's solicitor as agent for the seller, and must ultimately be held by a solicitor as stakeholder. Any deposit which is not used by the seller in a purchase must be held by the seller's solicitor as stakeholder with accrued interest being paid to the seller on completion.

The buyer's solicitor should always enquire as to whether the seller is to use the deposit under SC 2.2.5, and if he is then the buyer should also ask where the deposit has been sent.

Should the deposit cheque be dishonoured when first presented, SC 2.2.2 allows the seller, within seven working days of being notified that the cheque has been dishonoured, to give the buyer notice that the contract is discharged. This condition reflects the decision in *Millichamp* v. *Jones* [1983] 1 All ER 267. It should be noted that the Standard Conditions of Sale contain no obligation on the seller to re-present the cheque.

4.4.5.4   Pre-contract deposits

A buyer will sometimes pay a pre-contract deposit before exchange of contracts as a sign of good faith. In the majority of cases, these are paid to the estate agent when the buyer makes an offer. Once contracts have been exchanged, the question of the pre-contract deposit is to be governed by the terms of the contract. It would seem that the seller would be liable if the estate agent defaulted at this stage.

Under the Estate Agents Act 1979, pre-contract deposits paid to estate agents are to be held on trust for the person who is entitled to call for them to be paid over to him. Trust monies cannot be seized by the estate agent's trustee in bankruptcy.

4.4.5.5   Interest payable on the deposit

Under SC 2.2.6 interest is to be paid to the seller on a deposit held by the seller's solicitor as stakeholder.

4.4.6   Interest rate

The interest rate specified in the contract will be that which is payable on the balance of the purchase money should completion be delayed. It will usually be four per cent above the base lending rate of one of the clearing banks. There is a space on the front page of the standard form of contract to include an interest rate.

If no rate is specifically included, SC 1.1.1(e) provides that it will be the Law Society's interest rate from time to time in force. This is set at four per cent above the base lending rate of Barclays Bank plc.

It is important to ensure that the rate of interest in the contract is the same as that being imposed on any related transaction.

4.4.7 Encumbrances affecting the property

Existing encumbrances, such as restrictive covenants, must be disclosed in the contract and there is space to do this on the front page of the standard form of contract. The sale will then be subject to these.

As covenants may continue to bind the seller after completion, there is the possibility that he may later be sued for a breach committed by a successor in title. As protection, an indemnity covenant should be included. This will then allow the seller to be indemnified by the buyer should he be sued for breach of covenant.

Under SC 4.6.4 the purchase deed is to include a covenant by the buyer:

(a)   to indemnify the seller against liability for any future breach of a covenant for which the seller will remain liable after completion; and

(b)   to perform the covenant.

4.4.8 Insurance

4.4.8.1 Open contract

At common law the rule is that the risk in the property will pass to the buyer on exchange of contracts. Consequently, the buyer must insure from exchange of contracts as he will still have to complete if the property is damaged between exchange and completion unless the damage is due to a breach by the seller of his duty to take reasonable care.

In certain circumstances, the buyer may be able to claim against the seller's insurance policy under the Law of Property Act 1925, s.47.

4.4.8.2 Standard Conditions of Sale

Standard condition 5.1.1 provides that the buyer bears the risk from the date of the contract.

Even though the risk passes to the buyer on exchange, the seller may still have an obligation to insure the property between exchange and completion by virtue of SC 5.1.2. This provides that the seller is obliged to insure if the contract so provides or if the property is leasehold and the seller (whether as landlord or as tenant) is obliged to insure under the terms of the lease. Standard condition 5.1.3 sets out the seller's obligations where he is required to insure.

Under SC 5.1.4, where the property is leasehold and insurance is effected by the landlord or other third party, the seller is to use reasonable efforts to ensure that the insurance is maintained until completion and if, before completion, the building suffers any loss or damage, the seller is to assign to the buyer any rights that the seller may have in the policy monies.

Standard condition 5.1.5 clarifies the position as regards 'double insurance'. This is where both the seller and buyer insure the property between exchange and completion. Standard condition 5.1.5 provides that where a payment under the buyer's insurance is reduced because the property is covered under an insurance policy taken out by or on behalf of the seller, then, provided the seller is not obliged to insure the property under SC 5.1.2, the purchase price is to be abated by the amount of that reduction.

Standard condition 5.1.6 specifically provides that the Law of Property Act 1925, s.47 does not apply.

4.4.9 Fixtures and fittings

Fixtures are things which are or have become part of the property, e.g. fitted shelving. Fittings are chattels in the property which do not form part of the real property, e.g. carpets and curtains.

In the absence of anything to the contrary in the contract, fittings are not included in the contract for the sale of the property, while fixtures are.

It may sometimes be difficult to decide whether something is a fixture or a fitting. A chattel may be affixed to the land but may not be a fixture. To become a fixture a chattel must be affixed substantially to the land for the purpose of improving the land as land. For a decision on what is a fixture, see *TSB Bank plc* v. *Botham* (1997) 73 P & CR D1.

Because of this difficulty, fittings which are included in the sale should be set out in the contract, as should any fixtures which the seller wishes to remove. The Standard Conditions of Sale refer to 'contents' rather than 'chattels'. Special condition 3 of the standard form of contract makes clear which contents are included in the sale and which fixtures are excluded by reference to an attached list. The Protocol requires the seller's solicitor to obtain information relating to fixtures and fittings from the seller using the Fittings and Contents Form (TA10 Fittings and Contents Form). This is then sent to the buyer's solicitor as part of the contract bundle. There is also provision on the front page of the standard form of contract to state any separate consideration payable for any contents included in the sale. This is referred to as the 'Contents price'.

Ownership of the contents will pass to the buyer on completion under SC 9. This also provides that, whether or not a separate price is being paid for the contents, the contract will take effect as a contract for sale of goods. As a result, there will be an implied warranty under the Sale of Goods Act 1979, s.12 that the seller has the right to sell the contents.

4.5 SALE OF PART

On the sale of part of the seller's property, the seller's solicitor must consider:

(a)   the description of the property to be sold;
(b)   the description of the property to be retained by the seller;

(c)   the grant of easements to the buyer over the seller's retained land;
(d)   the reservation of easements to the seller over the part of the seller's land being sold;
(e)   the imposition of new covenants; and
(f)   obtaining the consent of the seller's lender to the sale.

4.5.1   The description of the property

It will be necessary to prepare an accurate description of the property to be sold. The description of the land in the seller's register of title, or title deeds, can be adapted for this purpose. The description should refer to a scale plan showing the extent of the property. As previously mentioned, this scale must be a metric one. If it is not possible to use a scale plan, then the measurements of the land must be included in the written description of the property being sold.

When preparing the description, the following matters should be considered:

(a)   Do the particulars accurately describe the property to be sold?
(b)   Do the particulars refer to a plan, and is this of sufficient size and scale accurately to identify the extent of the property to be sold and the routes of easements, etc.?
(c)   Is a scale plan required, and is it accurate?
(d)   If the plan is not to scale, is it referred to as being for identification purposes only?

4.5.2   Retained land

If the seller is granting and reserving easements, it will be necessary to include a description of the property which the seller is retaining. Again, reference should be made to a plan showing the extent of the retained land, and the plan used in the description of the land to be sold can be used to show the extent of the retained land as well. The Standard Conditions of Sale do not contain a definition of retained land.

4.5.3   The grant of new easements

Under an open contract the buyer may on completion obtain easements over the seller's retained land which:

(a)   are easements of necessity;
(b)   arise under the rule in *Wheeldon* v. *Burrows* (1879) 12 Ch D 31. This rule states that the buyer will be impliedly granted all quasi-easements which:

   •   are continuous and apparent;
   •   are necessary for the reasonable enjoyment of the land to be sold; and
   •   have been and are at the time of the sale used by the seller for the benefit of the land to be sold;

(c)   are created by the Law of Property Act 1925, s.62 where, at the time of sale, the land to be sold and the retained land are occupied by different persons.

There will always be doubt over the application of these rules and so in practice it is better to exclude them by special condition and then expressly grant the buyer specific easements necessary to fit the particular circumstances.

Examples of common easements which a buyer may need are:

(a)   a right of way so that the buyer has access to the property;
(b)   a right to lay new drains, cables and pipes;
(c)   a right to use and maintain existing or new drains, cables and pipes (including a right of access to maintain them);
(d)   a right of light; and
(e)   a right of support.

In the case of a right of way, the seller's solicitor should consider:

(a)   whether the right should be for a particular class of user, e.g. pedestrians; and
(b)   whether the right should be exercised only at specified times of day or only for a particular purpose.

In the case of all easements the following matters should be considered:

(a)   Is the route of the right of way or drain shown on the plan?
(b)   Who is to be responsible for repairs and maintenance?
(c)   Will the buyer have to enter the retained land in order to inspect, repair or maintain?
(d)   Is the buyer to have a restricted right of access to inspect, e.g. must he give 24 hours' notice unless it is an emergency?
(e)   Should the buyer be made to cause no unnecessary damage and to make good all damage caused while inspecting or maintaining?
(f)   In the situation where the buyer has to install a new cable or pipe, should he be made to finish the work within a specified period after completion?
(g)   Is the consent of the seller's lender required?

4.5.4 Rights of light and air

The buyer may acquire rights of light and air under the rule in *Wheeldon* v. *Burrows* or the Law of Property Act 1925, s.62. Such rights could restrict the future development of the retained land. Consequently, they are normally excluded by way of a special condition.

4.5.5 The reservation of easements

If the seller wishes to reserve easements over the land being sold, then express provision for these must be made in the contract, as neither the rule in *Wheeldon* v. *Burrows* nor the Law of Property Act 1925, s.62 apply to reserve easements.

In the case of reservations, the seller's solicitor should consider the following:

(a) Will the seller need to continue to use a right of way, or a drain, cable or pipe, passing through the property to be sold?

(b) If he does, then express reservations must be included in the contract by way of special condition. When drafting these, regard should be had to the considerations which apply to the drafting of easements.

(c) In addition, it may be considered necessary to include, for the seller's protection, a general reservations clause dealing with all easements, quasi-easements, etc., currently enjoyed by the property as a whole.

(d) Should rights of light and air be expressly reserved so that the seller's freedom to use the retained land in the future is preserved?

4.5.6 The imposition of new covenants

The seller may wish to impose covenants over the land which he is selling, e.g. covenants relating to the use of the land. Such covenants must be expressly provided for by way of a special condition, which will set out the covenants and provide that the buyer will enter into them in the purchase deed.

The wording of the covenants is important, as their enforceability against later owners depends on their being:

(a) negative in nature;

(b) expressly for the benefit of the retained land; and

(c) protected by way of a notice on the charges register of the buyer's title.

The burden of positive covenants does not run and their enforcement will depend on there being a chain of indemnity covenants.

Matters to be considered when drafting the contract are:

(a) Should new restrictive covenants be imposed? If so, what restrictions will protect the retained land without imposing unnecessary constraints on the buyer?

(b) Consider imposing restrictions in respect of:

- the erection of new buildings on the property;
- the use of the property;
- the repair and maintenance of buildings on the property;
- nuisance.

(c) Will the covenants be negative in nature?

(d) Does the wording of the covenants ensure that an enforceable obligation will be created?

4.5.7 Consent of the seller's lender

If the land being sold is mortgaged, then the consent of the seller's lender to the sale must be obtained. The seller's solicitor must approach the lender before exchange of contracts to make sure that the consent is forthcoming. A lender will normally give its consent provided the sale proceeds are used to repay the mortgage either in full or in part.

Where the land is unregistered, the lender will usually give its consent by way of a deed of release, though it may instead join in the purchase deed to release the land from the mortgage and to give a receipt for the money which it receives.

In the case of registered land, a Form DS3 will be used with a plan attached showing the land being released from the mortgage.

4.6 VOID CONDITIONS

Certain conditions will be void if included in the contract. These include a condition restricting the buyer's choice of solicitor, or a provision that the purchase deed or the registration of title shall be prepared or carried out by the seller's solicitor at the buyer's expense (Law of Property Act 1925, s.48). However, this will not prevent the seller from providing that the buyer will be supplied with a draft purchase deed and that the buyer will be charged a reasonable fee for this.

4.7 LEASEHOLDS

Drafting a contract for the sale of leasehold property is broadly the same as if the property were freehold, with the following differences.

4.7.1 Particulars

The legal description in the particulars will refer to the existing lease and also to the residue of the term of the lease.

4.7.2 Title to be deduced

In addition to complying with SC 4.1.2 which requires that the buyer must be supplied with official copies of the register, the title plan and any document referred to in the register of title and kept by HM Land Registry, the seller under SC 8.1.2 must supply the buyer with a copy of the lease. Standard condition 8.1.2 then provides that the buyer is treated as entering the contract knowing and fully accepting the terms of the lease.

If the seller's title is registered with good leasehold title, the buyer is not entitled to have the superior title deduced. A good leasehold title should be accepted only where paragraph 5.6.2 of the Lenders' Handbook, or paragraph D.3 of the BSA Mortgage Instructions, is satisfied. Accordingly, the buyer should usually insist that the superior title is deduced so that the good leasehold title can be upgraded to absolute leasehold. A special condition will need to be inserted in the contract to provide for this.

4.7.3 Licence to assign

The lease may contain a covenant to the effect that it may not be assigned without the consent of the landlord, although such a covenant is not usual in a long lease of residential property.

4.7.3.1 Open contract

If the landlord's consent is required, then under the open contract rules the seller must use his best endeavours to obtain it.

4.7.3.2 Standard Conditions of Sale

Standard condition 8.3.2 provides that the seller is to apply for the consent at his expense and is to use all reasonable efforts to obtain it. In addition, the buyer must provide all information and references as are reasonably required.

If at least three working days before the completion date (or before a later date on which the parties have agreed to complete the contract) consent is not granted, or has been granted subject to conditions to which a party reasonably objects, then SC 8.3.3 provides that either party may rescind the contract by giving notice to the other party. It also provides that if the contract is rescinded under these circumstances, neither party is to be treated as in breach of contract and SC 7.1.2 will apply. For these purposes 'consent' means consent in the form which satisfies the requirement to obtain it (SC 8.3.1(b)).

4.7.3.3 Statutory obligations on the landlord

If the landlord's consent is required, then:

(a)   no sum of money is to be paid for the consent except for reasonable legal and other expenses (Law of Property Act 1925, s.144);

(b)   the Landlord and Tenant Act 1927, s.19, provides that the consent must not be unreasonably withheld by the landlord;

(c)   the Landlord and Tenant Act 1988, s.1, provides that consent, unless it is reasonable to withhold it, must be given within a reasonable time. If consent is refused written reasons for the refusal must also be given. In addition, s.4 provides that damages are to be paid by a landlord who delays unreasonably.

4.7.4   Insurance

A lease will usually contain provisions as to who is to insure the property (see **15.3.5**).

4.7.5   Implied covenants for title

The same covenants may be implied as in the case of freehold land (see **4.4.1**). Additionally, on the assignment of the lease, the Law of Property (Miscellaneous Provisions) Act 1994, s.4 implies a covenant by the assignor that the lease is subsisting and there is no breach of covenant or event giving rise to forfeiture. This term (previously implied by the Land Registration Act 1925 or the Law of Property Act 1925) is intended to be varied by SC 3.2.2 so that it does not imply a covenant that the seller is liable for any breach of a repairing covenant. This must then be reflected in the transfer deed by including a clause stating that the covenants for title implied by the Law of Property (Miscellaneous Provisions) Act 1994, s.4 shall not be deemed to imply that any of the covenants contained in the lease on the part of the tenant for repair or decoration have been performed.

4.8   CONDITIONAL CONTRACTS

4.8.1   When are they used?

In certain situations the parties may decide that the contract is to be made subject to the satisfaction of a condition. If the condition is not fulfilled, the contract does not become binding and both parties are free to withdraw from the agreement, and the buyer is entitled to recover any deposit he has paid. Conditional contracts are not without risk and it may be preferable to delay exchange until the matter which was the subject of the condition has been resolved.

Examples of situations where a conditional contract may be used include:

(a)   where the buyer has not had an opportunity:

- to carry out preliminary enquiries and searches; or
- to have a survey carried out;

(b)   where the buyer has made an application for a mortgage but has not yet received an offer; and

(c)   where the buyer requires planning permission for development of the land before proceeding. If a condition is inserted that the contract is conditional upon planning permission being obtained, a date should be inserted into the contract by which time the planning permission should be obtained. If no time is specified, the permission must be obtained within a reasonable time from the date of the contract.

A conditional contract should not be used where either party has a related transaction. This is due to the obvious risk that a party could end up having to complete a dependent contract after the conditional contract has been rescinded for non-performance of the condition.

A conditional contract should be protected by registration as a notice in order to make it binding on a subsequent buyer of the property.

4.8.2   The condition must be certain

The terms of the condition must be certain. In *Lee-Parker* v. *Izzet (No.2)* [1972] 2 All ER 800, the contract was subject to the buyer obtaining a satisfactory mortgage. This was held to be void for uncertainty as the term 'satisfactory' was vague. However, in *Janmohamed* v. *Hassan* [1976] 241 EG 609, a contract which was subject to the buyer obtaining a mortgage which was satisfactory to him was not void. The effect of any condition is therefore a question of construction in any particular case. If the condition is void for uncertainty, the whole contract will fail.

4.8.3   When must the condition be satisfied?

The time for performance of the condition is of the essence and cannot be extended (*Aberfoyle Plantations* v. *Cheng* [1960] AC 115). The condition must be satisfied:

(a)   by the date specified in the contract for its satisfaction;
(b)   by the completion date; or
(c)   within a reasonable time where there is no completion date in the contract.

4.8.4   Waiver of the condition

A condition solely for the benefit of one party may be waived by that party.

4.9   UNFAIR CONTRACT TERMS

When drafting a contract, you should be aware of the possible application of Part 2 of the Consumer Rights Act 2015. This Act regulates contracts made between a 'consumer' and a 'trader'.

A 'consumer' is an individual acting for purposes that are wholly or mainly outside that individual's trade, business, craft or profession. 'Trader' means a person acting for purposes relating to that person's trade, business, craft or profession, whether acting personally or through another person acting in the trader's name or on the trader's behalf.

As a result, certain contracts for the sale of land will be caught by the Act. These will include a contract for the sale of a house or flat by a builder/developer to a private buyer, and a contract for the sale of a repossessed house or flat by a lender to a private individual.

Any contract caught by the Act must be both 'transparent' and 'fair'. To be 'transparent' a contract must be legible and expressed in plain and intelligible language. A contract term is unfair if, contrary to the requirement of good faith, it causes a significant imbalance in the parties' rights and obligations under the contract to the detriment of the consumer. An unfair term is not binding on the 'consumer'. The requirement for the contract to be 'fair' does not apply to the price specified in the contract, provided that the price is 'transparent' and prominent. Examples of terms that may be regarded as unfair can be found in Part 1 of Sched.2 to the Act.

4.10 PROCEDURE AFTER DRAFTING THE CONTRACT

When acting for the seller you should prepare and submit to the buyer's solicitor a contract bundle which includes:

(1)   The draft contract in duplicate.
(2)   Evidence of title:

- official copies of the register and title plan (including official copies of all filed documents);
- an official copy of any registered lease; and
- where appropriate, an explanation of the seller's title, for example, if the name of the registered proprietor is different from the name of the seller.

Note: At the time of submitting the contract bundle, entries in the register of title should be less than six months old, and if any information needs to be updated (e.g. change of name, death of proprietor) the register should be rectified.

(3)   Replies to enquiries with supporting documentation.
(4)   Replies to the TA10 Fittings and Contents Form.
(5)   Planning permissions and/or building regulations consents and completion certificates where any alterations or additions to the property have been carried out by the seller. Confirm that building plans will be delivered on completion where these are held.
(6)   Required consents (e.g. under restrictive covenants).
(7)   In addition, in relation to leasehold property:

- replies to the TA7 Leasehold Information Form;
- replies to enquiries made of the landlord/managing agents (where available) with accompanying documentation including three years'

      management accounts, a ground rent receipt, a buildings insurance policy with an up-to-date schedule and information about any required deed of covenant or other consent to assignment, etc.;

- official copies of the freehold and intermediate titles;
- a copy of the seller's share certificate for any landlord/management company where appropriate.

(8)   Any searches and enquiries made on behalf of the seller.

(9)   If provided by the seller, an EPC.

You should also consider preparing a draft transfer either to attach to the contract or to submit with the contract.

4.11 SUMMARY

- The seller's solicitor will draft the contract after investigating his client's title.
- A contract must be in writing, contain all agreed terms and be signed by all parties.
- A contract will comprise the particulars of sale, the standard conditions of sale and the special conditions of sale.
- A contract will incorporate the Standard Conditions of Sale (fifth edition – 2018 revision).
- The particulars of sale should contain a clear and concise description of the property and whether it is leasehold or freehold.
- The contract will need to include special conditions to vary or supplement the standard conditions, or to deal with transaction-specific matters.
- When acting for a buyer, you must review the draft contract and make any amendments you consider appropriate.
- If the sale is of part, a plan should be attached to the contract showing the extent of both the land being sold and the land being retained.
- On a sale of part, consideration should be given to easements, reservations and covenants to be created and imposed.
- New easements and covenants will be created and imposed in the transfer but they must be agreed in the contract.
- The procedures in selling a long residential lease are similar to those on a freehold transaction.
- You must check whether the landlord's consent to assign the lease is required, though this is unusual in a long residential lease.
- A conditional contract may be used where the buyer needs planning permission or is still waiting for the results of searches.
- The terms of any condition must be clear and certain if the contract is not to be void for uncertainty.
- A conditional contract should be protected by a notice on the register.

CHAPTER 5

Pre-contract enquiries and searches

5.1 INTRODUCTION

The buyer will wish to know as much as he can about the property before contracts are exchanged and he is committed to buying the property. We saw in the last chapter that the seller's duty of disclosure does not oblige the seller to disclose everything relating to the property, so the buyer will want to find out about anything which may have a bearing on whether he goes ahead with the purchase. To this end, the buyer's solicitor will carry out various searches and enquiries, some of which will be made in every transaction while others will be made only where appropriate. In this chapter we will consider these searches and enquiries.

Generally, the buyer's solicitor must make all the usual searches and enquiries, and he will be negligent if he falls short of this obligation and the buyer suffers loss as a result. Where the solicitor is acting for a lender, paragraph 5.4 of the Lenders' Handbook and paragraphs D.7–D.14 of the BSA Mortgage Instructions provide that conveyancers should carry out all appropriate searches and enquiries.

The usual searches and enquiries are:

(a)   enquiries of the seller;
(b)   local land charges search;
(c)   enquiries of the local authority; and
(d)   drainage and water enquiries.

In addition to these, there are other searches and enquiries which may need to be carried out depending on the circumstances of the transaction. A solicitor who fails to carry out a relevant search in circumstances where he should have done so may be liable in negligence to his client (*G & K Ladenbau (UK) Ltd* v. *Crawley & de Reya* [1978] 1 WLR 266).

If the buyer is obtaining a mortgage, a duty is owed to the lender to ensure that the searches are no more than six months old at the date of completion (see the Lenders' Handbook, paragraph 5.4.3 and the BSA Mortgage Instructions, paragraph D.10).

The usual method of carrying out the searches is by post. However, it is now possible to carry out searches electronically through NLIS. A solicitor can access NLIS through one of the channels which have been licensed to provide NLIS services. Other professional search providers also offer electronic searches.

As search results are not personal to the searcher, their benefit may be transferred to a third party. Thus, the seller may carry out pre-contract searches and pass the results to the buyer, and both the buyer and his lender may rely on these results. The buyer's solicitor must check that the seller has undertaken all the searches and enquiries which he deems necessary for the transaction, and if the seller has not, the buyer's solicitor must carry out any additional searches. If the buyer's solicitor is not satisfied with the results of the searches made by the seller, he should carry out new searches.

5.2　ENQUIRIES OF THE SELLER

These enquiries are intended to deal with matters which the seller is not obliged to disclose to the buyer but which may provide vital information in relation to the purchase of the property.

A buyer's solicitor will normally send two copies of his enquiries to the seller's solicitor. This allows the seller's solicitor to keep one copy of the enquiries together with his replies for his file.

5.2.1　Form of enquiries

Under the Law Society Conveyancing Protocol (2019), the seller's solicitor should ask his client to complete a TA6 Property Information Form (if the property is leasehold, a TA7 Leasehold Information Form should also be used) and a TA10 Fittings and Contents Form. These forms contain questions which are phrased in layperson's terms so that the seller can complete them with minimal help from his solicitor. The seller's solicitor should check the answers and endeavour to obtain any missing documentation. The forms are then submitted to the buyer's solicitor as part of the pre-contract package.

The Law Society also publishes LPE1 Leasehold Property Enquiries Form which captures information about a property held by the landlord, management company and managing agent; and LPE2 Buyers Leasehold Information Summary which is designed to improve the information given to leasehold buyers about the financial obligations they are taking on. LPE1 should only be completed by the seller where the seller is, or is appointed to represent, the landlord, the management company, managing agent or residents'/tenants' association. The information to be included in LPE2 will be taken from LPE1.

5.2.2　Summary of information to be obtained from the enquiries

Information obtained from the enquiries will include:

(a)　whether there are any disputes with neighbouring owners/occupiers;

(b)　who is in occupation of the property;

(c) whether there have been any alterations or other building work carried out on the property and, if so, whether planning permission and building regulations consent was obtained;

(d) whether there has been any change in the use of the property;

(e) whether any of the services to the property pass through adjoining land;

(f) whether services to other properties pass through the property.

5.2.3 Additional enquiries

The buyer's solicitor should consider making further enquiries and advising his client where a TA6 or TA7 has not been properly completed. Acceptance of an improperly completed form may amount to a failure to carry out all the usual enquiries and the solicitor will be in breach of his duty to the buyer client and to any lender client for whom he is also acting. Additional enquiries should only be raised where relevant and necessary to the particular transaction. Additional enquiries about matters that can be resolved by a survey or personal inspection of the property should not be raised. The seller's solicitor should take his client's instructions before answering any additional enquiries.

5.2.4 The seller's replies

The seller is not obliged to answer the buyer's enquiries, but if they are not answered there is always the possibility that the buyer will withdraw from the transaction. In practice the seller will therefore usually answer the enquiries. Where enquiries have been answered in the terms 'not so far as the seller is aware', this will imply that the seller and his solicitor have made investigations and have no actual knowledge of any defect (*William Sindall plc* v. *Cambridgeshire County Council* [1994] 3 All ER 932). To be adequate, these investigations must cover the seller's personal knowledge as well as the contents of such files, deeds, etc., as are in the firm's possession and any other reasonable investigations.

5.2.5 Incorrect replies

An incorrect reply may lead to liability in misrepresentation. A misrepresentation is an untrue statement made by one party, usually the seller, or his agent, which induces the other party, the buyer, to enter into the contract. The effect of an actionable misrepresentation is to make the contract voidable. A misrepresentation may be fraudulent, negligent or innocent. Under the Fraud Act 2006 if the requisite criteria are satisfied for fraud by false representation or fraud by failing to disclose information, the seller may also be guilty of the criminal offence of fraud.

A fraudulent misrepresentation is a false statement made knowingly or without belief in its truth, or recklessly careless as to whether it is true or false. The buyer may sue for damages in the tort of deceit and rescind the contract.

Negligent misrepresentation occurs where, although there is no fraud, the seller cannot prove that he had reasonable grounds to believe and did so believe in the truth of the statement up to the time that the contract was made. The buyer may under the Misrepresentation Act 1967, s.2, either:

(a) rescind the contract; or
(b) claim damages.

In addition, the buyer may be able to obtain damages under the principle laid down in *Hedley Byrne & Co. Ltd* v. *Heller & Partners Ltd* [1964] AC 465, where it can be shown that:

(a) the seller owed a duty of care to the buyer arising from a special relationship, i.e. where the seller had some special skill or knowledge and knew or reasonably should have known that the buyer would rely on that statement;
(b) the representation was a breach of that duty; and
(c) as a result of that breach, loss has been suffered by the buyer.

Innocent misrepresentation occurs where the misrepresentation is made neither fraudulently nor negligently but is still an untrue statement. The importance of the distinction is that the only remedy available is rescission. If the right to rescind has been lost, even through no fault of the buyer, he is left without a remedy. Where rescission is available, the court may award damages instead of rescission under the Misrepresentation Act 1967, s.2(2).

Any exclusion clause purporting to avoid or minimise liability for misrepresentation will be subject to the reasonableness test in the Unfair Contract Terms Act 1977, s.11 and cannot therefore be guaranteed to afford protection to the seller (see SC 7.1.1(b) and *Walker* v. *Boyle* [1982] 1 All ER 634). Where the erroneous reply stems from the seller's solicitor's negligence, he will be liable to his own client (*Cemp Properties (UK) Ltd* v. *Dentsply Research & Development Corporation (No.1)* (1989) 2 EGLR 192), but in this respect he does not owe a duty directly to the buyer (see *Gran Gelato Ltd* v. *Richcliffe (Group) Ltd* [1992] 1 All ER 865).

5.3 LOCAL LAND CHARGES SEARCH

5.3.1 The local land charges register

The Local Land Charges Act 1975, s.3 requires local authorities to maintain a local land charges register.

The Infrastructure Act 2015 provides that HM Land Registry will eventually take over responsibility as the sole registering authority for local land charges in England and Wales. HM Land Registry will become the statutory owner of a single digitised local land charges register, to which the local authorities will provide updated entries. The Act provides that HM Land Registry will take over responsibility for local land charges in stages.

The register is divided into 12 parts:

(i)   general financial charges;
(ii)   specific financial charges;
(iii)   planning charges;
(iv)   miscellaneous prohibitions and charges;
(v)   charges for improvement of ways over fenland;
(vi)   land compensation charges;
(vii)   new town charges;
(viii) civil aviation charges;
(ix)   open-cast coal mining charges;
(x)   listed building charges (buildings of special historic or architectural interest);
(xi)   light obstruction notices;
(xii)   land drainage scheme charges.

All charges are enforceable by the local authority except: (viii) and (ix), which are enforceable by statutory bodies; and (xi), which is enforceable by private individuals.

Matters which may commonly be revealed by the search include:

(a)   financial charges (e.g. for the adoption of estate roads);
(b)   tree preservation orders;
(c)   smoke control orders;
(d)   compulsory purchase orders;
(e)   any grants of planning permission which contain conditions;
(f)   any restrictions on permitted development (e.g. an Article 4 direction (see **6.2.2**));
(g)   conservation area designation orders made since 31 August 1974 (orders made before that day will be revealed by the enquiries of the local authority);
(h)   listed buildings registration.

The buyer's solicitor should advise the buyer of the entries affecting the property and their significance (e.g. if there is a tree preservation order, then the tree in question cannot be felled or lopped without permission). Consideration should also be given as to how the entries will affect the buyer's proposed use for the property.

The buyer's solicitor should check any planning permission to make sure that the buyer's proposed use is the authorised use for planning purposes and that there are no conditions in the planning permission which might interfere with that use. The seller should provide copies of planning permissions, otherwise it may be possible to obtain copies from the relevant local authority.

If financial charges are revealed, the seller should be requested to discharge these before completion, or to reduce the purchase price.

5.3.2 Searching the register

A search should be made in every transaction. The method of making a search will depend on whether the register for the relevant area is maintained by the local authority or HM Land Registry. This can be checked at **https://search-local-land-charges.service.gov.uk** and the search made via this link if the register is held by HM Land Registry.

Where the register is still held by the local authority, the search is made by submitting Form LLC1, in duplicate, to the unitary, district or London borough council for the area in which the property is situated, together with the fee. A search should be made in all 12 parts of the register. The local authority may require a plan of the property showing its location as well as the postal address, and so the best practice is to send such a plan with each search. Form LLC1 is always accompanied by the form of enquiries of the local authority and together these are referred to in practice as 'the local search'.

A separate search must be made for each parcel of land being purchased, i.e. for each piece of land in separate occupation or separately rated at the date of search, or each building or part of a building so occupied or rated.

There is a statutory right to make a personal search, but local authorities do not guarantee the accuracy of the result which depends on the ability and diligence of the searcher. The right of compensation on a personal search is narrower than with an official search. Personal searches will normally be used only if it is necessary to have the result of the search quickly, such as where the buyer wishes to exchange contracts in a short space of time. Alternatively, either the contract could be made conditional on the result of the search, although this would not be suitable where the transaction is part of a chain, or the contract could be exchanged without the search having been made and insurance taken out to provide protection against loss due to an adverse reply.

Personal searches carried out by search agents who are members of industry trade bodies are prepared in accordance with their own standards and codes of practice. The term 'regulated search' is used to describe such a personal search. Industry trade body members should be expected to maintain adequate and appropriate insurance to protect consumers, including £2 million minimum indemnity insurance, specialist search insurance for errors and omissions in local authority data and records, and run-off cover. Members of industry trade bodies should abide by the Property Ombudsman scheme (**www.tpos.co.uk**).

The limitations on personal searches also mean that some lenders will not accept them, although increasingly they are accepted by lenders particularly in relation to residential property. An individual lender's specific requirements in Part 2 of the Lenders' Handbook or in the BSA Mortgage Instructions should be checked.

Before a personal search is undertaken, clients should be advised of the limitations on personal searches and their possible implications, and a check of the search agent should be made to ensure that the search result will be backed by adequate indemnity insurance. The amount of the insurance cover and who can benefit should also be checked.

The buyer (or his agent, which includes his solicitor) may attend personally at the local authority offices and, after paying the prescribed fee, can personally search the register. In practice, personal searches are usually carried out by commercial personal search companies.

5.3.3 Search result

The result of the search is given in the form of an official certificate. This will state either that there are no subsisting entries relating to the property, or that there are a certain number of entries, and in this case copies of the relevant entries will be attached to the certificate.

5.3.4 The effect of registration

Registration of a local land charge is deemed to be notice of the charge to all persons for all purposes, and therefore the buyer will be bound by any registered charges whether or not he searches the register. To be validly registered the charge must be entered in the correct part of the register.

5.3.5 Compensation

Where a person suffers as a result of an error in an official certificate of search, compensation may be payable under the Local Land Charges Act 1975, s.10.

5.4 ENQUIRIES OF THE LOCAL AUTHORITY

A search in the local land charges register will reveal only those matters which are capable of registration. There are many other matters of concern to the buyer, such as responsibility for roads, environmental health, planning, building control and housing, which will not be disclosed by the search, and further enquiries are therefore required to elicit other relevant information about the property from the local authority.

The enquiries are made by submitting form CON 29 in duplicate to the appropriate unitary, district, metropolitan or London borough council with the local land charges search and the appropriate fee. The fees charged vary between different local authorities and so can be ascertained by contacting the relevant local authority. There is a single fee payable for all the CON 29 enquiries. An additional fee is payable for each CON 29O optional enquiry raised. A plan should always be submitted with the search. Some local authorities now accept electronic search requests.

While it is possible to carry out a personal search, the accuracy of the results will not be guaranteed and much of the information required to answer the enquiries may not be available to a personal searcher. A personal search should only be carried out where there is not enough time for an official search. A personal search may not be acceptable to a lender. See **5.3.2** for more information about regulated searches.

A buyer should also be advised that, generally, the CON 29 enquiries only reveal matters directly affecting the land and will not reveal matters relating to adjoining land which may indirectly affect the property.

5.4.1 The forms

CON 29 contains the standard enquiries that should be raised in every transaction, while CON 29O contains optional questions which will only be appropriate to particular types of property or location.

Both forms have boxes for the address of the property to be searched. It is important to include the correct address to be searched against, as, unless otherwise indicated, the replies will disclose matters only if they apply directly to the property described.

Any road, footway or footpath that abuts the property to be searched or which gives access to or egress from the property, but which is not included in the property address, should be set out in Box C on CON 29.

5.4.2 The enquiries

5.4.2.1 CON 29 Enquiries of the Local Authority (2016)

CON 29 contains a number of standard enquiries which are appropriate to every transaction, and are answered by the relevant local authority in return for payment of its standard fee.

The substance of these enquiries is as follows.

ENQUIRY 1.1: PLANNING AND BUILDING DECISIONS AND PENDING APPLICATIONS

This enquiry asks which of the following relating to the property have been granted, issued or refused or are the subject of pending applications:

(a) planning permission;
(b) listed building consent;
(c) conservation area consent;
(d) certificate of lawfulness of existing use or development;
(e) certificate of lawfulness of proposed use or development;
(f) certificate of lawfulness of proposed works for listed buildings;
(g) heritage partnership agreement;
(h) listed building consent order;

(i)   local listed building consent order;
(j)   building regulations approval;
(k)   building regulations completion certificate; and
(l)   any building regulations certificate or notice issued in respect of work carried out under a competent person self-certification scheme.

ENQUIRY 1.2: PLANNING DESIGNATIONS AND PROPOSALS

This enquiry seeks to find out what development plans affect the property, and what any such plan may indicate as the use for the area in which the property is situated.

ENQUIRY 2.1: ROADWAYS, FOOTWAYS AND FOOTPATHS

This enquiry asks which of the roads, footways and footpaths mentioned in Boxes B and C on the front of the enquiry form are:

(a)   highways maintainable at public expense;
(b)   subject to adoption and, if so, whether the agreement is supported by a bond or other financial security;
(c)   to be made up a local authority who will then reclaim the cost from the frontagers; and
(d)   to be adopted by a local authority without any cost to the frontagers.

ENQUIRIES 2.2–2.5: PUBLIC RIGHTS OF WAY

These enquiries seek information about existing and pending public rights of way which might cross or run alongside the boundary of the property. They also seek any information about legal orders created under any Act that might affect the current route of a public right of way.

ENQUIRY 3.1: LAND REQUIRED FOR PUBLIC PURPOSES

This enquiry seeks to find out whether the property is blighted in that it is required for public purposes, e.g. for the building of a new school.

ENQUIRY 3.2: LAND TO BE ACQUIRED FOR ROAD WORKS

This enquiry asks whether the property is to be acquired for highway construction or improvement.

ENQUIRY 3.3: DRAINAGE MATTERS

This enquiry asks about sustainable urban drainage systems (SuDS). SuDS are structures and techniques aimed at draining surface water efficiently and sustainably.

ENQUIRY 3.4: NEARBY ROAD SCHEMES

This enquiry asks whether any part of the property is within 200 metres of certain road schemes, e.g. new trunk roads. Where any such schemes are revealed, details and plans should be obtained.

ENQUIRY 3.5: NEARBY RAILWAY SCHEMES

This enquiry asks for details of any proposed railway, tramway, light railway or monorail within 200 metres of the property.

ENQUIRY 3.6: TRAFFIC SCHEMES

This enquiry asks whether certain traffic schemes, such as one-way driving, pedestrianisation, traffic calming works, residents parking controls, minor road widening or improvement, pedestrian crossings, cycle tracks and bridge construction, have been approved by the local authority in respect of any roads, footways and footpaths mentioned in Boxes B and C, which are within 200 metres of the boundaries of the property.

ENQUIRY 3.7: OUTSTANDING NOTICES

This enquiry asks whether there are any statutory notices relating to the property (other than any covered elsewhere in the replies to the CON 29) made under legislation relating to:

(a)   building works;
(b)   environment;
(c)   health and safety;
(d)   housing;
(e)   highways;
(f)   public health; and
(g)   flood and coastal erosion risk management.

Such notices may affect the way in which the property can be used and may impose obligations on the owner.

ENQUIRY 3.8: CONTRAVENTION OF BUILDING REGULATIONS

This enquiry asks whether the local authority has authorised any proceedings relating to contravention of the building regulations.

ENQUIRY 3.9: NOTICES, ORDERS, DIRECTIONS AND PROCEEDINGS UNDER PLANNING ACTS

This enquiry seeks details of any notices, orders, directions and proceedings under the Town and Country Planning Act 1990. Examples of the matters it may reveal include:

(a)   enforcement notices and stop notices;

(b)   listed building repairs notices;

(c)   Article 4 directions (see **6.2.2**) – if a direction has been made it will be shown in the Official Certificate of Search;

(d)   whether any orders have been made to revoke, vary or discontinue any planning permission or use; and

(e)   whether the council has resolved to make a tree preservation order.

ENQUIRY 3.10: COMMUNITY INFRASTRUCTURE LEVY (CIL)

This enquiry asks about the discretionary planning charge known as the Community Infrastructure Levy (see **6.3.10**).

ENQUIRY 3.11: CONSERVATION AREA

This enquiry asks whether the property is in a conservation area that was created before 31 August 1974, or whether since that date, a resolution has been made to designate the area as a conservation area but has not been implemented. Since 31 August 1974, conservation designation orders have been registrable as local land charges. An area may be designated as a conservation area to protect its character if this is considered to be of special architectural or historic interest. Where an area is a conservation area, there will be limitations on development.

ENQUIRY 3.12: COMPULSORY PURCHASE

This enquiry asks if the property is subject to a compulsory purchase order. It needs to be noted that electricity, gas and water companies also have compulsory purchase powers and enquiry may need to be made with them if thought appropriate. If the property is affected by a compulsory purchase order, this will have a major effect on the buyer's decision to proceed with the purchase.

ENQUIRY 3.13: CONTAMINATED LAND

The reply to this enquiry will relate both to the land and also to any adjoining or adjacent land that has been identified as contaminated land because it is in such a condition that harm or pollution of controlled waters might be caused on the property.

ENQUIRY 3.14: RADON GAS

This enquiry seeks to find out whether the property is situated in an area which is affected by radon gas. Areas affected include parts of Devon, Cornwall, Derbyshire, Northamptonshire and Somerset. If the property is situated in an area affected by radon gas, protective measures are required for new dwellings under the building regulations.

ENQUIRY 3.15: ASSETS OF COMMUNITY VALUE

A building or land can be nominated by a 'local group' as an asset of community value. When an asset of community value then comes up for sale or change of ownership, the local community group will receive an early warning of the impending sale, and may be able to delay the sale by six months to give them time to develop a competitive bid and to raise money to buy the asset, thereby keeping much loved sites in public use and part of local life.

Local authorities cannot list land or buildings on their own initiative, but they are under a statutory obligation to review and determine nominations and to keep and maintain a list of community assets. In addition, they must also keep and maintain a list of assets that have been nominated but not subsequently listed and this includes applications which fall into the 'excluded' category.

5.4.2.2 CON 29O

CON 29O comprises 19 optional enquiries, any of which should be asked if they are considered relevant to the transaction. An optional enquiry will be answered only if the buyer ticks the appropriate box on the front page of the form and pays an additional fee. If optional enquiries are to be asked, CON 29O should be completed and submitted to the local authority with CON 29.

The matters covered by these optional enquiries are (the numbering continues from CON 29):

(4) road proposals by private bodies;
(5) advertisements (entries in the register; and notices, proceedings and orders);
(6) completion notices under the Town and Country Planning Act 1990;
(7) parks and countryside (areas of outstanding natural beauty; and national parks);
(8) pipelines;

(9) houses in multiple occupation;
(10) noise abatement (noise abatement zone; and entries in register);
(11) urban development areas;
(12) enterprise zones, local development orders and business improvement districts (BIDs);
(13) inner urban improvement areas;
(14) simplified planning zones;
(15) land maintenance notices;
(16) mineral consultation and safeguarding areas;
(17) hazardous substance consents;
(18) environmental and pollution notices;
(19) food safety notices;
(20) hedgerow notices;
(21) flood defence and land drainage consents; and
(22) common land and town or village green.

5.4.2.3 Additional enquiries

The buyer can make other additional enquiries which will be answered at the council's discretion. An additional fee is payable for each enquiry raised.

5.4.3 Exclusion of liability

Subject to the validity of the exclusion clause printed on the front sheet, a local authority could be sued in negligence for an erroneous reply to the enquiries.

5.5 DRAINAGE AND WATER SEARCH

A drainage and water search using CON 29DW should be carried out with the water service company on all transactions at the same time as the local search is sent to the local authority. The enquiries should be submitted to the appropriate water service company for the area in which the property is situated together with the appropriate fee and a plan showing the location of the property.

The search will reveal matters such as:

(a) whether the property has foul water drainage and surface water drainage to the public sewer;
(b) whether there is a water main, public sewer, disposal main or lateral drain within the boundaries of the property; and
(c) whether the property is connected to the public water supply.

If the property does not drain into a public sewer, the buyer will be liable for the costs of maintaining the drains and sewers, and may be liable for the costs of bringing them up to adoption standard if the water authority decides to adopt them.

If there is a public sewer on the property, the water company's consent will be needed to any development over or within the vicinity of the sewer. The water companies now have ownership of and responsibility for existing private sewers (i.e. pipes serving two or more properties) and all new sewers. This means that a higher proportion of developments will now require consent from the water company. A buyer should be aware that water companies have statutory rights of access to properties on which they hold assets.

5.6   ENVIRONMENTAL SEARCH

The Law Society's Contaminated Land Practice Note (28 January 2020) provides that solicitors should consider whether land contamination is an issue in all conveyancing transactions. Enquiry 3.13 on CON 29 will help a buyer's solicitor to identify contaminated land, but is hardly in itself likely to be sufficient. If it appears that contamination is an issue, the practice note sets out the steps to be taken.

There are a number of professional search providers which provide environmental reports. These collate information from a variety of sources and are usually priced on a tariff relating to the value and nature of the property. If necessary, a specialist environmental consultant can be asked to prepare a more tailored and detailed report. These reports are usually referred to as 'desk-top' environmental searches. If an environmental search report reveals that the property is at risk of contamination, the buyer will need to decide whether he wishes to instruct environmental consultants to undertake an environmental survey of the land. This will involve samples of the soil being taken for testing in order to establish the extent and nature of any contamination.

Where there are unresolved contamination problems, the buyer's solicitor should consider advising the buyer to withdraw from the transaction. It is important that a note of the advice given to the buyer is made on the file. Alternatively, the solicitor could consider obtaining environmental insurance.

5.7   COMMONS REGISTRATION SEARCH

If the property or any land that abuts the property is affected by a registration under the Commons Registration Act 1965 or the Commons Act 2006, the land:

(a)   may be subject to rights of common, for example grazing rights;

(b)   may be impossible to develop;

(c)   may have access problems as there is no right to drive a vehicle over common land or land that is a town or village green;

(d)   will be 'access land' for the purposes of the Countryside and Rights of Way Act 2000.

The system of registration of common land and town and village greens under the Commons Registration Act 1965 is gradually being replaced by Part 1 of the Commons Act 2006.

A commons registration search should be carried out to find out whether the property or any land that abuts it is affected by a registration. In practice a search should be carried out where:

(a)   the property adjoins a village green or common;
(b)   the property is separated from a public highway by a strip of land which does not belong to the property; or
(c)   the land is undeveloped.

A search is made by raising Enquiry 22 'Common land and town or village green' on Form CON 29O. If the reply to Enquiry 22.1 is positive, copies of the registration should be obtained to establish what part(s) of the property are affected.

5.8   COAL AUTHORITY MINING SEARCH

A coal mining search should be carried out if the property is within an area of past, present or future coal mining. A check to see whether a property is affected by coal mining can be made at **www.gov.uk/check-if-property-is-affected-by-coal-mining**.

A standard form of search (CON 29M) is sent together with the appropriate fee and a location plan to the Coal Authority. An online search can be made at **www.groundstability.com**.

A mining report will reveal whether a property has been subject to a coal mining related subsidence damage notice or claim since 1984. It also provides information on past, current and proposed underground coal mining activity along with details of any recorded old coal mineshafts and licences for future mining. The report refers to any current or proposed opencast coal mining operations and whether the property was built over a worked out opencast site. The report also includes details of mine gas emissions and incidents dealt with under the Coal Authority's emergency Surface Hazard call-out procedure.

5.9   COMPANY SEARCH

Where the seller is a company, a company search should be made to check that the company:

(a)   exists;
(b)   has the power to buy and sell land;
(c)   has no undisclosed fixed or floating charge which affects the land being sold; and

(d)   is not in administration, receivership or liquidation.

A company search is a snapshot of the company at the time the search is carried out. The search should be carried out before exchange in order to identify any issues before the buyer is contractually bound, and then again before completion to make sure the results are as up to date as possible.

There is no standard company search, so the buyer's solicitor must decide which documents lodged at Companies House should be inspected. Copies of these documents can be obtained directly from the Companies House website for free (**www.gov.uk/government/organisations/companies-house**). Alternatively, a specialist firm can be instructed to obtain these and produce a company search report (a fee will be payable). A report will identify any existing mortgages or charges on a property and report on any adverse entries. The report will also usually include:

(a)   date of incorporation;
(b)   change of name history;
(c)   registered office address;
(d)   confirmation the company has power to buy and sell;
(e)   mortgage report; and
(f)   adverse information including petitions, meetings of creditors or other potential insolvency procedures.

5.10   CHANCEL REPAIR SEARCH

The obligation to repair the chancel (that part of the church containing the altar and the choir) of an Anglican church may not be apparent from the title deeds or known to the owner of the land. The costs associated with a chancel repair liability can be considerable. In the case of *Aston Cantlow and Wilmcote with Billesley Parochial Church Council* v. *Wallbank* [2003] UKHL 37 it was £186,000. Chancel repair liability does not apply to all churches; the liability relates to churches built before the Reformation. Chancel repair liability used to override both first registration and registered dispositions, but this overriding status ended on 13 October 2013.

Chancel repair liability can still be protected by notice in the register of the burdened property at any time until a transfer for value occurs on or after 13 October 2013. Once a transfer for value of the burdened property occurs on or after 13 October 2013, the liability will not bind any subsequent buyer unless it was already protected by notice. If no such transfer has occurred, a buyer's solicitor should carry out a screening search to find out whether the property is within a liable parish as there is a risk of being bound by a chancel repair liability protected by a notice entered after the buyer has completed his title investigation but prior to registration of his transfer. If the screening search result shows that the property is within a liable parish, insurance can be obtained against the potential liability. It is possible to make a personal search at the National Archives in Kew to ascertain whether a particular property is liable for chancel repairs, but insurance will usually be cheaper and quicker. In addition, if a personal search did find that a property had such a liability, it would not then be possible to obtain insurance against the liability and the property would be very difficult to sell.

If a transfer for value of the property on or after 13 October 2013 has occurred, the buyer should not be bound by a chancel repair liability unless a notice has already been entered in the register of title. Having said that HM Land Registry will continue to register unilateral notices to protect chancel repair liability, regardless of whether a transfer for value after 13 October 2013 has been made. The reasoning behind this is that HM Land Registry does not assess the legitimacy of a unilateral notice application. It leaves it to the registered proprietor to challenge the unilateral notice if he considers it does not protect a valid interest. Consequently, it may be advisable to carry out a screening search.

A person acquiring property without giving consideration (for example, by way of a gift) will retain any chancel repair liability. Such liability will remain until a sale (for value) to a third party occurs on or after 13 October 2013. This is so even if the obligation has not been protected as mentioned above.

5.11 FLOOD SEARCH

The Environment Agency estimates that one in six homes in England (approximately 5.2 million properties) are at risk from flooding. Flooding does not just occur in properties that are near to rivers or coasts. The Environment Agency estimates that 2.8 million homes are at risk of surface water flooding, which arises where heavy rainfall overwhelms the drainage capacity in an area. Flooding can also occur when sewers become blocked ('sewer flooding') or when underground water levels rise above surface level ('groundwater flooding'). The Law Society's Flood Risk Practice Note (31 January 2020) is available when you sign in with My LS at **www.lawsociety.org.uk**. The advice given includes the following:

(a)   In all conveyancing transactions, the solicitor should mention the issue of flood risk to his client and, if appropriate, make further investigations.

(b)   A solicitor should consider advising a buyer to do the following before exchange of contracts:

•   Establish the terms on which buildings insurance, including flood risk cover, is available. Where a property is at risk of flooding, insurers may charge high premiums or excesses, or decline insurance entirely.

•   Discuss the level of flood risk with his building surveyor or, if necessary, a flood risk consultant.

If, after discussion with the client, further investigations are deemed appropriate (or if they are required by a lender), the risk of flooding can be checked using the property's postcode on the 'flood risk maps' on the Environment Agency's website (**www.environment-agency.gov.uk**). This will show the extent of possible river and coastal flood plains (but not surface water flooding) and give a flood risk assessment for the area. HM Land Registry also provides a Flood Risk Indicator via its website (**www.gov.uk/search-property-information-land-registry**), which combines Environment Agency flood data with Land Registry property data to provide an indication of whether a piece of land is at risk of flooding. The Law Society's practice note states that neither the Environment Agency Flood Map nor the Flood Risk Indicator should be used as the sole means of assessing flood risk as neither is property-specific and neither shows groundwater flooding, surface water flooding or sewer flooding.

The possibility of a commercial flood search should be discussed with the client on every transaction, but specific instructions should be obtained before undertaking it due to the cost. Such searches vary in terms of their cost and the range of information provided. It is possible, however, to carry out commercial searches that will provide surface water and groundwater flooding information. The Law Society advises that the solicitor should consider the terms and conditions on which the search or report is given, including any limits on the liability of the provider. When reporting on the results of any flood search, the solicitor should make it clear he is not qualified to advise on technical matters regarding the search results. Any such question should be raised with the client's surveyor or the consultant who produced the report.

The TA6 Property Information Form asks for details of flooding that has affected the property. The Law Society states that the reply to this should not be the only source of information relied upon in relation to flooding risk.

5.12 ENQUIRIES OF OTHER BODIES

In appropriate circumstances enquiries will be made with other bodies, for example:

(a) If the property adjoins a railway line there might be any rights of way, or other easements or interests relevant to railway workings. There is no official railway search, but Network Rail does provide some information on its website. Searches are also available in relation to other railways, e.g. Tyne & Wear Metro, London Underground, Docklands Light Railway, Crossrail and HS2.

(b) If the property is in Cheshire, a search should be made to see whether the property is in the area of former brine extraction.

(c) Statutory undertakers such as the electricity or gas boards where their activities or conduits might affect the purpose for which the land is being bought.

(d) The Environment Agency is responsible for rivers, estuaries and harbours.

The Canal & River Trust is responsible for canals. Where the property adjoins a waterway, or has a waterway passing through it, a search should be made to establish:

- liability for maintenance of the river bank or of the canal;
- liability for flooding;
- whether there are any rights of way along the river banks or tow paths;
- whether there are any drainage rights;
- whether there are any fishing rights;
- whether there are any water abstraction licences.

(e) Where the property is situated in an area where tin, clay or limestone mining is known to have taken place or is still taking place, a search in respect of these should be carried out.

5.13 INSPECTION OF THE PROPERTY

The buyer should always inspect the property to check:

(a) whether there are any physical defects;
(b) that the boundaries are correct;
(c) whether there are any rights over the property; and
(d) whether anyone, other than the seller, occupies the property.

5.13.1 Physical defects

The maxim *caveat emptor* applies, which means that the seller has no duty to disclose any physical defects in the property. A buyer should therefore always have the property surveyed by a professional surveyor before exchange of contracts to ensure that it is structurally sound, and his solicitor should always strongly advise him to have such a survey carried out. Standard condition 3.2.1 provides that the buyer agrees to take the property in the physical state in which it is at exchange.

5.13.2 Boundaries

The buyer should inspect the property to make sure that:

(a) the boundaries are correct; and
(b) the contract description of the property is correct.

5.13.3 Rights over the property

As the seller is under no duty to disclose patent defects in title the buyer should inspect the property to see if there are any such defects, e.g. a right of way over the property. The necessity for such an inspection is emphasised by SC 3.1.2(b).

5.13.4 Third-party occupiers

The property should always be inspected to see whether there is anyone else, other than the seller, occupying the property. The buyer will be concerned that any such occupier may have an equitable interest in the property, e.g. as a result of having contributed to the purchase price, which will bind the buyer. In addition, a non-owning occupying spouse or civil partner may have protected his or her statutory right of occupation under the Family Law Act 1996.

The buyer should:

(a) Ascertain who is in occupation. Form TA6 asks the seller whether there is anyone else, aged 17 or over, living in the property, and if there is, whether they are tenants or lodgers, and whether they have agreed to leave prior to completion and sign the contract. The problem with this enquiry is twofold. First, an incorrect reply may only amount to a misrepresentation; and, secondly, under the Land Registration Act 2002, Sched.3, para.2, the enquiry must be made of the occupier.

(b) Having discovered that there is someone in occupation, the buyer must then find out what interests he or she has.

(c) If the occupier does have an interest, the buyer must then take steps to make sure that it is released.

5.14 SURVEYS

A buyer should have a survey carried out to ensure that there are no physical defects in the property.

5.14.1 Types of surveys

There are four main types of survey available to a buyer:

(a) a mortgage valuation report;
(b) a Level 1 Royal Institution of Chartered Surveyors (RICS) Condition Report;
(c) a Level 2 RICS HomeBuyer Report; and
(d) a Level 3 RICS Building Survey.

RICS has published a new professional statement, the *Home Survey Standard*, which is effective from 1 June 2020. This has replaced the RICS guidance, practice notes and professional statements relating to the Condition Report, the HomeBuyer Report and the Building Survey. The professional statement sets out mandatory requirements for all RICS members and regulated firms who provide condition-based residential property surveys, and also highlights areas of good practice.

5.14.2 Mortgage valuation report

Most domestic purchases are made with the assistance of a mortgage from a building society or bank. Before the lender agrees to advance the mortgage monies on a property, it will have the property valued to make sure that the property will be adequate security for the loan. The report is prepared for the lender and answers only the lender's questions about whether the property offers suitable security for the mortgage. While the cost of the report is borne by the buyer, it does not mean that the buyer should rely on it, as it may not be sufficiently detailed for the buyer to decide whether to proceed or not.

5.14.3 Level 1 RICS Condition Report

The RICS Condition Report aims to give buyers of conventionally built properties and newer homes a clear, concise picture of the state of a property. It is not an in-depth survey, but sets out clear 'traffic light' ratings of the condition of different parts of the building, services, garage and outbuildings, showing problems that require varying degrees of attention together with a summary of the risks to the condition of the building, and other matters including guarantees, planning and building control issues. The report does not provide a valuation, but is designed to complement a mortgage valuation.

The RICS Condition Report is aimed principally at buyers who would otherwise rely purely on a lender's mortgage valuation, but may be useful to landlords who wish to assess the condition of their investments and sellers looking to highlight any problems that may potentially have an impact on a future sale.

5.14.4 Level 2 RICS HomeBuyer Report

The RICS 'HomeBuyer Report' includes all the features of the RICS Condition Report together with a market valuation and insurance rebuild costs. It also includes advice on defects that may affect the value of the property, repairs and ongoing maintenance advice. It is an attractive option for a client who, for reasons of expense or otherwise, is reluctant to commission a RICS Building Survey. In many cases the buyer's lender will agree (for an additional fee) to instruct the lender's valuer to undertake the report concurrently with the mortgage valuation, with consequent savings in time and expense for the client.

This type of survey may provide adequate information for the client who is purchasing an ordinary suburban residential property built within the last 100 years, but the client should not be misled into thinking that the survey result is a comprehensive report on the state and condition of the property. An alternative option where the property is of conventional construction or relatively newly built is the RICS Condition Report, which should provide a clear, concise picture of the state of the property without including a valuation, and so it will complement a mortgage valuation. Although of much more value to the client than a mere valuation, these two types of survey are both still relatively superficial in scope.

5.14.5 Level 3 RICS Building Survey

This is the most detailed type of survey which can be carried out and is also known as a full structural survey. It is also the most expensive, as the fee will vary very much according to the property involved. Such a survey should disclose the true state and condition of the property and should be carried out where, for example, the property is more than 100 years old, the property is of high value, the buyer intends to alter or extend the property, the property is not of conventional brick and mortar construction, the property is located near something which may cause subsidence or other structural problems (e.g. clay subsoil), or the property is not detached.

5.14.6 Flats

Where the property is a flat (or is structurally attached to neighbouring property), a full building survey should be considered. The structural soundness of the property is dependent on the soundness of the neighbouring property, and so the surveyor should also inspect the structure of the building and, if possible, the adjoining property.

5.14.7 Liability of the surveyor

The surveyor owes a duty of care to the client to carry out the survey with reasonable skill and care. This is confirmed by the Supply of Goods and Services Act 1982, s.13.

Where a client suffers loss as a result of a negligent survey, an action can be sustained against his surveyor, subject to the validity of any exemption clause which may have formed part of the surveyor's terms of work. The normal rules relating to remoteness of damage apply; thus, the client will not sustain a successful action unless the area of the client's complaint lies within the scope of what the surveyor was instructed to do. It is therefore important to give full and explicit instructions when the survey is commissioned.

Where the client is a consumer (that is, an individual who is acting for purposes wholly or mainly outside his trade, business, craft or profession), the exclusion clause will be subject to the test of fairness in the Consumer Rights Act 2015, s.62. Where the client is not a consumer, the contract will be subject to the reasonableness test in the Unfair Contract Terms Act 1977, s.11.

Where the client suffers loss after having relied on a lender's valuer's report, an action in tort may lie against the surveyor. No action in contract can be sustained because, the survey having been commissioned by the lender, there is no contractual relationship between the buyer and the surveyor. The success of such an action may again depend on the validity of any exclusion clause contained in the valuation;

however, it was held by the House of Lords in *Smith* v. *Eric S Bush (a firm)*; *Harris* v. *Wyre Forest District Council* [1990] 1 AC 831 that a valuer instructed by a lender to carry out a mortgage valuation of a modest house, knowing that the buyer would rely on the valuation without obtaining an independent survey, owed a duty of care to the buyer to exercise reasonable care and skill in carrying out the valuation.

A complaint about a negligent valuation/survey made in-house by a lender may be investigated by the Financial Ombudsman Service, provided the complainant is an existing borrower from that lender.

5.15 RESULTS OF SEARCHES AND ENQUIRIES

The results of the searches and enquiries must be checked to make sure that the information supplied complies with the buyer's instructions. Any reply which is unclear must be followed up until a satisfactory explanation is received. Failure to pursue an unsatisfactory reply which results in loss being suffered by the buyer may result in the buyer's solicitor being liable to the buyer in negligence (*Computastaff Ltd* v. *Ingledew Brown Bennison & Garrett* (1983) 7 ILR 156).

Any reply which is not satisfactory must be referred to the client for further instructions. The contract should not be approved by the buyer's solicitor or exchanged until satisfactory results of all searches have been received. A summary of the information received from the searches should be provided to the buyer by his solicitor.

5.16 SUMMARY

- When acting for a buyer, you must carry out all appropriate searches and enquiries before exchange.
- You should always carry out a local land charges search, enquiries of the local authority, enquiries of the seller, and a water and drainage search on every transaction.
- Depending on the circumstances, additional searches may be required.
- Additional searches may include an environmental search, a mining search, a chancel repairs search, a company search, a flood search and searches and enquiries arising out of the location of the property.
- You must consider the results of all the searches and enquiries you carry out and report the results to your client.
- A buyer should consider a survey, as he must find out whether there are any physical defects in the property.
- There are different types of surveys available.

- A building survey should be considered where the property is of high value or is more than 100 years old; the buyer intends to alter or extend the property; the property is not of conventional brick and mortar construction; the property is located near something which may cause subsidence or other structural problems; or the property is not detached.

CHAPTER 6

Planning considerations

When advising a buyer, you will need to take account of the planning legislation which affects the use of property. We saw in the last chapter that enquiries will be made of both the seller and the local authority about planning matters, and this chapter outlines the legal background to these. Responsibility for planning matters lies with the local planning authority, which will usually be the appropriate district, unitary or London borough council. The local planning authority will be responsible for the grant or refusal of planning permission and enforcing planning control.

Of particular concern when acting for a buyer will be:

(a)   whether planning permission will be required for any use of the property which the buyer proposes;
(b)   whether the buyer intends to carry out alterations to the property, as he will need to be advised whether consent will be required for these; and
(c)   to check the contents of any existing planning consents affecting the property to see whether there are any onerous conditions attached to them. If there are any, then they must be reported to the client.

6.1   DEVELOPMENT

The Town and Country Planning Act 1990, s.57(1) provides that planning permission is required for any 'development' of land.

Section 55 defines 'development' as 'the carrying out of building, engineering, mining or other operations in, on, over or under land, or the making of any material change in the use of any buildings or other land', and provides that 'building operations' includes the demolition of buildings, rebuilding, structural alterations of or additions to buildings, and other operations normally undertaken by a person carrying on business as a builder.

In relation to change of use, only a 'material' change in use requires planning permission. There is no definition of 'material' and so this will be a question of fact and degree in each case. The use as two or more separate dwelling houses of any building which was previously used as a single dwelling house will involve a material change in the use of the building.

Section 55 also provides that the following do not involve development:

(a) maintenance, improvement or other alteration works which affect only the interior of a building or which do not materially affect the external appearance of a building;

(b) the use of any building or other land within the curtilage of a dwelling house for any purpose incidental to the enjoyment of the dwelling house as such (the 'curtilage' of a dwelling house is the land immediately surrounding the house; in most cases this will be the garden);

(c) change of use within the same use class as specified in the Town and Country Planning (Use Classes) Order 1987, SI 1987/764.

The Town and Country Planning (Use Classes) Order 1987 specifies different classes of use which include:

- *Class A1 shops* – use for the purpose of most types of retail shop, including use as an internet café.
- *Class A2 financial and professional services* – use for the provision of financial or professional services provided principally to the visiting public (e.g. banks and building societies).
- *Class A3 restaurants and cafes* – use for the sale of food and drink for consumption on the premises.
- *Class A4 drinking establishments* – use as a public house, wine-bar or other drinking establishment.
- *Class A5 hot food takeaway* – use for the sale of hot food for consumption off the premises.
- *Class B1 business* – use as an office other than one within Class A2 (e.g. the administrative offices of a business) and light industrial use.
- *Class B2 general industrial* – any use for the carrying on of an industrial process not covered by Class B1.
- *Class B8 storage or distribution* – use for storage or as a distribution centre.
- *Class C1 hotels* – this includes use as a hotel, boarding house or guest house where no significant element of care is provided.
- *Class C2 residential institutions* – use for the provision of personal care or treatment and residential educational institutions.
- *Class C2A secure residential institutions* – use for the provision of secure accommodation (e.g. prisons).
- *Class C3 dwelling houses* – the use of property for the accommodation of a family and the accommodation of up to six people as a single household.
- *Class C4 houses in multiple occupation* – use of a dwelling house by not more than six residents as a 'house in multiple occupation' (HMO).
- *Class D1 non-residential institutions* – e.g. medical centres, libraries and museums.
- *Class D2 assembly and leisure* – e.g. cinemas, swimming pools and bingo halls.

- *Sui generis* – certain uses do not fall within any use class and are considered '*sui generis*'. These uses include theatres, amusement arcades, scrap yards, petrol filling stations and shops selling and/or displaying motor vehicles, retail warehouse clubs, nightclubs, launderettes, betting offices, taxi businesses, pay day loan shops and casinos.

A change of use within a use class does not require planning permission. So, for example, a change of use from a newsagent to a greengrocer will not require planning permission as both uses are within Class A1. However, alterations to the premises to facilitate the change of use may require planning permission. A change of use from one use class to another will require planning permission if it amounts to a material change of use (but see **6.2.1** for permitted development).

6.2 REQUIREMENT FOR PLANNING PERMISSION

If a client is going to carry out development, then planning permission will be needed. This can be given either:

(a)   by a deemed permission under the Town and Country Planning (General Permitted Development) (England) Order 2015, SI 2015/596 or, where the property is in Wales, the Town and Country Planning (General Permitted Development) Order 1995, SI 1995/418; or

(b)   by a formal application for planning permission to the local planning authority.

6.2.1   Deemed permission

The General Permitted Development Orders specify categories of development for which blanket permission has been granted. Individual applications for permission are not required in any case which falls within one of the listed categories. These include:

(a)   the enlargement, improvement and other alteration of a dwelling house so long as certain restrictions as to the height and volume of the altered building are observed;

(b)   the erection or construction of a porch outside any external door of a dwelling house;

(c)   the painting of the exterior of any building, provided that this is not for the purpose of advertisement, announcement or direction.

Permitted development also includes some material changes of use, for example a change from class A1 (shops) to class A2 (financial and professional services).

A local planning authority can make a 'local development order'. Such an order will expand the permitted development rights and can be site specific or apply to the whole or part of the area covered by the local planning authority. There are limitations on the type of development that can be permitted under an order, and before an order can be made the local planning authority must consult with interested bodies, e.g. Natural England.

In addition, a neighbourhood development order deems planning permission to have been granted for specific types of development in a particular area. A community right to build order is a special type of neighbourhood development order which gives a community organisation a right to carry out a particular development in its local area without the need for planning permission.

6.2.2   Article 4 directions

A local planning authority can exclude the effect of all or part of the General Permitted Development Orders by making a direction under Article 4 of the relevant Order. An Article 4 direction deprives a landowner of the right to permitted development in respect of all or any of the classes specified in the Order, and allows the local planning authority to control development such as the installation of double glazing in a conservation area. Where an Article 4 direction has been made, a formal application for planning permission will need to be made for development covered by the direction. The existence of an Article 4 direction will be discovered in the results of a local search (see **Chapter 5**).

6.2.3   Demolition

The demolition of a building is specifically defined as a 'building operation' and so falls within the definition of development. Planning permission is therefore required. Certain demolition works are excluded from the definition of 'development' in England by the Town and Country Planning (Demolition – Description of Buildings) Direction 2014 and in Wales by the Town and Country Planning (Demolition – Description of Buildings) Direction 1995.

In *R (on the application of Save Britain's Heritage)* v. *Secretary of State for Communities and Local Government* [2011] EWCA Civ 334 it was declared that certain provisions of the 1995 Direction were unlawful. These provisions provide that the total demolition of the following categories of buildings does not constitute development:

- a listed building;
- a building in a conservation area;
- a building that is a scheduled monument; and
- a building other than a dwelling house or a building adjoining a dwelling house.

The effect of this is that the demolition of these buildings is not excluded from the definition of development and requires planning permission. However, deemed planning permission may be given by the Town and Country Planning (General Permitted Development) Order 1995.

6.3 PLANNING PERMISSION

If an application for planning permission is required, it should be made to the local planning authority and a fee is payable. An applicant need not be the freehold owner of the land, but if he is not, he must notify the owner of the application.

6.3.1 Outline planning permission

An application may be made initially for outline planning permission. This allows the applicant to 'test the water' and obtain approval for the development in principle without the expense of having to prepare detailed plans.

Outline applications may only be made for the erection of buildings, and if successful will be granted subject to the approval of reserved matters which will usually cover such considerations as access, landscaping and the external appearance of the building. When granting the permission, the local planning authority can impose such conditions as it sees fit.

In England, after an outline planning permission has been granted, application for approval of the reserved matters must be made within three years from the date of the outline planning permission, and development must start within two years of the final approval of the reserved matters. In Wales, after an outline planning permission has been granted, application for approval of the reserved matters must be made within three years from the date of the outline planning permission, and development must start within five years from the date of the grant of the outline planning permission or if later, the expiration of two years from the final approval of the reserved matters.

6.3.2 Full planning permission

An application for full planning permission must include all the information which the local planning authority will need, e.g. detailed plans. As with the grant of outline planning permission, the local planning authority can also impose such conditions as it sees fit.

A full planning permission is usually granted subject to a condition requiring the development to be started within a specified time. In England, this is usually three years from the date of the permission; in Wales it is usually five years.

6.3.3 Completion notices

Once the development has started, there is no time limit within which it must be completed. However, if development has not been completed within a reasonable time, the local planning authority may serve a completion notice terminating the planning permission after the expiration of a further period, being not less than 12 months from the date of service of the notice.

6.3.4 Register of planning applications

Each local planning authority must keep a register containing details of both pending applications and decided applications, together with the results of the applications. The register will give details of any conditions which attach to the planning permission. In addition, a condition prohibiting or restricting the use of land is registrable as a local land charge if imposed on or after 1 August 1977. Therefore, a search in the local land charges register should disclose the condition. Nevertheless, such an entry will not disclose the full details of the condition so the register of planning applications should always be checked even when it is known that the planning permission was granted on or after 1 August 1977.

6.3.5 Revocation, modification and discontinuance orders

Express planning permission can be revoked or modified. Compensation for loss resulting from such action should be claimed within six months of the order being made. A discontinuance order can discontinue the use, impose a condition or require the alteration or removal of a building or works. All three types of order are subject to the approval of the Secretary of State.

6.3.6 Tree preservation orders

A tree preservation order may refer to an individual tree or a group of trees and is subject to the approval of the Secretary of State. The usual form that the order takes is that it prevents the tree being cut down or lopped without permission unless it is in a dangerous state or dying. If the tree is cut down in defiance of an order or because it is dying, the owner of the land must replace the tree unless the local planning authority dispenses with this obligation.

6.3.7 Compensation

Compensation is paid when a decision of the Secretary of State has restricted the existing use development of the land, for example where the land is zoned for industrial development but planning permission is refused for a new factory. However, compensation is not always payable. The fact that compensation has been paid could affect any price payable under a compulsory purchase order.

6.3.8 Listed buildings

A building of special architectural or historic interest may be 'listed' by the Department for Digital, Culture, Media and Sport and Historic England (in Wales, the Welsh Assembly and Cadw). Once a building has been listed, special controls on development apply and listed building consent must be obtained for any development.

A buyer will be concerned to see whether any work has been carried out in contravention of these controls, or whether a notice has been served requiring that a building be returned to its original state. If a listed building is not being properly maintained, a repair notice can be served and, if necessary, a compulsory purchase order made.

The local planning authority may serve a building preservation notice relating to a building which it thinks should be listed and which is in danger of demolition or alteration. The notice lasts for six months, unless the decision about its listing is confirmed by the Secretary of State. During the duration of the notice the listed building controls operate.

6.3.9 Conservation areas

A local planning authority may designate any part of its area which is of special architectural or historic interest, the character or appearance of which it considers should be preserved or enhanced as a conservation area. Once an area has been designated, there will be restrictions on development. Conservation area consent is not required for the demolition of an unlisted building in a conservation area in England, but instead planning permission is required. In Wales, conservation area consent is required for the demolition of an unlisted building in a conservation area.

6.3.10 Planning obligations and the Community Infrastructure Levy

An applicant for planning permission, for example a developer, cannot be required to make a payment in return for the grant of planning permission. There will be situations, however, where a development could place demands on the local infrastructure that would legitimately require a developer to make such a payment, for example a housing development that creates a need for additional school classrooms. In such situations, a planning obligation under the Town and Country Planning Act 1990, s.106 may be used. This is a separate agreement entered into between the developer and the local planning authority, and will be a material consideration when deciding whether the planning permission should be granted.

In order to prevent abuse of planning obligations, the Community Infrastructure Levy Regulations 2010, SI 2010/948 provide that a planning obligation may constitute a reason for granting planning permission only if the obligation is:

(a)   necessary to make the development acceptable in planning terms;
(b)   directly related to the development; and
(c)   fairly and reasonably related in scale and kind to the development.

The Community Infrastructure Levy is a form of discretionary tax that a local planning authority may charge on developments which have an impact on local infrastructure. The Levy is based on a formula that reflects the size and type of development, and is set out in a charging schedule published by the local planning authority. The aim is that it will fund the infrastructure requirements currently dealt with by planning obligations, but in a more open and accountable way. Where the Levy is in use, planning obligations will continue to be relevant in dealing with site-specific matters, but their role and use will be significantly reduced. A local planning authority does not have to introduce a Community Infrastructure Levy. There will be no liability for the Community Infrastructure Levy unless there is a charging schedule in effect on the day planning permission for the Levy-liable development is granted. The Community Infrastructure Levy is registrable as a local land charge.

6.4 ENFORCEMENT

6.4.1 Enforcement notices

An enforcement notice may be served following a breach of planning control, either because a condition has been broken or because development has been carried out without permission. Notice is served on the owner, occupier and anyone else who has an interest in the land which is materially affected by the notice.

An enforcement notice must be served within 10 years of the breach, except in the following cases where notice must be served within four years of the breach:

(a) the carrying out of building operations, for example the erection of a new building; and

(b) changing the use of any building to use as a single dwelling house.

Non-compliance with a notice once it has taken effect is an offence, with the offender liable on conviction to an unlimited fine.

Before a notice comes into force, anyone on whom it has been served can appeal to the Secretary of State on any of the following grounds:

(a) planning permission ought to be granted;

(b) the matters alleged do not constitute a breach of planning control;

(c) the breach of control has not taken place;

(d) the relevant period within which enforcement action can be started has elapsed;

(e) the notice was not properly served;

(f) the steps required exceed what is necessary to remedy the breach; and

(g) the specified period for rectification falls short of what should reasonably be allowed.

A local planning authority can also apply to a magistrates' court for a planning enforcement order which allows enforcement action to be taken when the statutory time limits have expired and the breach of planning control has been concealed.

6.4.2 Stop notices

An enforcement notice has no effect while an appeal against it is pending. A local planning authority can therefore serve a stop notice to prevent the carrying on of any activity which is, or is included in, a matter alleged by an enforcement notice to constitute a breach of planning control. A stop notice must therefore always relate to an enforcement notice. A stop notice cannot relate to the use of a building as a dwelling house, and may also not prohibit any activity which commenced more than four years previously.

A local planning authority also has the power to serve a temporary stop notice which will prevent the carrying on of any activity specified in the notice while it considers whether further action should be taken. A temporary stop notice does not have to wait for an enforcement notice to be issued.

6.4.3 Breach of condition notice

A breach of condition notice is a notice which can be served by a local planning authority on a developer if a condition on a planning permission is not complied with. A breach of condition notice will outline the steps which should be taken in order to comply with the specific condition. If this notice is not complied with, the person served with the notice will be guilty of an offence and will be liable for a fine. There is no right of appeal against a breach of condition notice.

6.5 BUILDING REGULATIONS

In addition to an application for planning permission for development, an application may need to be made to the local authority for building regulations consent under the Building Regulations 2010, SI 2010/2214, as all building works must comply with these. The Regulations set standards for the design and construction of buildings to ensure the safety and health for people in or about those buildings. They also include requirements to ensure that fuel and power are conserved and facilities are provided for people, including those with disabilities, to access and move around inside buildings. A 'final certificate' is issued by the local authority on completion of the building works.

Many 'home improvement' works will require consent, for example replacement windows, new electrical installations and certain plumbing and drainage alterations. There are a number of 'self-certification' schemes which are regulated by the appropriate trade body and which allow contractors to self-certify their work. An example is the FENSA (Fenestration Self-Assessment) scheme which applies to replacement windows and doors. A contractor will issue a self-certification certificate on completion of the work and the appropriate trade body will then notify the local authority that the work has been completed. See 'Competent person schemes' at **www.gov.uk/building-regulations-competent-person-schemes** for details of other schemes.

The Regulations are enforced by the local authority which may serve an enforcement notice, prosecute in the magistrates' court and/or apply for an injunction. Even if a local authority does not prosecute or take enforcement action, it will not issue a 'final certificate'. This may cause problems on a subsequent sale, though it may be possible to obtain a 'regularisation certificate'.

An enforcement notice is served on a property owner and requires the removal or alteration of work that does not comply with the Building Regulations. An enforcement notice must be served within 12 months from the date of completion of the building work and gives the property owner 28 days to carry out the required work, failing which the local authority can carry out the work and charge the cost to the property owner.

Proceedings in a magistrates' court must be brought within six months from discovery of the breach provided that action is taken within two years of the completion of the offending work. An injunction may be applied for outside these time limits (*Cottingham* v. *Attey Bower & Jones (a firm)* [2000] EGCS 48).

6.6   SUMMARY

- When acting for a buyer, you should ensure that the property has all necessary planning permissions and building regulations approvals.
- Planning permission is required for any activity that amounts to 'development'.
- 'Development' includes building, engineering, mining or other operations, as well as a material change of use.
- Planning permission can be granted either by a deemed permission under the General Permitted Development Orders, or pursuant to an express application to the local planning authority.
- An application may be made for either full or outline planning permission.
- Enforcement action may be brought if there is a breach of planning control.
- Enforcement action must be brought within four years if it relates to building works or a change of use to a single dwelling, and within 10 years for other types of development.
- There are additional controls for listed buildings and buildings in conservation areas.
- Building regulations consent is required for building works.
- If building regulations are not complied with, doubt may be cast on the safety of the building works and may result in enforcement action.

CHAPTER 7

Investigating title

7.1 DEDUCTION OF TITLE

The seller is under an obligation either to prove ownership of the estate or interest which has been contracted to be sold, or to prove that someone else can be compelled to transfer that interest to the buyer. In other words, the seller must provide the buyer with a good title to the property.

There are no requirements as to title imposed by the Land Registration Act 2002, and so the parties are free to agree their own terms as to the title to be deduced. The Standard Conditions of Sale (fifth edition – 2018 revision), SC 4.1.2 provides that the seller must supply official copies of the title to the buyer. Under the Law Society Conveyancing Protocol (2019), the official copies should not be less than six months old.

Traditionally, under an open contract, the title was delivered to the buyer within a reasonable time after exchange of contracts. The modern practice is for title to be deduced before exchange of contracts, and this is reflected by SC 4.2.1 which provides that the buyer may not, after exchange of contracts, raise requisitions on a title which is deduced before exchange of contracts. The buyer may still raise requisitions on matters coming to his attention for the first time after exchange of contracts (SC 4.2.2). In the unlikely event of title being deduced after exchange of contracts, SC 4.3.1 sets out time limits for deducing title and raising requisitions.

7.2 INVESTIGATION OF TITLE

Once title has been deduced to the buyer, the buyer's solicitor will need to investigate the title to ensure that the seller owns the property and can transfer it to the buyer and that there are no defects in the title. Any problems which are discovered must be raised with the seller's solicitor by way of requisitions within the time limits specified in the contract for raising requisitions.

Title will also need to be investigated on behalf of any lender. Where the buyer's solicitor is also acting for the lender, title will be investigated once on behalf of both the buyer and the lender. If the lender is separately represented, its solicitor may either investigate the title or require the buyer's solicitor to provide a 'certificate of title'. This certifies that the borrower has a good and marketable title and is signed by the borrower's solicitor. The lender will then rely on this certificate of title in lieu of carrying out its own investigation of title.

7.3 HOW TO INVESTIGATE TITLE

Investigation of title comprises:

(a)   an examination of the official copies of the title supplied by the seller (including a copy of the lease where the title is leasehold and documents which are referred to on the register and evidence relating to matters as to which the register is not conclusive);

(b)   checking for evidence of overriding interests, as these are not entered on the register but are binding on the buyer irrespective of notice; and

(c)   pre-completion searches.

7.3.1 Official copies

It is good practice for you to check the following points when examining the official copies and title plan.

7.3.1.1   The property register

(a)   Does the description of the land accord with the contract description?
(b)   Does the title number correspond with that given in the contract?
(c)   Is the estate freehold or leasehold?
(d)   Which easements are enjoyed by the property?
(e)   Has any land been removed from the title? If so, does this affect the land being purchased?

7.3.1.2   The proprietorship register

(a)   Is the class of title correct?
(b)   Is the seller the registered proprietor? If not, who has the ability to transfer the land?
(c)   Are there any other entries such as restrictions, or pre-Land Registration Act 2002 cautions or inhibitions? What is their effect?

7.3.1.3   The charges register

(a)   Are there any incumbrances or other entries?
(b)   How do these affect the buyer?

(c)   Which of them will be removed or discharged on completion and how will their removal be effected?

7.3.1.4   The title plan

(a)   Is the land being purchased included within the title?
(b)   Check any colourings/hatchings which may indicate rights of way, the extent of covenants or land which has been removed from the title.

7.3.2   Adverse entries

The most commonly found entry on the proprietorship register will be a restriction. The wording of the restriction will indicate what procedure must be followed for a valid disposition of the land. The buyer must therefore either follow that procedure (e.g. payment of money to two trustees in the case of land held on a trust of land) or require the seller to procure the removal of the restriction from the register on or before completion.

A pre-Land Registration Act 2002 inhibition may also be found on the proprietorship register (usually in connection with the bankruptcy of the proprietor) and this will prevent any disposition of the land until it is removed. Similarly, a caution may have been entered on the register. Unless the caution is withdrawn, no dealing with the land can be registered until HM Land Registry has served notice on the cautioner giving him the opportunity to show cause why the dealing to the buyer should not proceed.

7.3.3   Overriding interests

The existence of most overriding interests can be discovered through:

(a)   disclosure in the contract by the seller;
(b)   pre-contract enquiries of the seller under which the seller will normally be asked to reveal details of adverse interests and occupiers' rights;
(c)   a local land charges search (local land charges not protected on the register are overriding interests);
(d)   inspection of the property before exchange which may reveal, e.g. occupiers, easements or adverse possession. The buyer's solicitor may also advise the buyer to re-inspect immediately prior to completion.

7.3.4   Documents referred to on the register

If any documents are referred to on the register as being filed with the title at HM Land Registry, a copy of such documents should be obtained and examined.

7.4 PROBLEM AREAS

The transaction with the seller and any past transactions revealed in the official copies should be considered to see whether they involve any problem areas, including those that follow.

7.5 TRUSTEES OF LAND

A restriction may be entered on the proprietorship register indicating what must be done to overreach the beneficial interests. A further restriction may also be entered reflecting any other limitations on the trustees' powers to dispose of the land. Provided the terms of any restriction are complied with, the buyer will get good title. Where trustees hold the land on trust for themselves as joint tenants in equity, no restriction is placed on the register and the buyer may safely deal with the survivor on proof of death of the other trustee.

7.6 PERSONAL REPRESENTATIVES

The term 'personal representatives' covers:

(a)   the executors of a deceased person's estate where there is a will; and

(b)   the administrators of a deceased person's estate where he has died intestate.

Only the personal representatives have power to deal with the legal estate of a deceased sole owner.

Following the death of a registered sole proprietor, his personal representatives can either apply to be registered as proprietors by sending the grant of representation to HM Land Registry, or sell the property in their capacity as personal representatives and provide the buyer with a certified copy of the grant. Personal representatives will only register themselves as proprietors if they are going to hold the land for some time, e.g. until the beneficiary reaches full age. Provided the buyer takes a transfer from all the proving personal representatives and submits an office copy or a certified copy of the grant with his application for registration, he will obtain a good title.

Personal representatives may assent the property to a beneficiary. An assent by personal representatives to a beneficiary must be in the prescribed form (e.g. form AS1).

7.7 CO-OWNERS

Where two or more people are beneficially entitled to the legal estate, it is vested in them as joint tenants upon a trust of land. The beneficial interest will be held by them either as joint tenants or as tenants in common.

Where the property is owned by two co-owners who are joint tenants in equity and one dies without severing the tenancy, the survivor is solely and beneficially entitled to the property and can deal with the legal estate. The buyer will require proof of death of the deceased co-owner, e.g. the death certificate.

Where the co-owners are tenants in common in equity, there will be a restriction on the proprietorship register. This will ensure that a second trustee is appointed to join with the surviving trustee in the sale. Alternatively, the buyer can deal with the survivor alone provided the restriction is removed, or the survivor provides the buyer with documentary evidence which will enable the restriction to be removed on the buyer's application for registration. Such proof might consist of a statutory declaration or statement of truth by the survivor that in stated circumstances the declarant had become entitled legally and beneficially to the registered estate and that he has not encumbered or dealt with his own share nor has he received notice of any incumbrance on or dealing with the deceased's share. In practice, it is better for the seller either to procure the removal of the restriction or to appoint a second trustee to act with the seller.

A second trustee can be appointed before exchange of contracts. The new trustee will then be a party to the contract. Alternatively, the sole trustee can enter into the contract on his own and then appoint another trustee prior to completion in order to receive the purchase price and thus ensure overreaching takes place. A special condition can be included in the contract requiring the seller to appoint the new trustee, although he would be under an obligation to do so anyway in order to comply with the duty to make good title.

7.8 SALES BY LENDERS

A lender may sell mortgaged property by exercising its power of sale. Such a power must exist, have arisen and become exercisable. The principles apply equally to registered and unregistered land.

7.8.1 Power of sale

Under the Law of Property Act 1925, s.101, every lender whose mortgage is made by deed has a statutory power of sale once the legal date for redemption has passed. This date is normally specified in the mortgage deed as a date within the first six months of the mortgage.

The power of sale cannot be exercised until one of the following conditions laid out in s.103 has been fulfilled:

(a)   notice has been served on the borrower requiring the repayment of all mortgage monies and this has not been complied with within three months of service of the notice;

(b)   some interest due on the mortgage has not been paid and two months have elapsed since the date for payment; or

(c)   the borrower has breached some provision of the Act or of the mortgage deed, not being a covenant for the payment of the mortgage sum or interest, e.g. where the borrower's statutory power of leasing is excluded and the borrower has let the mortgaged premises without the knowledge and consent of the lender.

7.8.2   Protection given to a buyer

Section 104 of the Law of Property Act 1925 provides that a buyer from a lender selling under a statutory power of sale does not have to enquire whether the power has become exercisable. The buyer merely has to ensure that the power of sale has arisen. This will be discovered by checking the mortgage deed.

7.8.3   Effect of sale

The effect of a sale by a lender is that the legal estate will be conveyed free from subsequent mortgages, but subject to any prior mortgages.

7.9   POWERS OF ATTORNEY

A power of attorney is a deed by which the donor gives someone else, the attorney, power to dispose of the donor's property or otherwise to act on behalf of the donor, e.g. a seller may appoint an attorney to execute the transfer where he will be abroad at the time the deed needs to be executed.

   There are five types of power of attorney:

(a)   a general power of attorney under the Powers of Attorney Act 1971, s.10 which entitles the attorney to deal with all of the donor's assets;

(b)   a special power of attorney which allows the attorney to deal only with certain specified assets or categories of assets;

(c)   a trustee power of attorney which is used where property is held on trust;

(d)   an enduring power of attorney made before 1 October 2007 under the Enduring Powers of Attorney Act 1985 which endures through the donor's mental incapacity (subject to registration); and

(e)   a lasting power of attorney which replaced an enduring power of attorney as from 1 October 2007.

When dealing with an attorney, or where a document of title has been executed by an attorney, the buyer's solicitor must check that the power has been correctly executed, that it gives the attorney power to dispose of the property and that it has not been revoked. The buyer is entitled to a certified copy of any power of attorney which affects the title.

7.9.1 Formalities

The Powers of Attorney Act 1971, s.1 provides that a power of attorney must be executed as a deed.

When a trustee executes a power of attorney, this is done by deed under the Trustee Act 1925, s.25. Written notice of the delegation must be given before or within seven days of its execution to the other trustees and the person(s), if any, who has (have) power to appoint new trustees. However, failure to give the notice does not invalidate the power of attorney.

7.9.2 General power of attorney

The general power of attorney set out in the Powers of Attorney Act 1971, s.10(1) is often used. This authorises the attorney to do on behalf of the donor anything which can be lawfully done by an attorney, and can be used by a sole beneficial owner of land.

7.9.3 Trustee power of attorney

Where there is a single trustee in respect of a trust, the Trustee Act 1925, s.25 allows the trustee to grant a power of attorney delegating his functions as a trustee. Section 25 sets out a short form of power of attorney by which a trustee can delegate his trust functions under a single trust to an attorney. The short form power would not be appropriate where the trustee wished to delegate his functions under several trusts to one attorney, or wished to limit the range of functions to be delegated.

Section 25 contains the following safeguards for the beneficiaries:

(a)   the trustee may only delegate his functions as a trustee for a period up to 12 months;

(b)   the trustee must, either before or within seven days after giving the power of attorney, give notice to his co-trustee(s) and anyone who is entitled to appoint a new trustee; and

(c)   the trustee is liable for the acts and defaults of his attorney.

Where there is more than one trustee, the requirements vary according to the date of the transaction:

(a)   Before 1 March 2000, a co-owner who wanted to appoint an attorney to act for him on the sale had to use a specific trustee power of attorney under the Trustee Act 1925, s.25. This power was only effective for a period of 12 months. Under a Trustee Act power, a co-owner or trustee could not appoint his sole co-trustee to be his attorney. If a co-owner wished to appoint his sole co-trustee, an enduring power of attorney under the Enduring Powers of Attorney Act 1985 should have been used.

(b) On or after 1 March 2000, a co-owner who has a beneficial interest in the land can use a general power of attorney and can appoint his sole co-trustee to be his attorney (Trustee Delegation Act 1999, s.1).

(c) Under the Trustee Delegation Act 1999, trustees who are not beneficially entitled to the land may use a general trustee power (Trustee Delegation Act 1999, s.5). However, the general trustee power is only effective for a period of 12 months. The trustee can appoint his sole co-trustee to be his attorney under the general trustee power.

However, whether a general power or general trustee power is used, if a sole co-trustee has been appointed to act as attorney, he cannot give a valid receipt for capital money. Overreaching cannot operate in these circumstances. So, if one of two owners wishes to appoint an attorney to execute the purchase deed, he should therefore appoint a third party to act as attorney. From 1 March 2000, enduring powers of attorney cannot be used to appoint a sole co-trustee to be an attorney.

7.9.4 Enduring power of attorney

Enduring powers of attorney were governed by the Enduring Powers of Attorney Act 1985. This has been repealed in full by the Mental Capacity Act 2005, s.66. Schedules 4 and 5 to the Mental Capacity Act 2005 contain provisions that apply to enduring powers of attorney created before 1 October 2007.

A power of attorney is an enduring power of attorney if it is in the prescribed form, executed by the donor and the attorney in the prescribed manner and incorporates the prescribed explanatory information to the effect that the power is intended to continue despite the supervening incapacity of the donor (Mental Capacity Act 2005, Sched.4, para.2).

Until the incapacity of the donor, the power takes effect as an ordinary power of attorney. Once the attorney has reason to believe that the donor is or is becoming mentally incapable, an application must be made by the attorney to the Office of the Public Guardian to register the power. An attorney may not act under the authority of a power when the donor is mentally incapable unless or until the power has been registered, or the attorney is taking action under the power to maintain the donor and protect his property. A buyer from an attorney under an enduring power should search at the Office of the Public Guardian in order to find out whether an application to register has been made or is pending.

Since 1 March 2000 an enduring power of attorney cannot be used for the general delegation of a trustee's powers (Trustee Delegation Act 1999, s.4). This means that a sole co-trustee cannot be appointed as attorney for the other trustee under an enduring power of attorney. Prior to 1 March 2000 such delegation had been permitted.

7.9.4.1   The effect of registration

Once the power is registered:

(a)   the donor cannot validly revoke it unless the court confirms the revocation;
(b)   the attorney cannot validly disclaim the power until the court is given notice of disclaimer; and
(c)   the donor cannot extend or restrict the scope of the authority.

These restrictions apply for as long as a power is registered under the Act even though the donor may no longer be mentally impaired.

7.9.4.2   Protection given to third parties

If the donor has become mentally incapable and no application has been made for registration by the attorney, the Powers of Attorney Act 1971, s.5 will apply to protect a person who without knowledge of incapacity deals with the attorney. It is as though the power had not been revoked.

If an application to register the power has been made but registration has not yet been completed, the attorney may only act under the power during this period to the extent that it is necessary in order to maintain the donor and to prevent loss to the donor's estate (Mental Capacity Act 2005, Sched.4, para.1(2). However, a person dealing with an attorney who is unaware that the attorney is acting outside Sched.4, para.1(2) is protected as the transaction is as valid as if it were one within para.1(2) (Sched.4, para.1(3)).

7.9.4.3   Protection where the power is invalid or revoked

The Mental Capacity Act 2005, Sched.4, para.18 provides that where:

(a)   a registered power did not create a valid enduring power;
(b)   had the power been valid it would have been revoked; or
(c)   it would have expired,

the transaction between the attorney and another person shall, in favour of that person, be as valid as if the power had been in existence unless that person knew that:

(a)   the instrument did not create a valid enduring power;
(b)   an event has occurred which would have revoked a valid enduring power; or
(c)   the power would have expired before that date if it was a valid enduring power.

In favour of a buyer from a person who dealt with the attorney, there is a conclusive presumption that that person did not know of any of the above matters, provided that either:

(a)   the transaction between the attorney and that person took place within 12 months of the date of registration of the power; or

(b) that person makes a statutory declaration, before or within three months of the completion of the transaction, that, at the time, the person had no reason to doubt that the attorney had the authority to carry out the transaction.

7.9.5 Lasting power of attorney

From 1 October 2007, the Mental Capacity Act 2005 has replaced enduring powers of attorney with lasting powers of attorney. There are two types of lasting powers of attorney:

(a) A lasting power of attorney that grants authority in relation to the donor's property and affairs – for example, it may allow the attorney to sell the donor's property. The attorney may use the lasting power of attorney while the donor still has capacity, unless the donor specifies otherwise in the lasting power of attorney.
(b) A lasting power of attorney that grants authority in relation to the donor's personal welfare. This type of lasting power of attorney may not be used until the donor loses capacity (or the attorney reasonably believes that the donor has lost capacity).

A lasting power of attorney must be made using the prescribed form and be executed following the prescribed procedure.

7.9.5.1 The effect of registration

A lasting power of attorney does not have to be registered as soon as it is made, but the attorney must not act under a lasting power of attorney until it has been registered. A lasting power of attorney may be registered at any time after it is made. Registration is with the Office of the Public Guardian.

7.9.5.2 Protection given to third parties

A third party dealing with an attorney should ensure that:

(a) The lasting power of attorney is registered and is still in force. A register of lasting powers of attorney is kept by the Office of the Public Guardian and can be searched to check that the lasting power of attorney remains in force.
(b) The identity of the attorney is clear.
(c) The attorney is acting within the scope of their authority.

7.9.5.3 Protection where the power is invalid or revoked

If a lasting power of attorney is invalid, a transaction between an attorney and a third party will be valid, in favour of the third party, unless the third party knew that the lasting power of attorney was invalid or was aware of circumstances that would have terminated the attorney's authority to act under the lasting power of attorney (Mental Capacity Act 2005, s.9).

A buyer who subsequently buys from the third party (in good faith and for valuable consideration) can rely on the presumption that the transaction between the attorney and the third party will be valid (by virtue of the Mental Capacity Act 2005, s.14) if either of the following applies:

(a)   the transaction between the attorney and the third party was completed within 12 months of the date on which the lasting power of attorney was registered;

(b)   the third party makes a statutory declaration, either before or within three months of completion of the purchase, that they had no reason to doubt that the attorney had authority to dispose of the property at the time of the transaction.

7.9.6   Proof of power

A power of attorney becomes a document of title and, under the Law of Property Act 1925, s.125(2) a buyer is entitled to have, free of charge, either the original or a copy of any power of attorney which affects the title. A photocopy of the power will suffice provided that it is certified by a solicitor as being a true and accurate copy of the original.

HM Land Registry will require the original or a certified copy of the power on registration of a disposition made in exercise of the power.

If the transaction between the attorney and the buyer is not made within 12 months of the date on which the power came into operation, HM Land Registry may require evidence to satisfy it that the power has not been revoked. This must be either a statutory declaration or a statement of truth by the buyer or a certificate given by the buyer's conveyancer. A form of statutory declaration and certificate are set out in Appendix B to HM Land Registry Practice Guide 9 (Powers of Attorney and Registered Land).

7.10   DISCHARGED MORTGAGES

A mortgage which has been discharged will be deleted from the charges register and is therefore of no further concern to the buyer.

As far as the seller's existing mortgage is concerned, the buyer should raise a requisition requiring this to be removed on or before completion. Discharge of a mortgage of registered land is effected by filing a completed Form DS1 at HM Land Registry or by use of the electronic discharge (ED) or e-DS1 system.

7.11 TRANSACTIONS AT AN UNDERVALUE

Where a prospective buyer has notice that the land has been the subject of an undervalue transaction, it may be necessary to consider whether the court's powers to set aside, under the Insolvency Act 1986, s.238 (insolvent companies) or s.339 (insolvent individuals), apply.

An undervalue transaction may be the result of a gift; a partial gift (made for a consideration but a substantially below market value one); financial arrangements following a marriage breakdown; or a deed of variation in relation to an inheritance.

If s.238 or s.339 do apply, it will then be necessary to see whether the protection provided by ss.241(2) and 342(2) operates. The powers of the court under ss.238 and 339 are exercisable where the completed transaction at an undervalue took place within the two-year period leading up to the start of the administration or liquidation (insolvent companies), or the five-year period leading up to the bankruptcy (insolvent individuals), but the provisions of the Insolvency Act protect a subsequent buyer of the property who was not a party to the undervalue transaction and who acquires in good faith and for value during those periods.

7.11.1 Transactions by an individual

Wide-ranging provisions affecting transactions at an undervalue are contained in the Insolvency Act 1986, ss.339–342 as amended by the Insolvency (No.2) Act 1994.

If a donor becomes bankrupt after having made a transaction at an undervalue, the transaction may be set aside by the donor's trustee in bankruptcy if it was made within the last two years. This means that it is unsafe for a buyer to proceed until at least two years have passed since the voluntary disposition.

If the transaction at an undervalue was made within between two and five years ago, a current buyer will be protected, provided he acquires the property in good faith and for value. There is a presumption that a buyer is not in good faith where:

(a)   when he acquired the property, he had notice of the bankruptcy proceedings and that the disposition to the donee was at an undervalue; or

(b)   he was an associate of either the donor or the donee. The term 'associate' is widely defined in s.435 to include a spouse, relative, partner, an employer or employee.

The buyer's solicitor should make a Land Charges Department search against the donor in a transaction at an undervalue to find out whether he has become insolvent within five years of the transaction.

7.11.2 Transactions by a company

There are similar provisions relating to voluntary dispositions by a company contained in the Insolvency Act 1986, ss.238–341. If a company has made a voluntary disposition within the two years prior to the current transaction to a person connected with the company, it may be set aside by the liquidator should the company subsequently become insolvent. A 'person connected' is defined as a director of the company, an associate and a company within the same group. The practical effect of this is that the current transaction cannot proceed until two years have elapsed since the voluntary disposition.

If, however, the voluntary disposition was made to a person not connected with the company, the liquidator can only set it aside if the current buyer has notice of the insolvency proceedings and of the voluntary disposition. A buyer should therefore carry out a company search to make sure that there were no insolvency proceedings within the two years after the voluntary disposition.

After the buyer's solicitor has examined the title which has been deduced, any doubt or objection to the title should then be raised with the seller's solicitor by means of a written requisition. This will be more than just a question about an alleged defect; it will also require the seller to remove the alleged defect from the title.

7.12 REQUISITIONS ON TITLE

The purpose of raising requisitions on title is to require the seller's solicitor to clarify, and if necessary to rectify, matters on the title supplied which the buyer's solicitor finds unsatisfactory. In practice, requisitions are commonly used also to resolve administrative queries relating to the arrangements for completion.

In some cases, the replies given to requisitions may be construed as undertakings, e.g. to discharge the seller's outstanding mortgage on the property. Where such an undertaking is given, the seller's solicitor should ensure that he has only committed himself to do what is within his power to do; an undertaking to discharge the seller's mortgage(s) on the property or one which is simply worded 'confirmed' or 'noted' will be interpreted as meaning that all subsisting charges will be removed. The seller's solicitor should therefore ensure that he is fully aware of the details of all such charges before committing himself to such an undertaking. Alternatively, the seller's solicitor or licensed conveyancer may prefer to undertake to discharge certain named charges only.

7.12.1 Standard form requisitions

Most law stationers produce a standard form which includes many commonly asked questions and deals with the administrative arrangements for completion. Under the Law Society Conveyancing Protocol (2019), the TA13 Completion Information and Undertakings form must be used. Where the title has been investigated before exchange, the only question relating to title is to ask the seller to confirm that nothing has altered since contracts were exchanged. Queries which are specific to the property may either be added to the end of the standard form or typed on a separate sheet. The buyer's solicitor should send two copies of the form to the seller's solicitor, who will return one copy with his answers. The buyer's solicitor should make sure that the answers given by the seller's solicitor are satisfactory. Any unsatisfactory answers should be taken up with the seller's solicitor.

7.12.2 Time for raising requisitions

The modern practice is for the seller's evidence of title to be sent to the buyer together with the draft contract. Any doubts which the buyer has on the title can then be raised before exchange of contracts. Standard condition 4.2.1 then prohibits the buyer from raising requisitions after exchange of contracts. This means that the buyer must investigate title and raise any requisitions before exchange of contracts. Notwithstanding this, if a title matter comes to the buyer's attention after exchange of contracts which had not been previously disclosed, he can raise requisitions on that matter within six working days of it coming to his attention (SC 4.2.2).

If the seller does not supply his evidence of title before exchange of contracts, the timetable for raising requisitions is contained in SC 4.3.1. The buyer must raise requisitions within six working days of either the date of the contract or the date of delivery of the seller's evidence of title, whichever is the later. The seller must then reply in writing to any requisitions within four working days after receiving the requisitions. The buyer may then make written observations on the seller's replies within three working days after receiving the replies. These time limits are based on there being a period of 15 working days between exchange of contracts and completion; if there is not, then SC 4.3.4 provides for the time limit to be reduced.

If the seller supplies incomplete evidence of his title, then the time limit within which requisitions must be raised is postponed until the missing evidence is delivered, but only as regards matters disclosed by this missing evidence. However, matters which are apparent from an imperfect abstract must be taken up within the ordinary time period.

Time is of the essence when raising requisitions, and if the buyer does not keep to the time limits, the seller is under no obligation to answer the requisitions and the buyer could be liable for damages should completion be delayed.

7.12.3 Vendor and purchaser summons

If the seller's solicitor refuses to answer a proper requisition, the buyer can compel an answer by means of the vendor and purchaser summons procedure under the Law of Property Act 1925, s.49 which provides a summary method of resolving disputes between the parties. This procedure is intended to be used to resolve an impasse between the parties where agreement cannot be reached over a specific point in relation to the title and not as a general sounding-board to test the validity of the whole title or of the contract.

7.12.4 Right to rescind

The Standard Conditions of Sale do not allow the seller to rescind the contract where the buyer raises a requisition with which the seller is unable or unwilling to comply.

If the seller has not answered a requisition by the contractual completion date, it might be possible for the buyer to treat the contract as discharged by a breach of condition or to serve a notice to complete under SC 6.8.

7.13 SUMMARY

- Title is deduced before exchange of contracts by the seller supplying official copies of the register.
- When acting for a seller, you must investigate before drafting the contract; and when acting for a buyer, you must investigate title before exchange of contracts.
- If your investigation reveals a problem, you should raise a requisition with the seller's solicitor.
- If a problem with the title cannot be resolved, it may be possible to take out defective title indemnity insurance.
- You should check the official copies and title plan, and also check for any interests that override.
- If buying from trustees, the buyer must pay the purchase money to all the trustees, being at least two in number, or a trust corporation.
- Where a sale is by personal representatives, you must check the grant of representation and purchase from all proving personal representatives.
- If a co-owner has died, the buyer must ask for evidence of the death and if the co-owners held as tenants in common, a second trustee must be appointed.
- When buying property from a lender, you must check that the power of sale has arisen.
- When acting for a buyer, you must ensure that all subsisting mortgages are discharged on or before completion, or an undertaking provided on completion.
- If an attorney is selling, the buyer must be satisfied that the power of attorney authorises the attorney to sell the property, and that the power is valid and subsisting.
- Where property was previously sold at an undervalue, the buyer should carry out bankruptcy searches against the individual or company who sold at an undervalue for the period of five years (in the case of an individual) or two years (in the case of a company) from the date of the undervalue transaction.

CHAPTER 8

Mortgages

If the buyer is obtaining a mortgage to assist with the purchase, it is common for the buyer's solicitor to be instructed by the lender also to act on its behalf. It is possible in these situations for the buyer's solicitor to act for the lender. Some lenders prefer to instruct their own solicitor, or have a restricted panel of solicitors who can act for them, and in this case the buyer's solicitor must ensure that the lender's solicitor is satisfied with the title to the property before exchange of contracts. UK Finance has a set of standard instructions for a solicitor acting just for the lender and these are set out in Part 3 of the Lenders' Handbook.

Where the solicitor acts for both buyer and lender, then care must be taken to comply with the solicitor's professional duty not to act for persons where there is a conflict of interest.

In this chapter we look at the steps which need to be taken in connection with a mortgage where the buyer's solicitor is also acting for the lender.

8.1 LENDERS' PANELS

A firm which wishes to act for lenders in conveyancing transactions will have to apply for membership of that lender's panel. The criteria applied to determine an application to a panel may differ from lender to lender.

Many lenders have made the Law Society's Conveyancing Quality Scheme (CQS) accreditation a prerequisite for a firm wishing to join or remain on their conveyancing panels.

Lender Exchange (**www.lenderexchange.co.uk**) is an internet application to help certain lenders manage their conveyancing panels.

8.2 PRE-CONTRACT MATTERS

8.2.1 Mortgage offer

Before contracts are exchanged, the buyer must be sure that he will be able to complete, and therefore if a mortgage is needed he must have received and, if necessary, accepted a mortgage offer. If a formal acceptance is required, the buyer must be advised to do this within the time limit stipulated by the lender, otherwise the mortgage funds may not be available for completion.

The mortgage offer must be considered carefully to ensure that any conditions attached to it are satisfactory. Conditions may either be standard, in that they apply to all mortgages granted by that lender, or be particular to that mortgage offer only. Common conditions include:

(a) *Details of any repairs which the lender requires, including the time by which they must be completed.* The lender may decide to make a retention from the advance until the work has been completed. The buyer must be advised of the fact that the lender is making a retention and that the money being retained will not be released until the necessary work has been completed. This may cause the buyer financial difficulties as he will still have to pay the seller the full purchase price. It may be possible to negotiate a reduced price with the seller, bearing in mind the work which has to be carried out. In any event, the buyer must be advised to obtain estimates for the work before contracts are exchanged, as it may well be that the cost of carrying out the work exceeds the amount of the retention and this could cause further financial difficulties for the buyer.

As an alternative, the buyer may be able, with the seller's permission, to carry out the work before completion so that the lender can release the money in time for completion. Where the buyer is considering such action, advice must be given that it would be extremely risky for the buyer to do this as the seller may refuse to complete once the work has been carried out.

Some lenders, rather than making a retention, may just require the buyer to undertake in writing to carry out the work within a specified period after completion.

(b) *The lender will, where the loan is more than the lender considers advisable (e.g. it is a large percentage of the purchase price), take out a mortgage guarantee policy which will give it protection should the property be sold and the sale price not be sufficient to repay the mortgage.* A single 'once and for all' premium is payable by the buyer for this insurance. This premium will either be added to the loan or be deducted from the amount of the advance. In the event of the latter, the buyer must be advised of the need to make up the amount deducted from his own funds.

(c) *If the mortgage is an interest-only mortgage, the buyer will usually also take out a separate investment vehicle, such as an endowment policy, an Individual Savings Account (ISA) or a pension plan, and the lender may impose conditions relating to this.* If a new policy is being issued, the buyer's solicitor may be required to ensure that it is in force at exchange of contracts. Existing policies must be checked to make sure that they are not already mortgaged, or if they are that they will be released on completion, and also that the amount of cover is sufficient.

(d)   *If the lender is insuring the property, the offer will set out details of the amount of cover and when the cover will start.* The buyer's solicitor must make sure that the cover starts in accordance with the provisions in the contract.

The buyer must also have the repayment terms explained to him.

8.2.2   Mortgage instructions

The buyer's solicitor will receive formal instructions from the lender, and these must be carefully considered like any other set of instructions. The solicitor must act strictly in accordance with the instructions given; in particular, the instructions may specify exactly the circumstances when the lender's funds may be used. Along with the instructions, the solicitor will also receive copies of the lender's standard mortgage documentation, e.g. mortgage deed, report on title.

The lender may have adopted either the Lenders' Handbook or the BSA Mortgage Instructions, both of which contain a set of standard mortgage instructions. The lender's instructions will specify whether the solicitor is being instructed in accordance with the Lenders' Handbook or the BSA Mortgage Instructions.

If during the course of the transaction anything comes to the attention of the solicitor whereby the buyer will be in breach of the mortgage offer – e.g. the purchase price as stated on the offer is not the true price – it must be reported to the lender. However, before doing this the buyer's solicitor must obtain the buyer's consent, otherwise there will be a breach of the solicitor's duty of confidentiality to the buyer. If the solicitor does not report such a matter to the lender and the buyer is perpetrating a fraud, then it is possible that the solicitor will be criminally liable and subject to disciplinary proceedings.

The buyer's solicitor must also inform the lender of any matters revealed in the replies to the pre-contract searches and enquiries which could affect the lender's offer.

8.2.3   Acting for both lender and borrower

In residential transactions, the buyer's solicitor will very often act for both the buyer and the buyer's lender (see **3.5.3**).

8.3   PRE-COMPLETION

8.3.1   Investigation of title

The same investigation of title must be carried out for the lender as is carried out for the buyer. The official search of the register should be made on behalf of the lender. This will protect both the lender and the buyer, whereas a search carried out on behalf of the buyer will only protect the buyer.

It must also be established whether anyone else other than the buyer and the lender will acquire an interest in the property as this could affect the lender's right to possession. Enquiries must be made with the buyer to see whether there will be anyone else living in the property or contributing to the purchase price. If there will be, it must be reported to the lender, and the person will usually be required to execute a deed postponing his or her interest to that of the lender. Before executing such a deed, the person who is to execute must be advised to take independent legal advice. Additionally, or alternatively, the lender may require that the buyer appoints a second trustee to receive the mortgage advance and thereby overreach the other person's interest.

If the other person knew about the mortgage then, following *Paddington Building Society* v. *Mendelsohn* (1985) 50 P & CR 244 and *Abbey National Building Society* v. *Cann* [1991] 1 AC 56, they will not be able to argue that their interest takes priority over the lender's.

8.3.2 Investigation of the buyer

The lender's solicitor must also investigate the buyer by making a bankruptcy-only search of the Land Charges register against the buyer's full name. If the search reveals an adverse entry, it must be reported immediately to the lender and further instructions requested.

8.3.3 The mortgage deed

As already mentioned, the lender's solicitor will receive copies of the lender's standard mortgage deed as part of the documentation sent with the instructions to act. Usually the solicitor has to complete the deed by inserting the required information in the blank spaces, although some lenders now supply already completed mortgage deeds which the solicitor just has to check to make sure that the details of the buyer and the property are correct. The deed must then be executed by the buyer. This must be done before completion, otherwise the lender will have no security for the loan.

The mortgage deed must be explained to the buyer, including such matters as:

(a) the amount of the repayments and the initial rate of interest, which will vary;
(b) the legal redemption date, which is the date on which the lender's power of sale arises;
(c) any exclusion of the statutory right to lease; and
(d) any penalties for early repayment.

8.3.4 Endowment mortgages

In the case of an endowment mortgage, the buyer is also offering the lender the endowment policy as additional security for the loan. A lender may insist that a mortgage deed is executed in relation to the policy, but the more usual modern practice is just to deposit the policy with the title deeds. Whichever method is used, a notice of assignment or deposit of the policy must be prepared in duplicate if required by the lender. A standard form of notice will be included with the bundle of documentation sent with the mortgage instructions if its use is required.

8.3.5 Report on title

The lender's solicitor must report to the lender that the title is satisfactory and that the mortgage deed has been executed. In residential transactions, the form of certificate approved by the Law Society and UK Finance will be used.

It is important to note that the report on title contains important promises by the solicitor that he has investigated the title and has complied with all the lender's instructions, and failure to do so can lead to legal action and professional disciplinary sanctions. Sufficient time must be allowed for the lender to dispatch the mortgage money in time for completion.

8.4 POST-COMPLETION

8.4.1 Report of completion

The lender's solicitor must report to the lender that completion has taken place. Some lenders provide a standard form for this purpose.

8.4.2 Stamp duty land tax and registration

The lender will be concerned to ensure that the buyer has good title, that any SDLT has been paid and that the transaction is registered. The mortgage deed must be registered at HM Land Registry at the same time as the transfer.

8.4.3 Endowment mortgages

The notice of assignment or deposit must be served in duplicate on the life assurance company. One copy will be subsequently returned duly receipted by the company, and this should be placed with the title deeds.

8.4.4 Custody of title deeds

Once registration has been completed, the documents should be dealt with as required by the lender. A schedule in duplicate listing the documents may be required by the lender. One copy of this will be returned duly receipted. This should be placed on file.

8.5 SUMMARY

- A lender will issue a 'mortgage offer' indicating the terms on which it is willing to lend.
- You should check the mortgage offer and advise the buyer of any terms and conditions attached to the offer – for example, if there is a retention, whether the buyer has to pay for a mortgage guarantee policy and whether the buyer must formally accept the offer.
- It is usual for a solicitor to be instructed to act for the buyer as well as the lender.
- When acting for both buyer and lender, you must consider the risk of a conflict of interest and be aware of your duty of confidentiality.
- You will usually have to act in accordance with standardised instructions as set out in either the Lenders' Handbook or the BSA Mortgage Instructions.
- When acting for a lender, you must confirm that the property has a good and marketable title.
- You will need to complete a mortgage deed in the lender's standard form and you must explain the nature and effect of the mortgage documentation to the borrower.

CHAPTER 9

Exchange of contracts

This chapter will look at the action to be taken by each party's solicitor in readiness for exchange; the requirements for the formation of a valid contract; the methods of exchanging contracts; and the position of the parties after exchange.

9.1 PREPARING FOR EXCHANGE – ACTING FOR THE BUYER

9.1.1 Replies to pre-contract searches and enquiries

The replies to the pre-contract searches and enquiries must be checked to make sure that they are satisfactory. Any matters arising out of the replies must be resolved before exchange.

9.1.2 Mortgage arrangements

Before contracts are exchanged, the buyer's solicitor must ensure that the buyer will have sufficient funds to complete the purchase. In the majority of purchases of residential property the buyer will be obtaining a mortgage. Before exchange, a satisfactory mortgage offer must have been made and, if required by the lender, accepted by the buyer.

The terms of the mortgage offer must be carefully considered by the buyer's solicitor, particularly any special conditions attached to the offer, e.g. a retention from the advance, to make sure that they can be complied with and that they will not cause the buyer any problems.

9.1.3 The deposit

The deposit will be paid by the buyer either from his own funds, e.g. where the buyer is a first-time buyer, or alternatively, where the buyer has a related sale, it is usual to use the deposit received on the sale transaction as the deposit on the purchase and, as we have seen, this is allowable under the Standard Conditions of Sale (fifth edition – 2018 revision), SC 2.2.5 provided that the requirements specified are fulfilled.

Where the deposit is to be paid from the buyer's own funds, it must be obtained in sufficient time to allow funds to clear before exchange.

If the funds available either from the buyer or from the deposit on the related transaction are less than a full 10 per cent deposit, then either:

(a)   the buyer must make up the difference; or

(b)   the payment of a reduced deposit must be agreed with the seller, and a special condition to this effect included in the contract.

Possible ways of making up the deposit include:

(a)   *Bridging finance.* Where the buyer has a related sale, his bank may be prepared to make available funds which are then repaid on completion. Before such a loan is made, the buyer's solicitor will have to undertake with the bank to repay the loan out of the sale proceeds. A standard form of undertaking has been agreed by the Law Society with the banks for use by solicitors when giving undertakings in relation to bridging loans. An arrangement fee will be payable by the buyer, and the interest payable will be high. The buyer must be advised that there are risks involved in taking out bridging finance, especially if the buyer's sale does not proceed to completion.

(b)   *A deposit guarantee.* These are not very common and involve the buyer taking out an insurance policy in lieu of paying a deposit. Should the buyer then default after exchange, the seller can recover the amount of the deposit which should have been paid from the insurance company. As a deposit is not actually paid on exchange where such a policy is used, the seller's consent must be obtained before the policy is taken out, and a provision included in the contract to allow the policy to be used instead of paying a deposit.

9.1.4   Insurance

Arrangements must be made to insure the property from exchange of contracts.

9.1.5   Report to the buyer

When the buyer's solicitor has completed his investigations, he should report to the buyer. This report should either include or deal with the following:

(a)   a description of the property (including a copy of the title plan);

(b)   whether the title is freehold or leasehold, and the grade of registration;

(c)   details of any rights passing with, or over, the property;

(d)   an explanation of any covenants affecting the property;

(e)   a summary and explanation of the results of the searches and enquiries carried out;

(f)   an explanation of the main terms of the contract, e.g. purchase price, deposit, completion date, insurance, etc.;

(g)   an explanation of the terms of any mortgage.

9.1.6 Approval and signature of the draft contract

The buyer's solicitor must carefully consider the terms of the draft contract in the light of the title and all the searches and enquiries to make sure that the property is suitable for his client's use and enjoyment.

When looking at a clause in the draft contract, the buyer's solicitor should consider:

(a)   Does it accord with the buyer's instructions?
(b)   Does it do what it is intended to?
(c)   Does it represent a fair balance between the interests of the parties?

If it does not, then it should be amended until it does.

One matter in particular which the buyer's solicitor must consider is whether there are any restrictive covenants affecting the property which may affect the buyer's use of the property. If this is the case, then the following options should be considered:

(a)   *Obtain the consent of the person with the benefit of the covenant.* In the case of an old covenant this will not be easy, unless it was imposed by someone such as the Duke of Northumberland. A fee may be payable for the consent.

(b)   *Take out insurance against breach of covenant.* This is appropriate where the person with the benefit of the covenant cannot be found and not in the situation where he or she has been found but refuses to give consent. This type of insurance is offered by several insurance companies. Initial contact should be made to find out exactly what information the company will require in order to decide whether to accept risk. A single premium will be payable, and the benefit of the policy will normally be capable of being passed on to a subsequent buyer. It is important that any lender involved is informed that a policy is being applied for as it will usually wish to approve the terms of the policy.

(c)   *Apply to the Lands Chamber of the Upper Tribunal under the Law of Property Act 1925, s.84.* The Upper Tribunal has the power to discharge or modify a restrictive covenant in certain circumstances.

(d)   If none of the above is possible, the buyer's solicitor should advise his client of the risks of proceeding.

Once agreement has been reached on the terms of the contract and the buyer has given instructions to proceed, the buyer's solicitor will return one copy of the contract to the seller's solicitor and both parties will then sign their respective parts of the contract in readiness for exchange.

Before the buyer signs his part of the contract, his solicitor must ensure that the buyer fully understands the terms of the contract and the results of the searches and enquiries. The contract is not dated until exchange.

9.1.7 Completion date and synchronisation

Before exchange, a completion date should be agreed by the parties. This is then inserted into the contract just before exchange.

If the buyer's purchase is dependent on the sale of another property, then the exchange of contracts for each property must be synchronised and the same completion date agreed for both transactions.

9.2 PREPARING FOR EXCHANGE – ACTING FOR THE SELLER

9.2.1 Mortgage arrangements

The seller's solicitor may at this stage write to the lender to obtain details of the amount required to redeem the seller's mortgage on completion so that he can then ensure that there will be sufficient funds available on completion to redeem the mortgage.

9.2.2 Approval and signature of the draft contract

Any amendments made to the draft contract by the buyer's solicitor must be approved before the seller signs the contract. As with the buyer, the terms of the contract must be explained to the seller before the seller signs it. The contract is not dated until exchange.

9.3 FORMATION OF THE CONTRACT

As with any other contract, there must be an offer and an acceptance, an intention to create legal relations and consideration must be present. In addition, the requirements of the Law of Property (Miscellaneous Provisions) Act 1989, s.2 must be complied with.

9.4 SIGNATURE OF THE CONTRACT

9.4.1 Signature by the client

The contract should usually be signed by the client in the presence of the client's solicitor. This will enable the solicitor to:

(a)   explain the terms of the contract to the client and to ensure that the client understands them; and

(b)   answer any queries which the client might have.

However, in practice it is not always convenient for the client to attend the solicitor's offices. In this case, the contract may be sent out to the client with a covering letter containing:

(a)   an explanation of the terms of the contract;
(b)   details of how and where the client must sign; and
(c)   a request for a deposit, if appropriate.

9.4.2   Signature by an agent

If an agent signs the contract he must have authority to do so, whether expressly, impliedly or ostensibly. When an agent signs the contract it should be made clear that it is being signed by him as agent so that the agent will incur no personal liability on the contract. The words 'X as agent for Y' are usually used.

A solicitor, when instructed to act in the sale of a property, has no implied authority to sign a contract, although he may be given express authority to do so. Such authority should be given in writing and the client advised of its effect, i.e. that the solicitor can commit the client to a binding contract. It is important to obtain authority from all those for whom the solicitor is to sign otherwise the solicitor may be liable for breach of warranty of authority (see *Suleman* v. *Shahsavari* [1989] 2 All ER 460).

9.5   METHODS OF EXCHANGE

A binding contract may be entered into by any method allowed by contract law, but the usual practice is for the contract to be formed by an 'exchange' of two identical parts. In this case, neither party is actually bound until the contracts have been exchanged.

There are three customary methods of exchange:

(a)   in person;
(b)   by post or document exchange; or
(c)   by telephone.

9.5.1   Exchange in person

Exchange takes place by the buyer's solicitor attending the seller's solicitor's office and actually handing over his part of the contract and receiving in exchange the seller's part. The contract will become binding at the time of the exchange. This method is now rarely used as it is only practicable where the offices of the solicitors involved are close to each other and the transaction is not part of a larger chain of transactions.

9.5.2 Exchange by post

After the contract has been signed, the buyer's part of the contract, together with a cheque for the deposit, is posted to the seller's solicitor. On receiving the buyer's part of the contract, the seller's solicitor will insert the agreed completion date, date both parts of the contract and then send the seller's signed part to the buyer's solicitor to complete the exchange. Exchange by post can cause problems where there is a chain of transactions.

9.5.3 Exchange through the document exchange

Where rather than using the post to exchange the solicitors use the document exchange, SC 2.1.1 provides that the contract will be made when the seller's part is deposited at the document exchange.

9.5.4 Exchange by telephone

This is now the most common method of exchanging contracts. In *Domb* v. *Isoz* [1980] Ch 548, the Court of Appeal said that a solicitor, acting for either a seller or a buyer of a house, who holds his client's signed part of the contract has ostensible authority to effect exchange of contracts and that the exchange can be effected in any manner recognised by the law as amounting to exchange. A telephone call between the solicitors for the seller and the buyer purporting to exchange contracts may create a binding contract. Where a solicitor has ostensible authority to deliver that document to another solicitor, if he gives an undertaking to hold that document to the order of the other solicitor, this binding undertaking constitutes constructive delivery of that document.

It was recommended in *Domb* v. *Isoz* that this method of exchange should be carried out only by partners in the firm, and that both parties to the telephone call should agree and record identical attendance notes.

Standard condition 2.1.2 appears to provide that telephone exchange must be carried out by the parties' conveyancers (as defined by SC 1.1.1(f)).

This method is not without its problems and the Law Society has produced three formulae for solicitors to use when exchanging over the telephone in an attempt to reduce the risks, explained in the next section.

9.6 LAW SOCIETY FORMULAE

9.6.1 Formula A

This formula is used where one solicitor (normally the seller's solicitor) holds both signed parts of the contract. Both solicitors agree a completion date, and the solicitor holding the contracts must confirm that both parts are identical and that the agreed completion date will be inserted into both parts.

Exchange then takes place at an agreed moment during the telephone conversation, and the solicitor holding the contracts acknowledges that he holds the part signed by his client to the order of the other party and that this part will be sent to the other party that day by first-class post, through the document exchange or by hand delivery, together, if he is the buyer's solicitor, with any deposit.

This is the safest of the formulae as the seller's solicitor can ensure that both parts of the contract are identical, and he will also have the deposit cheque in his possession.

9.6.2 Formula B

This is for use when each solicitor holds his own client's signed part of the contract. A completion date is agreed and each solicitor undertakes to hold his signed part to the other's order so that there is an immediate exchange. They also undertake to forward their respective parts to the other party in the ways mentioned for Formula A, and the buyer's solicitor agrees to forward the deposit with the buyer's part of the contract.

The possible problems which may arise with the use of this formula include that:

(a)   the parts of the contract might not be identical;
(b)   one of the parts might not be signed; and
(c)   the buyer's solicitor might not send the deposit.

9.6.3 Memorandum of exchange

When using either Formula A or Formula B, each solicitor should make a note recording:

(a)   the date and time of exchange;
(b)   the formula used and any agreed variations to it;
(c)   the completion date;
(d)   the amount of the agreed deposit; and
(e)   the names of the parties to the conversation.

9.6.4 Formula C

This formula has been introduced to deal with the risks which arise where there is a chain of transactions and exchange must be synchronised.

The formula is in two stages. First, the solicitors must confirm that they each hold their client's signed part of the contract. The buyer's solicitor then undertakes:

(a)   to exchange if, by an agreed time later that day, the seller's solicitor telephones him and requests an exchange;
(b)   that he or some other named person in his office will be available up to the

final time for exchange to activate the second part of the formula when the seller's solicitor telephones.

The seller's solicitor is then free to exchange on the seller's related transaction. Having done this, he will telephone the buyer's solicitor and request exchange. The second part of the formula is now activated: both solicitors undertake to hold their client's part of the contract to the other's order, so that exchange takes place, and that they will dispatch their respective parts to the other party in the same way as for the other formulae. The buyer's solicitor also undertakes to forward the deposit, either to the seller's solicitor or to some other solicitor whom the seller's solicitor nominates. The deposit must be held on 'Formula C terms', which means that it is to be held as stakeholder or as agent for the seller with authority to forward it only to another solicitor as a deposit in a related transaction on the same terms.

Two memoranda are required when using Formula C. The first one will cover the first part of the exchange and should record:

(a)   the date and time when it was agreed to use Formula C;
(b)   any variations to the formula;
(c)   the final time for exchange;
(d)   the completion date;
(e)   the name of the solicitor to whom the deposit is to be paid; and
(f)   the names of the parties to the conversation.

The second memorandum will record the request of the seller's solicitor to exchange.

Before a solicitor uses Formula C his client's written irrevocable authority should be obtained, as a solicitor has no automatic authority to exchange on a Formula C basis. A form of authority is included in the formula.

9.7   EXCHANGE BY FAX OR EMAIL

It is not possible to exchange contracts by fax as SC 1.3.3 provides that fax is not a valid method of service of a document where delivery of the original is essential, nor would it be a valid exchange for the purposes of the Law of Property (Miscellaneous Provisions) Act 1989, s.2. Neither is it possible to exchange contracts for the sale of land by email as this would also not satisfy s.2. Fax and email can, however, be used to transmit messages which activate the Law Society formulae.

9.8   PROTECTING THE CONTRACT

If the title is registered and there is likely to be a long delay between the date of the contract and completion, or the buyer has reason to suspect that the seller may try to sell the same property to someone else, the contract should be protected by a notice. If the buyer is in occupation, he may have an overriding interest.

9.9 POSITION OF THE PARTIES AFTER EXCHANGE OF CONTRACTS

9.9.1 The seller's position

After exchange of contracts, the seller holds the legal estate as a qualified trustee for the buyer who is the beneficial owner. This trusteeship differs from an ordinary trusteeship in several ways:

(a)   the seller is entitled to the rents and profits from the property until the date fixed for completion and must pay the outgoings (e.g. council tax, ground rent where applicable) until then;

(b)   he has a right to retain possession of the property until the purchase monies or the balance of the purchase monies are paid;

(c)   he has a lien over the property in respect of any unpaid part of the purchase monies;

(d)   he owes a duty to take reasonable care of the property.

9.9.2 The seller's lien

The seller has a lien over the property for the balance of the purchase monies. This lien arises independently of any agreement between the parties and may be enforced by the seller against the buyer and, after the buyer's death, the buyer's personal representatives. The lien will be lost if the seller agrees to take a mortgage of the property in lieu of the outstanding monies. It is also subject to the limitation period.

9.9.3 The duty to take reasonable care

The seller is bound to take reasonable care of the property. This extends to keeping the garden in good order. The seller will be liable to the buyer if the seller culpably lets the property fall into disrepair, or in any other way fails to prevent loss or damage to the property where reasonable care would have prevented this.

The duty lasts as long as the seller remains in possession, even where this may be extended as a result of the buyer failing to complete on the agreed date. In *Lucie-Smith* v. *Gorman* [1981] CLY 2866, the seller, who left the property in winter with the water not turned off, was liable in respect of damage caused by burst pipes.

9.9.4 The buyer's position

After exchange of contracts the buyer is beneficially entitled to the property, and is therefore also entitled to any increase in the value of the property between contract and conveyance. However, the buyer will have to bear any loss or damage sustained during that period subject to the right to sue the seller for damage resulting from breach of the seller's duty of care.

The buyer also has a lien over the property, similar to the seller's, in respect of any part of the purchase price which is paid before completion, such as the deposit. This right is likened to the seller executing a mortgage of the property to the buyer for the monies which the buyer has paid to the seller. This lien (like the seller's lien) can be enforced by a court order for the sale of the property, the lien being discharged out of the proceeds of sale.

9.9.5 The position if the buyer takes possession before completion

The seller may allow the buyer access to the property after exchange in order to clean and decorate, and he may in certain circumstances let the buyer take actual possession. This could cause problems for the seller if the buyer later claims to be a tenant and refuses to vacate the property or complete the purchase.

Under SC 5.2 'Occupation by buyer', the buyer may be allowed possession as a licensee and not a tenant. The terms of the buyer's licence are set out in SC 5.2.2.

One of the terms of the licence is that the buyer is to keep the property in as good a state of repair as it was in when the buyer went into occupation (fair wear and tear excepted).

Termination of the licence is dealt with by SC 5.2.4, and by SC 5.2.6 the buyer's right to raise requisitions is not affected.

It should also be noted that SC 5.2 will not apply if the buyer is merely exercising rights of access given solely to do work agreed by the seller, which will cover the situation where the seller lets the buyer in to clean and decorate (SC 5.2.3).

9.9.6 Bankruptcy

9.9.6.1 Bankruptcy of the seller

The normal principles of bankruptcy apply so that the seller's trustee in bankruptcy stands in the shoes of the seller and can therefore compel the buyer to complete the contract. If a date has been fixed for completion and time is of the essence of the contract (which is not normally the case) then, should a bankruptcy petition be presented against the seller, the buyer can rescind the contract and recover the deposit if on the completion date there is no trustee in bankruptcy able to complete the sale.

Once a buyer is aware of a bankruptcy petition registered against the seller, he cannot safely take a conveyance from the seller as it will not be binding upon the trustee in bankruptcy (Insolvency Act 1986, s.284).

The seller's trustee in bankruptcy is obliged to complete the sale if the buyer tenders the purchase monies or the balance of them on the completion date.

An onerous contract can be disclaimed by the trustee in bankruptcy. However, when the trustee in bankruptcy takes over the property from the seller, it is taken subject to the buyer's equitable interest in the property. As a result, the only way the trustee in bankruptcy can effectively disclaim the contract is by disclaiming any interest in the property, and so effectively giving it to the buyer without the buyer having to pay the outstanding monies.

9.9.6.2 Bankruptcy of the buyer

When a buyer is declared bankrupt all the buyer's property vests in his trustee in bankruptcy. The trustee in bankruptcy can then compel the seller to complete the transaction by paying the outstanding monies on the day fixed for completion.

If the seller wishes to go ahead with the sale and the trustee in bankruptcy is reluctant to, the trustee in bankruptcy has the right to disclaim onerous contracts and the seller is then entitled to keep any deposit which has been paid. The seller can serve a notice on the trustee in bankruptcy requesting that the contract be either performed or disclaimed. If the trustee in bankruptcy does not then disclaim the contract within 28 days, the trustee in bankruptcy is deemed to have adopted the contract.

Where the seller knows that bankruptcy proceedings are pending against the buyer, but the buyer has not yet been formally declared bankrupt, the seller should not complete the contract as it will not be binding on a trustee in bankruptcy if the buyer is subsequently adjudged bankrupt.

9.9.7 Death

9.9.7.1 Death of the seller

The personal representatives of a deceased seller are entitled to, and can be compelled to, transfer the property to the buyer. The purchase monies will be paid to the personal representatives who hold the monies in accordance with the terms of the will if there is one, or in accordance with the rules relating to intestacy if there is no will.

9.9.7.2 Death of the buyer

The personal representatives of a deceased buyer are also entitled to complete the purchase of the property and can be compelled to do so by the seller. The beneficiary who is entitled to the property takes it subject to a charge for the unpaid purchase monies, but this does not affect the seller's right to obtain payment from the personal representatives.

9.10 SUMMARY

- A deposit will be paid on exchange as an indication of the buyer's commitment to the purchase.
- The deposit is usually 10 per cent of the purchase price, and there are risks for the seller in accepting a lesser deposit which must be explained to a seller client.
- A deposit is usually held by the seller's solicitor as stakeholder.
- There are risks if the deposit is held as agent, and these risks must be explained to the buyer.
- The buyer's insurance must be in place immediately on exchange.
- A buyer must be advised about all restrictive covenants affecting the property, especially if they are being breached by the seller or are likely to be breached by the buyer.
- It may be possible to insure against losses arising from the successful enforcement of a restrictive covenant. Alternatively, you seek the consent of, or release from, the person with the benefit of the covenant. Another option is an application to the Upper Tribunal.
- All outstanding queries must be resolved before exchange.
- The contract can be signed by the client or the client's solicitor.
- You must explain the effect of the exchange to the client before you exchange.
- Contracts may be exchanged in person, by telephone or by post.
- Telephone exchange is the most common method, but there are risks and the Law Society has produced three formulae, based on mutual undertakings, to reduce these risks.
- Any departure from, or variation of, the formula being used must be agreed between the solicitors for both parties and recorded in writing.
- After exchange, the buyer is the beneficial owner of the property and the seller is the legal owner.
- When acting for the buyer, you should consider whether it is necessary to register the contract as a notice.
- A buyer is not usually allowed to enter or occupy the property until after completion, but if the seller agrees to allow this, it may be possible to use SC 5.2.2 to protect the seller's interests; otherwise, alternative provisions will have to be agreed in the contract.
- If one of the parties dies after exchange, the personal representatives of the deceased person are bound to complete, and this will usually delay completion.
- As there may not be enough time between exchange and completion to carry out the pre-completion tasks, you should consider carrying out some or all of these tasks before exchange.

CHAPTER 10

Pre-completion

Before completion takes place, there are a number of matters which both parties need to deal with to ensure that completion proceeds smoothly. This chapter contains a summary of the matters to be dealt with at this stage.

10.1 ACTING FOR THE BUYER

When acting for the buyer you should:

(a) draft the transfer deed and forward it to the seller's solicitor together with TA13 Completion Information and Undertakings (both should be sent in duplicate);

(b) ensure the transfer deed has been approved and the TA13 has been satisfactorily answered;

(c) engross the transfer and mortgage deeds;

(d) arrange for the buyer to execute the mortgage deed, transfer deed and plan (if necessary);

(e) send the executed transfer deed to seller's solicitor so that the seller can execute it in readiness for completion;

(f) make pre-completion searches and ensure their results are satisfactory;

(g) submit your report on title to the lender and request the mortgage advance in time for completion;

(h) where appropriate, receive the completion statement and copies of last receipts in support of apportionments from the seller's solicitor and check they are correct;

(i) advise the buyer of arrangements for completion;

(j) agree the form of wording of any undertaking which needs to be given by the seller's solicitor on completion (e.g., in relation to the discharge of the seller's mortgage);

(k) make sure that any life insurance policy required by the lender has been obtained and check with the buyer that any other insurances required for the property have been taken out;

(l) check your file to ensure that all outstanding queries have been dealt with;

(m)   prepare a financial statement and bill for the client and submit them to the buyer with a request that the balance due is to be paid in sufficient time for the funds to be cleared before completion;

(n)   receive the mortgage advance from the lender and balance of funds from the buyer and pay these into the client account and clear funds before completion;

(o)   prepare a list of matters to be dealt with on completion;

(p)   check the arrangements for vacant possession and handing over the keys;

(q)   instruct the seller's solicitor to act as your agent on completion if completion is not to be by personal attendance;

(r)   make final arrangements with the seller's solicitor for time and place of completion;

(s)   make arrangements to send the completion money to the seller's solicitor; and

(t)   ensure that the relevant SDLT forms have been completed and signed.

10.2   ACTING FOR THE SELLER

When acting for the seller you should:

(a)   approve the draft transfer deed and reply to the buyer's TA13 Completion Information and Undertakings form;

(b)   when you receive the engrossed transfer deed, check that the buyer has executed it, if appropriate, and any plan;

(c)   arrange for the seller to execute the transfer deed in time for completion;

(d)   obtain redemption figure(s) for seller's mortgage(s);

(e)   obtain last receipts, etc. (e.g. rent receipts for leasehold property) where apportionments are to be made on completion;

(f)   where relevant, prepare the completion statement showing the amount due on completion and send it to the buyer's solicitor;

(g)   remind the seller to organise final meter readings;

(h)   draft any undertaking which needs to be given on completion, e.g., for discharge of the seller's mortgage if also acting for the lender;

(i)   contact the lender to confirm final arrangements for the discharge of the seller's mortgage;

(j)   check your file to ensure all outstanding queries have been dealt with;

(k)   prepare a list of matters to be dealt with on completion;

(l)   check which deeds and documents, if any, will need to be inspected or handed over on completion and prepare certified copies for the buyer of those documents which are not being handed over together with a schedule, in duplicate, of those deeds and documents which are to be handed over;

(m)   prepare a financial statement and bill for the client and submit them to the seller;

(n)   prepare an inventory of any chattels included in the sale and a receipt for money payable for them;

(o)   check the arrangements for vacant possession and handing over the keys, and inform the estate agents of the completion arrangements;

(p)   obtain the estate agent's bill and the seller's instructions to pay the estate agent's fees from the sale proceeds;

(q)   receive instructions from the buyer's solicitor to act as his agent on completion and clarify these with him if necessary; and

(r)   make final arrangements with the buyer's solicitor for the time and place of completion.

10.3   TRANSFER DEED

10.3.1   Procedure

The buyer's solicitor usually prepares the draft transfer in duplicate and submits it to the seller's solicitor. Sometimes the seller may reserve the right in the contract to prepare the transfer, e.g. where the sale is of a new house (the right is set out in the Law of Property Act 1925, s.48(1)).

The buyer's solicitor will prepare the transfer after exchange of contracts and send it to the seller's solicitor with TA13 Completion Information and Undertakings. This is done either within the time limit stipulated in the contract, if there is one, or in an open contract after a good title has been deduced by the seller. The Standard Conditions of Sale (fifth edition – 2018 revision), SC 4.3.2 provides that the draft is to be sent to the seller's solicitor at least 12 working days before completion (note that this is reduced under SC 4.3.4 if the time between exchange and completion is less than 15 working days).

When drafting the transfer, the buyer's solicitor will need to bear in mind the terms of the contract and the official copies.

The seller's solicitor then approves or amends the transfer. It should be checked to make sure it reflects the terms of the contract. The top copy is then returned with any amendments which the seller's solicitor thinks it is proper to make marked in red. The form of the transfer is for the buyer's solicitor to determine and the seller's solicitor must refrain from making purely formal alterations. Under SC 4.3.2 the seller's solicitor is to approve or return the revised draft document four working days after delivery of the draft transfer by the buyer's solicitor.

When the transfer is settled, the buyer's solicitor will arrange for it to be engrossed, i.e. a copy is made which incorporates any agreed amendments. If the buyer's execution is necessary (i.e. the buyer is entering into a covenant or making a grant to the seller), this is attended to and the transfer is then forwarded to the seller's solicitor for the seller to execute. It is then retained by the seller's solicitor until completion, when it will be dated and handed over to the buyer's solicitor in return for the purchase money.

10.3.2   Form of transfer

The Law of Property Act 1925, s.52 provides that a deed is necessary to pass the legal estate (though there are exceptions to this, e.g. assents, surrenders by operation of law and leases for three years or less complying with the Law of Property Act 1925, s.54(2)).

A standard form of transfer is usually used, and the Land Registration Rules 2003, SI 2003/1417 lay down standard forms of transfer. Form TR1 is the standard form of transfer used where the whole of the land in a title is being transferred. It is designed to be able to be reproduced and completed electronically. HM Land Registry has issued guidance on completing form TR1; see HM Land Registry's 'Guidance: how to complete form TR1 (updated 17 June 2019, available at **www.gov.uk/government/publications/registered-titles-whole-transfer-tr1/ guidance-completing-form-tr1-for-the-transfer-of-registered-property**).

If only part of the land within the seller's title is being sold, form TP1 is used. The following points must be borne in mind when preparing a transfer of part:

(a)   The title number inserted in the transfer will be the one relating to the seller's title. HM Land Registry will issue a new number in respect of the land transferred when the transfer is registered.

(b)   The property must be described by reference to a plan, which must be signed by the transferor and by the transferee or his solicitor.

(c)   The transfer must include all easements being granted to the buyer and reservations being taken by the seller. Any new restrictive covenants must also be set out in the transfer.

Form TR1 will also be used where the property is leasehold, except that there will be reference to the unexpired term of the lease, and the covenants for title must be modified. The Standard Conditions of Sale, SC 3.2.2 and 3.2.3 provide for this and the Land Registration Act 1925, s.24 implied on the transfer of pre-1996 leases a similar covenant to that implied by the Law of Property Act 1925, s.77, whether or not the transfer is for value. This is continued so far as such leases are concerned by the transitional provisions of the Land Registration Act 2002. No such covenant applies to leases granted since the Landlord and Tenant (Covenants) Act 1995 came into force.

10.3.3   Execution and delivery

Section 1 of the Law of Property (Miscellaneous Provisions) Act 1989 provides that a deed must:

(a)   make clear that it is intended to be a deed;
(b)   be signed by the parties in the presence of a witness; and
(c)   be delivered.

The transfer deed must always be executed by the seller in order to transfer the legal estate (Law of Property Act 1925, s.52). The buyer need only execute the transfer if he is either making a declaration (e.g. as to co-ownership) or entering into new covenants (e.g. an indemnity covenant).

The transfer deed must make clear that it is intended to be a deed. This can be done either by describing the document as a deed or by expressing that the document is executed or signed as a deed.

The transfer deed must also be delivered. This means that the parties must intend to be bound by it. A deed takes effect on its delivery. When the buyer delivers the engrossed transfer to the seller for execution by him, he does not normally intend the transfer to become effective at that time. It is therefore common practice for the transfer to be delivered to the seller 'in escrow', i.e. conditionally, so that the operation of the transfer is postponed until completion. On fulfilment of the condition, the deed is an effective deed from the original date of delivery (see *Alan Estates Ltd* v. *WG Stores Ltd* [1981] 3 WLR 892). The following cases have discussed the question of what, in such a case, is the condition of the escrow:

(a) *Kingston* v. *Ambrian Investment Co. Ltd* [1975] 1 WLR 161. Where a seller executes a conveyance in advance of completion, he ordinarily does so subject to a condition to be fulfilled afterwards. In the Court of Appeal, Buckley and Scarman LLJ said this condition was that completion should take place 'in due course'. Lord Denning MR in the case amplified this as 'simply that the purchaser should pay the purchase price and costs within a reasonable time'.

(b) *Glessing* v. *Green* [1975] 1 WLR 863. In this case, where the seller executed the conveyance in advance of completion, the court explained further the nature of the implied condition. There was 'an implied condition that [the transaction] would be completed in due course in accordance with normal conveyancing practice'. Once a notice to complete (see **11.6.1**) had been validly served and had expired, it was impossible for the buyer to satisfy the condition by tendering the purchase money and offering to complete.

A company can also deliver a deed in escrow (see *Beesly* v. *Hallwood Estates Ltd* [1961] Ch 105).

10.3.3.1 Deeds executed by an individual

It is no longer necessary for a deed to be sealed, but it must be signed by the parties in the presence of a witness and delivered.

The witness must attest the signature he is witnessing by signing his name and then writing his name, address and occupation underneath his signature. A witness should be independent of the party signing and be of full age. The same person need not witness all the signatures. Alternatively, a deed may be executed by someone else signing at the direction of, and in the presence of, the person who is executing it and in the presence of two witnesses who each attest the signature. 'Signature' also includes a person making his mark.

A deed by an individual must be delivered. If another person is authorised to deliver a deed, then this authority need not be given by deed. If a deed is delivered on a person's behalf by a solicitor, licensed conveyancer or their agent or employee, then it shall be conclusively presumed in favour of a buyer that the person was so authorised – provided that this is done in the course of, or in connection with, a transaction involving the disposition or creation of an interest in land.

10.3.3.2 Deeds executed by companies

Section 44 of the Companies Act 2006 provides that a company can execute a deed in one of three ways:

(a) By affixing the company seal. A deed executed in this way is deemed, in favour of a buyer, to have been duly executed, provided that the seal purports to have been affixed in the presence of and attested by two members of the board of directors or a director and the secretary.

(b) By the deed being signed on behalf of the company by a director and the secretary or by two directors.

(c) By the deed being signed on behalf of the company by a director of the company in the presence of a witness who attests the signature.

In favour of a buyer in good faith for valuable consideration, a document is deemed to have been duly executed if it purports to be signed in accordance with (b) and (c) above (Companies Act 2006, s.44(5)).

The deed must also be delivered as such. A document which makes it clear on its face that it is intended to be a deed is presumed to have been delivered on execution: this presumption can be rebutted by a contrary intention.

10.3.3.3 HM Land Registry requirements

There are prescribed execution provisions for transfers of registered land (see HM Land Registry Practice Guide 8 (Execution of Deeds)).

10.3.3.4 Deeds executed by an attorney

Where a deed is executed by an attorney under a power of attorney, the attorney may either:

(a) sign in the name of the person who granted the power, e.g. 'Keith Green by his attorney Andrew White', or

(b) sign in his own name, e.g. 'Andrew White as attorney for Keith Green'.

10.3.4   Explaining the transfer to client

You must make sure that the client understands the nature and contents of the transfer before executing it. If you cannot see the client in person and have to send the transfer to the client, you should send a covering letter which should:

(a)   explain the purpose and contents of the transfer;

(b)   contain clear instructions as to the execution of the transfer;

(c)   tell the client when the signed transfer must be returned to the solicitor; and

(d)   ask the client not to date the transfer.

10.4   COMPLETION INFORMATION AND UNDERTAKINGS

Once contracts have been exchanged, the practical arrangements for completion need to be agreed. The buyer's solicitor will do this by sending TA13 Completion Information and Undertakings in duplicate to the seller's solicitor. In practice this is often referred to as raising 'requisitions on title'. This goes back to when title was deduced after exchange of contracts and so the buyer's solicitor would raise 'requisitions on title' requiring the seller's solicitor to deal with unsatisfactory title matters. Modern practice is for title to be supplied with the draft contract, and the contract will contain a clause excluding the buyer's right to raise requisitions following exchange (see SC 4.2.1). If, however, after exchange the buyer's solicitor discovers an undisclosed incumbrance or other defect, he will still be able to require it to be remedied or assert his remedies for non-disclosure. Under SC 4.2.2 the buyer must raise any further title requisitions within six working days of any matter coming to his attention, and under SC 4.3.1 the seller's solicitor must reply four working days after receiving any further title requisitions.

The TA13 form deals with the administrative arrangements for completion, including the method of payment of money, the place for completion, whether completion can take place by post, and the arrangements for the keys. The form also deals with the discharge of the seller's existing mortgage and contains a request for confirmation that existing mortgages will be discharged on completion. The answer to this question takes effect as an undertaking to discharge the mortgages referred to, and so avoids the need for such an undertaking to be handed over on completion.

The buyer's solicitor should ensure that the replies to the TA13 are satisfactory, and any that are not must be taken up with the seller's solicitor until they are resolved.

10.5 PRE-COMPLETION SEARCHES

10.5.1 Official search of the register

A buyer will have received an official copy of the register of title showing the exact state of the register at the date it was issued. The official search procedure provides a means to:

(a)   update the details of the official copy by checking the up-to-date subsisting entries in the register of title;

(b)   obtain the details of any relevant pending application or priority official search entered on the day list since the search from date; and

(c)   ensure, where appropriate, that no adverse entries are made in the register before a protectable disposition is completed by registration.

10.5.1.1 Procedure

An application for an official search must be made either on or in the correct form. A paper search must be made using Form OS1 for a search of the whole of the land in a title, or using Form OS2 for a search of part of the land in a title. Where a search is lodged by another method, the application must contain the same information as included in the paper form. A fee is payable whichever method is used. The application must give details of the title number of the property to be searched, the address of the property including its postcode, and the names of the registered proprietors. The applicant's name must also be given, together with the reason for making the search, i.e., he intends to purchase, take a lease or take a registered charge. A search must include a 'search from date', which is shown on the official copies.

A search may be lodged by post or DX, or electronically through Business e-services, Business Gateway or NLIS. Lodgement through Business e-services and Business Gateway is only available to Land Registry account holders.

A plan (in duplicate) must accompany the OS2 search unless the property is part of a registered building estate and can be described by reference to a plot number on the approved layout plan.

If the buyer is obtaining a mortgage, then the application should be made on behalf of the lender. There is no need to search on behalf of the buyer since the search on behalf of the lender will provide protection for them both. This means that the lender, not the buyer, should be named as the applicant on the search form. A search made on behalf of the buyer will not protect the lender.

10.5.1.2 Effect of the search

The buyer will receive an official search certificate which:

(a)   will contain a statement that there have been no adverse entries since the search from date or details of any relevant adverse entries made in the register on or after the search from date;

(b)   is not conclusive, although the buyer will be entitled to compensation for any entries which exist at the time of the search but which are not revealed by the search; and

(c)   gives the buyer a 'priority period' of 30 business days. This means that the register is in effect 'frozen' and the buyer will not be bound by any application made during this priority period provided that the buyer's application for registration is made within the priority period and is completed in due course by registration.

If completion is delayed, a further priority period can be obtained by making a further search. The second official search certificate will extend the priority afforded by the first and will not provide priority over any application lodged before its priority period commences.

10.5.1.3 *'Without priority' searches*

It is possible for anyone to apply for an official search without priority using Form OS3. A fee is payable.

10.5.2   Central land charges search

This will only be relevant:

(a)   when the title is possessory, where a search should be made against any previous estate owner; or

(b)   when the title is good leasehold, where a search should be made against the estate owners of the unregistered freehold title, if this is possible.

10.5.3   Search in the companies register

A buyer will only be bound by charges entered into by a corporate seller if they are protected by a notice on the register of title. Therefore, a company search is not required in order to discover charges. However, it would reveal whether a resolution has been passed to put the company into voluntary liquidation or whether the company has been removed from the register, and the buyer should therefore search if there is any suspicion about these matters. If a company search was carried out as one of the pre-contract searches, it should be updated to make sure that nothing has changed.

In addition, where the transaction is for a particularly high value, or there is reason to be concerned about the solvency of a corporate seller, a telephone search at the central registry of winding up petitions at the Companies Court should be carried out on the day of completion. This will reveal recent winding up and administration orders and applications and petitions for winding up/administration.

153

10.5.4 Bankruptcy search

Where the buyer is obtaining a mortgage, the lender will require a clear bankruptcy search before releasing the mortgage funds.

10.5.5 Enduring and lasting powers of attorney

Where the transfer deed is to be executed by a person who is acting under an enduring or lasting power of attorney, a search should be made with the Office of the Public Guardian to check whether or not registration of the power has been effected or is pending.

In the case of an enduring power, unless a registration is pending, the transaction may proceed, provided the buyer has no actual knowledge of any circumstances that would revoke the power. If the power has been registered, the attorney may deal with the land and, provided the donor is still alive, completion may take place. A copy of the power should be obtained from the Office of the Public Guardian. A lasting power only comes into effect when registered with the Office of the Public Guardian and, if the power is registered, a copy should be obtained.

10.5.6 Local land charges search

A further search would only be necessary where the original search was carried out a long time ago. The buyer will be bound by any charges registered since the original search was carried out. In practice, searches up to three months old are usually relied on. There is no 'hard and fast' rule, and in a large-scale or commercial purchase more frequent searches may be carried out.

10.5.7 Inspection of the property

The buyer should inspect the property to ensure that there is no evidence of any overriding interests, e.g. third-party occupation.

10.6 THE MORTGAGE

10.6.1 Acting for the seller

A redemption figure should be obtained from the seller's lender showing the amount required to discharge the mortgage on the day of completion. This may be calculated in one of two ways, depending on the lender:

(1) It may be calculated as an amount for the whole of the month in which the date for completion lies. This means that the mortgage may be redeemed at any time during that month and the figure will remain the same, so if completion is

delayed for a few days, the figure does not need to be recalculated provided completion takes place within the same month.

(2)   The more usual method is for the redemption figure to be calculated up to the date for completion and a daily interest rate provided so that the redemption figure can be adjusted for each day that completion is delayed.

The seller's solicitor may have to prepare the form of discharge of the mortgage for execution by the lender following redemption. This will depend on whether a paper or electronic discharge is being used. If a paper discharge is to be used, then the seller's solicitor must complete the appropriate form. Form DS1 will be used for a discharge of the whole of the land charged, and Form DS3 for a discharge of part of the land charged. If the lender is using an ED (electronic discharge) or an eDS1, there is no need for the seller's solicitor to prepare a DS1. A seller's solicitor will be notified by a lender in the redemption statement if the lender intends to use either of these instead of a DS1.

An ED is a discharge of a registered charge sent electronically by the lender's computer system direct to HM Land Registry. For an ED, the HM Land Registry computer system makes a number of checks and, if everything is in order, cancels the charge entries automatically and, in most cases, immediately on receipt of the discharge. An ED can only be used for a discharge of the whole of the land charged. An ED does not require a separate formal paper application to discharge the charge, nor does it need any manual intervention. It is completely automated between various computer systems. The lender will issue notification of the discharge of the mortgage to the seller's solicitor.

An e-DS1 is an electronic form of discharge submitted by a lender through the HM Land Registry portal. The e-DS1 acts as both the evidence of discharge and the application to remove the charge from the register. An e-DS1 can only be lodged for a discharge of the whole of the land charged. Once the mortgage has been discharged, the lender will issue notification of the discharge of the mortgage to the seller's solicitor.

Further details about discharges of mortgages can be found in HM Land Registry Practice Guide 31 (Discharges of Charges).

10.6.2   Acting for the buyer

The mortgage deed should be prepared and executed by the buyer. The lender may require that it is executed by the buyer in the presence of his solicitor. The solicitor also needs to report to the lender that the title is in order, marketable and acceptable as security for the loan. The form of certificate of title approved by the Law Society and UK Finance will be used. At the same time, the mortgage advance will be requested from the lender in time for completion. Where the mortgage advance is to be sent by CHAPS, it should be requested, wherever possible, that it is sent one working day before completion. The buyer should also be notified, if applicable, that the lender may charge interest from the day of transmission.

10.7 AMOUNT DUE ON COMPLETION

The seller's solicitor must advise the buyer's solicitor of the amount due on completion in his replies to the TA13 Completion Information and Undertakings. Usually this will just be the balance of the purchase price.

However, where outgoings are being apportioned, a completion statement showing the amount due on completion will be required. While council tax and water rates can be apportioned, it is better practice to advise the relevant authority after completion of the change of ownership and request it to send out apportioned accounts. Standard condition 6.3 deals with apportionments and allows a provisional apportionment to be made where exact figures are not available at completion. The seller must produce the last demands or receipts for all sums which are to be apportioned so that the calculations of the amounts due or to be allowed on completion may be made. Copies of these receipts should be sent to the buyer with the completion statement to allow him to check them.

10.8 LAND TRANSACTION RETURN

After completion, the buyer's solicitor will need to submit a land transaction return using form SDLT1 to HMRC giving details about the transaction and the buyer. Form SDLT1 should be completed and signed by the client before completion to avoid delays after completion. An additional fee may be charged for completing and submitting the form.

Where the buyer is obtaining a mortgage, the land transaction return must be completed and signed by the buyer before the loan is used. If it is left until after completion, there is a risk that the buyer may refuse to co-operate and it will then not be possible for the transaction to be registered at HM Land Registry. The lender will then have no security for its loan, and the solicitor could be held liable for any loss suffered. Both the Lenders' Handbook and the BSA Mortgage Instructions require the mortgage to be registered at HM Land Registry.

10.9 FINANCIAL STATEMENT

The buyer's solicitor should prepare a financial statement which shows the total amount due from the buyer in order to complete and how it has been calculated. This, together with the solicitor's bill, should be sent to the buyer in sufficient time before completion to allow the buyer to forward the required balance of funds so that those funds can be cleared by completion.

When calculating the net mortgage advance, the buyer's solicitor must take into account any retentions and other deductions from the mortgage advance.

If the buyer has a dependent sale, then the financial statement should include any balance from the sale which is being used towards the purchase.

The seller's solicitor should also prepare a financial statement for the seller.

10.10   SYNCHRONISATION

Where a client has a dependent sale and purchase which are both being completed on the same day, arrangements for completion must be agreed beforehand so as to ensure that the money is received from the sale before the purchase is completed.

10.11   SUMMARY

- The buyer's solicitor normally prepares the transfer.
- The transfer must always be executed by the seller.
- The buyer will execute the transfer where it contains a covenant or declaration by the buyer.
- When you are acting for the buyer, you should send a TA13 Completion Information and Undertakings form to the seller's solicitor to check that nothing has changed in the information provided before exchange, and to find out the arrangements for completion.
- Pre-completion searches should be carried out to check that nothing adverse to the buyer has happened to the property or the seller since exchange, and to protect the buyer against any adverse change.
- An OS1 search protects the buyer by providing a priority period during which no other entries may be registered.
- The purchase must be completed within the priority period.

CHAPTER 11

Completion

Completion is the occasion for the following rituals:

(a) the settling of the financial account between the seller and the buyer; and
(b) the completion of the legal work and handing over of the executed purchase deed and any other relevant documents to the buyer's solicitor.

The buyer is also entitled to possession of the property on completion, and although the buyer's solicitor will not usually oversee the transfer of possession, he needs to ensure that satisfactory arrangements have been made for this.

This chapter looks at the mechanics of completion, and the position should a party delay or fail to complete.

11.1 THE DATE, TIME AND PLACE OF COMPLETION

The date for completion will usually be stated in the contract. If it is not, the Standard Conditions of Sale (fifth edition – 2018 revision), SC 6.1.1 provides that the completion date is 20 working days after exchange. Time is not of the essence in relation to the completion date.

There is no provision in the Standard Conditions of Sale setting the time for completion. In the absence of contrary provision, SC 6.1.2 provides that if completion does not take place by 2.00 pm on the day of completion, completion is treated as taking place on the next working day. Standard condition 6.1.2 does not apply where the sale is with vacant possession and the seller has not vacated the property by 2.00 pm on the date of actual completion. This condition affects only the payment of compensation for late completion and does not make it a term of the contract that completion shall take place by a specified time, and if this is required a special condition to this effect must be added to the contract.

Where a purchase is dependent on the receipt of money from a related sale, you must make sure that the sale will be completed before the purchase as otherwise there will not be sufficient funds available to complete the purchase, and that there is a sufficient interval between the two transactions to allow the money received from the sale to be available for the purchase.

Usually completion will take place at the office of the seller's solicitor, and SC 6.2.2 provides that completion is to take place in England and Wales, either at the seller's conveyancer's office or at some other place which the seller reasonably specifies. For example, if there is an outstanding mortgage on the property and the lender will not release the deeds to the seller's solicitor until after the mortgage has been discharged, completion will take place at the offices of the lender's solicitor. Standard condition 6.2.1 provides that the buyer's conveyancer and the seller's conveyancer are to co-operate in agreeing arrangements for completion. Most completions now take place using the Law Society's Code for Completion by Post (2019). The actual place of completion is therefore of little significance as long as both parties' solicitors are able to contact each other by telephone or email to confirm the transmission and receipt of funds on the day of completion.

On the day before completion or as early as reasonably possible on the day of completion, you should consider whether there is likely to be any delay. If there is, you should notify the other party's solicitor and agree how communication will be handled during the course of the day until completion has taken place.

11.2   COMPLETION MONEY

Standard condition 6.7 provides for payment to be made only by a direct transfer of cleared funds from a solicitor's account held at a clearing bank and an unconditional release of a deposit held by a stakeholder.

The seller's solicitor will provide details of the amount required to complete and the account to which the money is to be sent in his replies to the TA13 Completion Information and Undertakings form. The buyer's solicitor will then instruct his bank to send the money from his client account to the account nominated by the seller's solicitor. This electronic transfer is often referred to as a 'telegraphic transfer'. The buyer's solicitor should inform the seller's solicitor of the commitment of funds to the banking system or instructions given to the bank. Instructions to the bank must be given sufficiently early on the day of completion so that the money arrives before the time limit for receipt of funds in SC 6.1.2 expires.

The seller's solicitor should ask his bank to telephone him to inform him of the receipt of the funds immediately they arrive. The seller's solicitor should then inform the buyer's solicitor of the receipt of the money and completion can then take place.

11.3   THE METHODS OF COMPLETION

Completion may take place in one of three ways:

(a)   by personal attendance;
(b)   by post; or

(c)   by an agent.

11.3.1   Personal completion

11.3.1.1   The purchase money

The buyer's solicitor will arrange with his bank to send the balance of the purchase money to the seller's solicitor's account.

11.3.1.2   Documents handed over

The buyer's solicitor will receive the following:

(a)   The transfer deed, which should be checked to ensure that it is correctly executed by the seller. It should also be dated with the date on which completion takes place.
(b)   A Land Registry discharge form, or an appropriate undertaking, in respect of any mortgage.
(c)   Other documents, such as a National House Building Council (NHBC) certificate if the house was built within the last 10 years, any planning permissions and building regulations approvals and, if appropriate, a receipt for the money, if any, paid for chattels.
(d)   The keys may be handed over, but this is not usual and they will normally be held by either the seller or the estate agents, who should be contacted to authorise them to release the keys to the buyer.

11.3.1.3   Discharge of the seller's mortgage

The seller's solicitor must supply a discharge in Form DS1, or an undertaking to discharge the mortgage and forward the DS1 on receipt of it from the lender. If an ED or an e-DS1 is being used, the seller's solicitor will merely hand over an undertaking that he will send the money required to discharge the mortgage to the lender and forward a copy of the lender's letter confirming successful redemption of the mortgage and lodgement of an electronic discharge at HM Land Registry on receipt of it from the lender.

The buyer's solicitor must check the terms of the undertaking being proposed by the seller's solicitor to ensure that it is acceptable. The Law Society has recommended a form of undertaking and this will usually be adopted though it may need to be amended to fit the circumstances of each transaction. Where an ED or e-DS1 is being used, the undertaking will need to be revised. There are risks in accepting an undertaking from the seller's solicitor.

If there is a second mortgage on the property, the buyer's solicitor must ensure that the undertaking which is given by the seller's solicitor adequately covers this second mortgage.

11.3.1.4 Sale of part

On a sale of part, arrangements must be made by the seller's solicitor for the release of the land being sold from the mortgage. A Form DS3 accompanied by a plan showing the land being sold is used.

11.3.1.5 Land Registry early completion policy

HM Land Registry's early completion policy applies to all applications to discharge the whole of a registered mortgage where other applications are made, e.g. to register a transfer of the property, but no evidence of discharge of the mortgage is supplied. Unless there is a restriction on the register preventing a disposal or the registration of a new mortgage without the consent of the existing lender, HM Land Registry will reject the discharge application but complete the other applications. Accordingly, a buyer purchasing with a new mortgage will be registered as the proprietor, but the seller's mortgage will remain on the title and until evidence of discharge is provided, the buyer's mortgage will rank in priority behind the seller's mortgage on the register. Where there is a restriction on the register preventing a disposal or the registration of a new mortgage without the consent of the existing lender, proof of discharge of the mortgage or evidence of compliance with the restriction must be provided to HM Land Registry within 20 working days (which can be extended to 40 working days on application). If this is not done, HM Land Registry will cancel the buyer's applications for discharge, transfer and charge.

Further details of the early completion policy can be found in HM Land Registry Practice Guide 31 (Discharges of Charges). See also the Law Society's Land Registry Early Completion Practice Note (10 June 2020).

11.3.2 Postal completion

Modern practice is that the buyer's solicitor does not attend in person to complete and that completion takes place through the post. The buyer's solicitor will send the purchase money to the seller's solicitor by electronic transfer, and in return the seller's solicitor will send the transfer deed, an undertaking for the mortgage and any other relevant documentation.

11.3.2.1 Undertakings

Problems can arise with a postal completion, and a Privy Council case from Hong Kong, *Edward Wong Finance Co. Ltd* v. *Johnson Stokes & Masters (a firm) (Hong Kong)* [1984] AC 296, illustrates these problems. In that case, the buyer's solicitors paid the purchase price in reliance on an undertaking from the seller's solicitors that they would pay off the mortgage. The seller's solicitors then disappeared with the money. It was held that the buyer's solicitors had been negligent as they should have taken steps to ensure that the seller's solicitors had the lender's authority to receive the money. The reality of this risk is illustrated by *Patel* v. *Daybells (a firm)* [2001] EWCA Civ 1229 where the Court of Appeal decided that the acceptance of a solicitor's undertaking to redeem the mortgage will not normally be negligent. In the light of this decision, the Law Society issued guidance (May 2002) in which it stated that it would not be normal or advisable to rely on an undertaking in two situations:

(a)   where the amount required to redeem the mortgage exceeds the minimum level of solicitors' indemnity insurance (currently £2,000,000 per claim); and

(b)   where the lender is not a member of the Council of Mortgage Lenders (now UK Finance).

11.3.2.2   The Law Society's Code for Completion by Post

The Law Society's Code for Completion by Post (2019) provides a procedure for postal completion. Under the Law Society Conveyancing Protocol (2019), if completion is to be by post, the parties must comply with the Code without variation unless instructions are given by the seller and are specific to the needs of the individual transaction. General exclusions of liability for obligations within the Code will be viewed as a breach of the Protocol. The Code is intended to provide a fair balance of obligation between seller's and buyer's solicitors and to facilitate professional co-operation for the benefit of clients.

   Under the Code:

(a)   The seller's solicitor acts on completion as agent for the buyer's solicitor for no fee. Instructions may be sent by the buyer's solicitor to the seller's solicitor confirming what is to be done on completion, e.g. which documents are to be examined and marked, and what memoranda are to be endorsed.

(b)   The seller's solicitor confirms by way of undertaking that on completion he will have the seller's authority to receive the purchase money and the authority of the proprietor of each mortgage to be redeemed or discharged, and which he has previously specified in writing to the buyer's solicitor, to receive the sum intended to repay it.

(c)   The buyer's solicitor will usually send the completion money by electronic transfer to the seller's solicitor's bank. The seller's solicitor must arrange for his bank to inform him by telephone as soon as the money is received. Completion will then take place when the seller's solicitor becomes aware of the receipt of the sum required to complete, unless the buyer's solicitor has notified the seller's solicitor that the money is to be held to the buyer's solicitor's order or it has previously been agreed (preferably in writing) that completion takes place at a later time. Once completion has taken place, all the documents to be handed over are held by the seller's solicitor to the order of the buyer's solicitor.

(d)   As soon as possible after completion, and in any event on the same day, the seller's solicitor must confirm to the buyer's solicitor by telephone, fax or email that completion has taken place; and must also as soon as possible after completion, and in any event by the end of the working day following completion, forward the documents to the buyer's solicitor by first-class post or document exchange. Once posted or delivered to the document exchange, the documents are then at the risk of the buyer's solicitor.

The notes to the Code refer to some of the points in the Code that solicitors may wish to consider before adopting it.

It should also be noted that adopting the Code will not in itself absolve the buyer's solicitor from any potential negligent practices involved in informal completions, e.g. sending the completion money without examining the title deeds, ensuring vacant possession is available or ensuring that the seller's solicitor has had the purchase deed executed.

11.3.3   Agency completion

Where the solicitors are in different localities, rather than complete through the post the buyer's solicitor could appoint a local solicitor to attend the seller's solicitor's office and complete on his behalf. The disadvantage of this is that the agent will charge for his services. If an agent is used, then full instructions will have to be given to him and arrangements made to send him the completion money.

11.4   EFFECT OF COMPLETION

Once completion has taken place, the contract for sale is said to be extinguished and to merge with the purchase deed. This means that, to the extent that merger operates, any action for damages against the seller by the buyer must be under the covenants for title implied into the purchase deed and the buyer cannot sue on the contract.

The effect of the doctrine of merger is to extinguish the contract only to the extent that the deed is intended to cover the same ground (see *Palmer* v. *Johnson* (1884) 13 QBD 351). This means that if the contract covers some collateral matter, then to that extent an action may be brought on the contract to enforce that stipulation notwith-standing completion. The most common example is where the seller has in the same contract as for the sale of the land also contracted to build a house. Thus, a stipulation, e.g. that the house is to be built to a specified standard, may be enforced even after completion (*Lawrence* v. *Cassel* [1930] 2 KB 83). In the same way, in *Feldman* v. *Mansell* (1962) 106 SJ 591 a term in the contract that the seller would provide the buyer with copies of specified leases could be enforced after completion.

Once the contract is completed by vesting the seller's legal estate in the buyer, the contract is said to be executed. The court has held that the Law of Property (Miscellaneous Provisions) Act 1989, s.2 does not apply to executed contracts. The effect of this is that terms in the contract concerning matters other than the transfer of the legal estate may then be enforced, even though the contract did not comply with the formalities required by s.2 (see *Tootal Clothing Ltd* v. *Guinea Properties Management Ltd* [1992] 41 EG 117).

11.4.1 Merger under Standard Conditions of Sale

Standard condition 7.3 provides that 'completion does not cancel liability to perform any outstanding obligation under this contract'. The effect of this clause is that the doctrine of merger has no application to a conveyancing contract which includes the clause. An example of this is shown by considering how SC 3 works. This provides for the seller to sell free from encumbrances. Where the doctrine of merger applies, an action after completion is only for breach of the implied title guarantee. Where SC 7.3 applies, then there can be an action after completion for breach of contract if SC 3 has been infringed.

11.5 LEASEHOLDS

11.5.1 Preparing for completion

11.5.1.1 Seller's solicitor

The completion statements prepared by the seller's solicitor will need to deal with any apportionment of ground rent, and service charge. Standard condition 6.3 deals with the methods of apportionment.

11.5.1.2 Buyer's solicitor

The buyer's solicitor must ensure that he has funds available to pay any apportionments in favour of the seller. In addition, the client's bill must include the costs of any fees which are charged by the landlord or his solicitor/agent for recording notices.

11.5.2 Completion

At completion the buyer's solicitor should check the receipts for the last payments of ground rent and any service charge, and collect the following:

(a) the lease, the transfer duly executed by the seller, the discharge or an undertaking in respect thereof, any duplicate notices and, where the title is good leasehold, a marked abstract of the freehold title if relevant;

(b) consent to assign, if required;

(c) transfer of share in any resident's company duly completed and signed, and the seller's share certificate;

(d)   any other documents, such as NHBC certificate, planning permissions and building regulations approvals.

11.6   FAILURE TO COMPLETE

If a party does not complete on the date for completion, then the other party can either serve a notice to complete, or apply for a decree of specific performance.

11.6.1   Notice to complete

Time is not of the essence in connection with the date for completion unless there is a special condition to that effect, or it is a necessary implication from the facts. Consequently, failure to complete by the contractual date does not entitle the innocent party to treat the contract as repudiated by delay. In order to terminate the contract the innocent party must serve a notice to complete which indicates to the other party that unless he completes by the date stated in the notice the first party will treat the contract as discharged. This notice will have the effect of making time of the essence so that failure to complete by the specified date will be a repudiatory breach.

In this situation, the innocent party has two problems:

(a)   How long after the delay in completion does he have to wait before serving the notice?
(b)   Having served the notice, how long should the period of notice be?

Under an open contract, the notice can only be served once the delay in completing is such that it would be unfair to require the innocent party to wait any longer. The period of notice within which completion should take place must be a reasonable time, taking into account the steps necessary to complete the transaction (see *Crawford* v. *Toogood* (1879) 13 Ch D 153). In *Nott* v. *Riccard* (1856) 22 Beav 307, a notice of 14 days was upheld, whereas in *Pegg* v. *Wisden* (1852) 16 Beav 239, six weeks' notice was insufficient.

The party serving the notice must, at the date of service, be ready, willing and able to complete the transaction or the notice will be ineffective. In *De Medina* v. *Norman* (1842) 11 LJ Ex 320, 'ready and willing' was defined as having 'not only the disposition but also the capacity to act'. Therefore, a seller who has not proved a good title to the land may not, by serving a notice to complete, seek to force a dubious title on the buyer (*Horton* v. *Kurkze* [1971] 1 WLR 769).

The difficulties caused by the open contract position do not occur under the Standard Conditions of Sale. Standard condition 6.8.1 provides that at any time after 2.00 pm on the date for completion, a party who is ready, able and willing to complete may serve a notice to complete on the other party. The parties are then to complete within 10 working days of giving the notice to complete, excluding the day on which the notice is given, and time is of the essence. It was confirmed in

Country & Metropolitan Homes Surrey Ltd v. *Topclaim Ltd* [1997] 1 All ER 254 that SC 6.8 'Notice to complete' sets out in full the rights and obligations of the parties as regards notice to complete following a party's failure to complete on the contractual completion date and is not an addition to the rights available under the general law.

Standard condition 1.1.3 provides that a party will be ready, able and willing if he could be but for the default of the other party; and the seller will be ready, able and willing even if there is a mortgage on the property, provided that the amount of the completion monies will enable this mortgage to be redeemed.

Once a notice to complete has been served, it is then binding on both parties. In *Oakdown Ltd* v. *Bernstein & Co. (a firm)* (1984) 49 P & CR 282, the notice to complete expired on a public holiday and the party which served it was in breach when it refused to complete on the day before the public holiday on religious grounds.

If a notice to complete is not complied with, the position is dealt with by either SC 7.4 or SC 7.5:

(a) If the buyer fails to comply, then SC 7.4 provides that the seller may rescind the contract and forfeit the deposit and accrued interest, resell the property and claim damages. The buyer must return any documents which he has received from the seller and cancel any registration of the contract. The seller retains his other rights and remedies.

(b) Should the seller fail to comply with a notice, then under SC 7.5 the buyer may rescind the contract and the seller must return the deposit with accrued interest. The buyer must return any documents which he has received from the seller and, at the seller's expense, must cancel any registration of the contract. The buyer retains his other rights and remedies.

11.6.2 Specific performance

This is an equitable remedy and is therefore discretionary.

11.7 LATE COMPLETION

If completion takes place after the date specified in the contract, the position under an open contract is that the parties are treated as if completion had taken place on the date specified in the contract. This means that the buyer will be entitled to the income of the property and must bear all outgoings. If the seller remains in possession, he must pay an occupation rent to the buyer unless the delay is the buyer's fault. The seller will, however, be entitled to interest on the outstanding purchase monies. If the delay is the seller's fault, then the buyer can keep the interest and the seller can keep the income if the interest exceeds the income. The innocent party will also be entitled to damages, e.g. the cost of finding temporary alternative accommodation. The normal contractual rules will apply when quantifying these damages.

If the Standard Conditions of Sale apply, then under SC 7.2.1 a party which delays in completing because of default in its obligations under the contract must pay compensation to the other party. If both parties are in default, then the party whose period of default is the greater must pay compensation. Compensation is calculated under SC 7.2.2 at the contract rate of interest on the purchase price or, where the buyer is in default, the purchase price less the deposit paid, for the period by which the paying party's default exceeds that of the other party or, if shorter, the period between the date for completion and actual completion. If the innocent party claims damages, under SC 7.2.3 these will be reduced by the amount of any compensation paid under SC 7.2.1.

11.8 SYNCHRONISATION

If either party is both buying and selling it will be necessary to synchronise the two completions so that the sale completes before the purchase. This will mean that the sale proceeds will then be available to be used towards the purchase price. Synchronisation can be achieved by amending SC 6.1.2 in the contract relating to the sale to provide for an earlier time for completion.

Usually, in a 'chain' the completion monies will be sent along the chain; and in practice this invariably causes delays, especially where the chain is lengthy. A possible solution to this would be to send the money 'up' the chain and miss out the parties in between, but the problem with this is usually that the purchase prices of the properties involved will not be the same and so there will be balances to be dealt with.

11.9 SUMMARY

- On completion, the transfer will be dated and the completion monies paid to the seller.
- Completion will take place in person or by post.
- The Law Society's Code for Completion by Post (2019) will be used where completion is by post.
- Compensation may be payable under the contract by a defaulting party if completion is delayed beyond the time and date specified in the contract.
- Under the Standard Conditions of Sale, either party may be liable to pay contractual compensation.
- If completion is delayed, the party who is ready, able and willing to complete may serve a notice to complete on the defaulting party.

- A notice to complete will make time of the essence, and if completion does not take place within 10 working days of the service of the notice, the aggrieved party may terminate the contract.
- If the buyer fails to comply with the notice to complete, he will forfeit his deposit.

CHAPTER 12

Post-completion

Once completion has taken place there are still certain matters for the solicitors acting for both parties to deal with, and in this chapter we look at these matters.

12.1 THE SELLER'S SOLICITOR

12.1.1 Report to the client

The seller's solicitor must confirm to the seller that the transaction has been completed and also account to the seller for the net sale proceeds. In certain situations, e.g. where the seller is selling as mortgagee in possession, the seller will not be entitled to the net sale proceeds and these will be payable either to a subsequent lender, or to the mortgagor.

Where the solicitor is also acting for the lender, the lender should be informed of completion.

The seller should be reminded to notify the local authority and water undertaker that the property has been sold and to cancel any insurance over the property and contents.

12.1.2 Contact the estate agents

The estate agents should be advised that completion has taken place and that the keys can be released to the buyers. If authorised by the seller, pay the estate agent's commission.

12.1.3 Contact the buyer's solicitor

The buyer's solicitor should be notified that completion has taken place and the keys have been released.

12.1.4 Send documents to the buyer's solicitor

Send the transfer, any title deeds and other relevant documents to the buyer's solicitor by first-class post or document exchange.

12.1.5 Discharge the mortgage

The seller's solicitor must, immediately after completion has taken place, send the amount required to redeem the seller's mortgage to the lender together with Form DS1 (or Form DS3 if it is a sale of part). If the lender has insured the property, it should be asked to cancel the insurance cover. The lender will then discharge the mortgage and return the Form DS1 or DS3 duly receipted. On receiving the relevant document, the seller's solicitor must check it to make sure it has been properly receipted before forwarding it to the buyer's solicitor in accordance with the undertaking given on completion. The buyer's solicitor should be requested to acknowledge receipt and confirm that the undertaking is discharged.

A lender using an e-DS1 will, on receipt of the amount required to redeem the seller's mortgage, arrange for the e-DS1 to be submitted to HM Land Registry. The lender will then notify the seller's solicitor that the mortgage has been discharged once it receives confirmation from HM Land Registry of completion of the registration of the e-DS1. The seller's solicitor should then notify the buyer's solicitor when confirmation is received from the lender. If none is received, the seller's solicitor must contact the lender to obtain such confirmation.

If the seller has an endowment mortgage, the mortgage of life policy deed, if applicable, should be sent to the lender along with the mortgage deed or a discharge form so that the policy can be re-assigned to the seller by the lender receipting the deed. When it is returned, the seller's solicitor must then serve notice on the life assurance company advising it that the policy has been re-assigned to the seller.

12.1.6 Transfer of costs and closure of file

The seller's solicitor must make sure that his costs are transferred from the client account to the office account. The file can then be closed after a final check to make sure that all outstanding matters have been dealt with.

12.2 THE BUYER'S SOLICITOR

12.2.1 Report to the buyer

The buyer's solicitor must advise his client that completion has taken place. Where the buyer has obtained a mortgage then the lender must also be informed of the completion. The lender may provide a standard form for this.

12.2.2 Complete the documents

The mortgage deed should be completed by inserting the date. File copies of the mortgage, transfer deed and other relevant documents should also be completed.

12.2.3 Stamp duty land tax

The buyer must deal with any liability for SDLT on the transaction. SDLT is a compulsory tax and a buyer must account for SDLT on a self-assessment basis. SDLT is a tax on 'land transactions' which include a sale, purchase, grant, creation, lease, variation, surrender or other transaction of any estate, interest, right or power in or over land.

Copies of all relevant forms and further information on SDLT can be found on HMRC's 'Stamp duty and other tax on property' website at **www.gov.uk/stamp-duty-land-tax**.

12.2.3.1 Procedure for SDLT

Where a buyer is liable to pay SDLT, it must be paid within 14 days of the 'effective date' of the transaction. The 'effective date' will usually be the date of completion, but may be where the contract is substantially performed before the completion date, e.g. where the buyer takes possession before completion.

A land transaction return (SDLT1) must be completed in all cases apart from transactions which are not notifiable (see **12.2.3.2**). This means that where a transaction is below the appropriate threshold and no SDLT is payable, a land transaction return must still be completed.

In some cases supplementary returns may need to be completed, for example:

(a)   SDLT2 – if there are more than two sellers or two buyers;
(b)   SDLT3 – where more than one property is purchased and all the address details cannot be fitted into the space provided on the SDLT1 form.

A land transaction return must be submitted in respect of:

(a)   a transfer of a freehold or the assignment of a lease for consideration, whether or not there is a charge to SDLT;
(b)   any transaction for which relief is being claimed;
(c)   the grant of a lease for a term of seven years or more, or which gives rise to a charge;
(d)   any other transaction which gives rise to a charge.

The land transaction return may be submitted by post or, more usually, online. Any SDLT can be paid as soon as the return has been submitted. Once the return has been submitted, a certificate in Form SDLT5 is issued confirming that the return has been submitted. Without this certificate, the transaction cannot be registered at HM Land Registry. Where the return is submitted online, the certificate can be printed off immediately. If the return is submitted by post, the certificate is returned by post and this may cause a delay with registration.

Payment of SDLT can be made in a variety of ways:

(a) by cheque;
(b) by electronic transfer of funds;
(c) at a bank; or
(d) at the Post Office.

12.2.3.2 Transactions which are not notifiable

Not all transactions have to be notified to HMRC. The following transactions will not need to be notified:

(a) freehold transactions with a consideration of less than £40,000;
(b) transactions involving a lease for a term of seven years or more if the consideration is less than £40,000 and the annual rent is less than £1,000;
(c) transactions involving a lease for a term of less than seven years if the consideration does not exceed the zero rate threshold.

12.2.3.3 Penalties for filing or paying late

The land transaction return and payment of any SDLT should be submitted to HMRC by the filing date otherwise there will be an automatic penalty.

If HMRC does not receive the land transaction return or any payment of the SDLT due within 14 days of the effective date, there will be an automatic £100 penalty. If the land transaction return is more than three months late, a £200 penalty is charged. If tax is paid late, interest will be charged. If the land transaction return is more than a year late, a tax-based penalty may also be levied, which can be up to the amount of SDLT due on the land transaction return.

12.2.3.4 Enquiries

As SDLT operates on a self-assessment basis, HMRC may start an enquiry into a land transaction return in the nine months after the filing date. Records of the transaction should be kept for six years from the effective date of the transaction.

12.2.4 Seller's mortgage

On receipt of the completed Form DS1 from the seller's solicitor, check it to make sure it is correct, acknowledge its receipt and release the seller's solicitor from the undertaking given on completion. The buyer's solicitor must request that the seller's solicitor explain the reason for delay if the discharge of the seller's mortgage is not received prior to the lodgement of the application for registration at HM Land Registry.

12.2.5 Registration at Companies House

If the buyer is a company or a limited liability partnership and has bought the property with the aid of a mortgage, then the mortgage must be registered at Companies House within 21 days of the date of its creation using Form MG01 (Form LL MR01 for a limited liability partnership). A certified copy of the mortgage deed must accompany the application. A fee is payable. The application can be made by post or online.

The 21-day time limit is absolute and cannot be extended without an order of the court. Failure to register within the time limit may prejudice the lender's security. It renders the charge void against the company's liquidator or administrator, and also against the company's other creditors.

12.2.6 Registration of title

The buyer's solicitor must apply to register the buyer as the new proprietor otherwise the legal estate will not pass to the buyer. The application must be made within the priority period of the search which was carried out before completion otherwise the buyer may lose priority to another application. The application must be received by 12.00 noon on the day on which the priority period expires, in order to preserve the applicant's priority over the registration of other interests. The priority period cannot be extended, though a second search conferring a separate priority period can be made.

Application may be made either by post or document exchange, or electronically. HM Land Registry's e-document registration service allows Land Registry business users to submit the majority of applications electronically. An application by post or document exchange must be delivered to the proper Land Registry office. All 14 Land Registry offices have been designated as proper offices for the receipt of paper applications, but HM Land Registry requires applications to be sent to its standard addresses rather than to an individual office – see **www.gov.uk/guidance/ hm-land-registry-address-for-applications**.

12.2.6.1 Registration of a dealing

Application to register a dealing is made using Form AP1 accompanied by the relevant documents. It is not necessary to send original documents with the application and certified copies should be sent instead.

The relevant documents are:

(a) A certified copy of the transfer.
(b) A certified copy of the mortgage deed. If the borrower is a company, a certified copy of the certificate of registration issued by Companies House, and the conveyancer's/lender's written confirmation that the certified copy of the mortgage deed is the same as that filed at Companies House and is the mortgage to which the certificate of registration relates.

(c)   A certified copy of the Form DS1 in respect of any mortgage which has been discharged. If an electronic means of discharge has been used no documentation will be submitted in respect of the discharged mortgage and all that is required is for reference to be made in the applications panel of Form AP1 to the use of electronic means of discharge.

(d)   The land transaction return certificate, if appropriate.

(e)   A certified copy of the grant of representation where the seller was the personal representative of the deceased proprietor.

(f)   A certified copy of any power of attorney under which the transfer has been executed.

(g)   If a registered proprietor has died, an office copy of the death certificate and, if there was a tenancy in common, a certified copy of the deed of appointment of the second trustee.

(h)   Form DI. In order to reduce the number of overriding interests, an applicant must complete Form DI setting out any overriding interests which affect the title so that they can be entered on the register and cease to be overriding (see **2.9.2.3**).

(i)   The correct fee, which is based on the value of the property and is ascertained by checking the current Land Registry Fee Order (see **www.gov.uk/ government/collections/fees-hm-land-registry-guides**).

When registering transfers, charges, leases and other dispositions, or giving effect to a discharge or release of a registered charge, HM Land Registry relies on the steps that a solicitor has taken to verify the identity of his clients. These checks reduce the risk of property fraud. Where the land is worth more than £5,000 in value, a solicitor is also required to say who acted for the other persons involved in the transactions to be registered. If no conveyancer is acting, the solicitor must either confirm that he is satisfied that sufficient steps have been taken to verify the identity of the unrepresented person, or lodge evidence of their identity. This will then help HM Land Registry decide what checks, if any, it may need to take before completing a registration. See HM Land Registry Practice Guide 67 (Evidence of Identity: Conveyancers) for further information.

12.2.6.2   Early completion

HM Land Registry's early completion policy applies to applications to discharge the whole of a registered charge where other applications are made (e.g. an application to register the transfer of the property to the buyer) but no evidence of satisfaction of the charge is supplied. HM Land Registry will reject the discharge application but complete the other applications. The effect of this is that a buyer purchasing a property with a new mortgage will be registered as the proprietor, but the seller's mortgage will remain on the title until evidence of discharge is provided, and the buyer's mortgage will rank in priority behind the seller's mortgage. Where there is a restriction on the register preventing a disposal or the registration of a new charge without the consent of the existing lender, proof of satisfaction of the charge or evidence of compliance with the restriction must be provided to HM Land Registry within 20 working days (which can be extended to 40 working days on application), otherwise the buyer's applications for discharge, transfer and charge will be cancelled. See HM Land Registry Practice Guide 31 (Discharges of Charges); and the Law Society's Land Registry Early Completion Practice Note (10 June 2020) for further information.

12.2.7   Notice of assignment of life policy

If the buyer has an endowment mortgage then, if required, notice of the assignment of the life policy must be given to the life assurance company. The notice will be given in duplicate and the life assurance company will return one copy duly receipted which should be placed with the deeds. Some lenders do not require a life policy to be assigned and it will simply need to be placed with the deeds.

12.2.8   Leasehold land

Where the land is leasehold, the terms of the lease may require that notice of any dealings with the land has to be given to the landlord or his agent. This should be sent in duplicate together with the appropriate registration fee. As with the notice of assignment of a life policy, the duplicate notice of dealing should be placed with the title deeds when it is returned.

12.2.9   Custody of the title deeds

When the registration at HM Land Registry has been completed the buyer's solicitor will receive a title information document which will comprise a copy of the register and, where the registration has resulted in the preparation of a new or amended title plan, a copy of that title plan. The title information document is issued for information only and is not a document of title. On receipt of the title infor-mation document, it should be checked carefully to ensure that there are no errors. If there are errors, then HM Land Registry should be requested to correct these.

The buyer's solicitor should also:

- Supply a copy of the title information document to the buyer and remind the buyer to keep the address for service up to date.
- Ask the buyer to check the contents of the title information document.
- Advise the lender of completion of registration.

If there is no mortgage, instructions should be taken from the buyer as to the safe custody of any pre-registration deeds and any other documents, e.g. mortgage loan agreements, planning permissions, indemnity policies, etc. The buyer should be informed of the need to keep these documents safe so that they can be available on a sale of the property. The buyer may wish for these to be held by the solicitor, or his bank, or may even wish them to be sent to him so that he can keep them. If the latter, then the buyer should be advised that they should be kept safe. Where there is a mortgage, any such documents should be dealt with in accordance with the lender's requirements. If any are to be sent to the lender, the lender will usually have a standard form of schedule to accompany them. This schedule should be completed to include all the documents being sent to the lender. A copy of the schedule will then be receipted by the lender and returned to the buyer's solicitor.

12.2.10　Transfer of costs and closure of file

If not already done, send a bill of costs to the client. Where money is being held by the solicitor on account of costs, it can be transferred to the office account, provided that the client has expressly or impliedly agreed to this being done. The file can then be closed after a final check to make sure that all outstanding matters have been dealt with.

12.3　SUMMARY

- When acting for the seller, you must advise the client, the estate agent and any lender that completion has taken place. You must also forward the relevant documentation to the buyer's solicitor and ensure that the seller's mortgage is discharged.
- When acting for the buyer, you must pay any SDLT payable within 14 days of completion. You must also register the transfer at HM Land Registry within the priority period.
- When acting for the lender, you must make sure that the mortgage is registered at HM Land Registry within the same priority period.

CHAPTER 13

Remedies

In this chapter we will consider the remedies which may be available to either of the parties in a conveyancing transaction, as a contract for the sale of land is subject to the general law of contract which provides remedies, for example in cases of misrepresentation, undue influence and fraud.

13.1 DAMAGES

13.1.1 Entitlement to damages

A buyer may be entitled to damages where there has been:

(a)   a misrepresentation by the seller;
(b)   a misdescription in the contract;
(c)   non-disclosure of a defect in title;
(d)   a failure by the seller to complete.

A seller may be entitled to damages where the buyer fails to complete.

13.1.2 Assessment of damages

The ordinary contractual principles as to remoteness of damages under *Hadley* v. *Baxendale* (1854) 9 Exch 341 apply to the assessment of the damages. An innocent party can therefore claim:

(a)   losses arising naturally from the breach; or
(b)   losses which ought reasonably to have been contemplated by the parties at the date of the contract as the probable result of the breach.

The operation of these principles is illustrated by the following cases:

(a)   *Beard* v. *Porter* [1948] 1 KB 321. The seller in breach of contract could not give the buyer vacant possession of the property. The buyer had to purchase another property instead and could recover as damages the difference between the contractual purchase price and the market value of the property at the time of the breach, together with the expenses of his lodgings while finding another property and his legal costs on the other purchase.

(b)   *Diamond* v. *Campbell-Jones* [1961] Ch 22. The seller failed to complete. The buyer sought as damages his loss of profit on a sub-sale. The seller was unaware that there was a sub-sale and the buyer could not recover in respect of this head of damages.

(c)   *Cottrill* v. *Steyning & Littlehampton Building Society* [1966] 1 WLR 753. In contrast the buyer in this case could recover as part of his damages loss of his expected profit where the seller was aware of his intention to redevelop the property.

In ordinary cases the damages will be assessed as at the date of the breach (*Johnson* v. *Agnew* [1979] 1 All ER 883). However, where the ordinary rule might cause injustice, the court has the power to fix some other date. For example, in *Johnson* v. *Agnew* where one party had refused to comply with an order of specific performance, the date fixed was the date when the possibility of performance of the contract was 'lost' as a result of the seller's lender entering into a binding contract for the sale of the property.

13.1.3   Standard Conditions of Sale

The Standard Conditions of Sale (fifth edition – 2018 revision), SC 7.1.1(a) limits the right to damages for misrepresentation to situations where there is a material difference between the description or value of the property as represented and as it is.

13.2   SPECIFIC PERFORMANCE

13.2.1   Nature of the remedy

Specific performance is an equitable remedy which is available in respect of a breach of contract by either the seller or the buyer in a contract for the sale of land. It is an order of the court to the party in breach compelling performance of the contract.

A party can apply for specific performance before the contractual completion date. In *Hasham* v. *Zenab* [1960] AC 316, where the seller signed the contract but then tore it up, the buyer applied for specific performance.

Specific performance may be refused by the court if the contract is illegal, or if there is no mutuality between the parties (i.e. the remedy is not available to both parties). In *Flight* v. *Bolland* (1818) 4 Russ 298, specific performance was held not to be available in favour of a minor since it could not be ordered against him. It may also be refused where the contract is affected by fraud, mistake, misrepresentation, inequitable conduct, hardship to the other party or delay in pursuing the remedy.

13.2.2 Delay

Where the buyer has taken possession and then seeks to obtain an order for specific performance for the seller to convey the legal title, the seller cannot claim 'laches' (i.e. delay) as a bar to the remedy. This was so held in *Williams* v. *Greatrex* [1957] 1 WLR 31, because the buyer should not be prejudiced as he had relied on his equitable title and the seller's acquiescence in his possession. In *Lazard Bros & Co.* v. *Fairfield Properties Co. (Mayfair) Ltd* (1977) SJ 793, Megarry J held that even in the absence of possession, delay in itself is not enough to bar the remedy. The delay must have been such as to prejudice the other party.

13.2.3 Specific performance plus indemnity

In *Grant* v. *Dawkins* [1973] 3 All ER 897, Goff J awarded the buyer an indemnity in addition to specific performance. The property sold was subject to mortgages, but the amounts owed under these totalled more than the purchase price. The buyer could abate the price, and that being insufficient he was able to recover as damages or indemnity the excess required to redeem the mortgages.

13.2.4 Specific performance and damages

Where one party obtains an order for specific performance this does not prevent him from applying to the court for damages, e.g. if he cannot enforce the order for specific performance (*Johnson* v. *Agnew* [1979] 1 All ER 883).

If a party does apply for damages the court could award common law damages, and the court will order damages if it is equitable to do so, because once the matter was in the hands of a court of equity it should thereafter be dealt with on equitable principles. Thus, in *Johnson* v. *Agnew*, the seller was awarded damages because it was the buyer's fault that the decree of specific performance had not been complied with.

It should be noted that in the circumstances discussed above the claimant will ordinarily have to make an election whether to pursue the remedy of specific performance when the action is commenced.

The court can award damages in lieu of, or in addition to, specific performance under its general jurisdiction in the Senior Courts Act 1981, s.50.

13.3 RESCISSION

13.3.1 Nature of the remedy

Rescission is a remedy whereby the parties to the contract are restored to their original position. The contract is 'undone' and the property or money which has passed under it is returned.

An action for rescission may be brought:

(a)   following a breach of contract by the other party; or

(b)   on the grounds of misrepresentation, mistake, fraud, equitable fraud or any other ground on which a court of equity is prepared to set the contract aside.

Rescission may take place:

(a)   by agreement between the parties;

(b)   where a contractual provision entitles one party to rescind the contract on specified terms in certain circumstances, e.g. where one party fails to complete by the stated date when time has been made the essence of the contract;

(c)   where a breach of contract by one party entitles the other to treat the contract at an end, such as in *Pips (Leisure Productions) Ltd* v. *Walton* [1981] 260 EG 601, where, on a contract for the sale of a lease, forfeiture proceedings had been commenced against the seller and the buyer was able to rescind even before the contractual completion date;

(d)   where one party applies to the court for the remedy of rescission to be awarded.

13.3.2   Rescission and damages

In *Horsler* v. *Zorro* [1975] Ch 302, Megarry J held that a claimant could not seek rescission and damages as alternatives. This statement of principle has been much criticised since. The principles have been restated disapprovingly by Goff LJ in *Buckland* v. *Farmer & Moody* [1979] 1 WLR 221, and on this point Goff LJ's judgment was approved by the House of Lords in *Johnson* v. *Agnew* [1979] 1 All ER 883.

The principles are as follows:

(a)   Where rescission is sought as a remedy in itself, e.g. for mistake, then damages cannot also be sought at the same time. The effect of rescission in such a case is to annul the contract *ab initio*, which means that the claimant loses the right to damages. In the case of misrepresentation, however, it may be that a claimant is able both to sue for damages under the Misrepresentation Act 1967, s.2(1) and to claim rescission.

(b)   Where the contract has been rescinded by the claimant because of the other party's breach, or where rescission is sought as an affirmation that the contract has been repudiated by the other's breach, then damages may be sought. Thus in *Buckland* v. *Farmer and Moody* [1979] 1 WLR 221, where the seller had written to the buyer saying that the contract was rescinded following the buyer's failure to complete, he was still entitled to maintain an action for damages.

The following two examples further illustrate these principles:

(a)   S contracts to sell a property to B. S then sells it to X. This is a fundamental breach of contract by S which terminates the contract. B may treat the contract as rescinded and sue S for damages.

(b) S contracts to sell a property to B and refuses to complete on time. B serves a valid notice to complete and when this has expired, he may rescind the contract and sue for damages.

13.3.3 Effect of rescission

Each party is required to return any benefit which he has received under the contract (but see **13.6** for a discussion of the Law of Property Act 1925, s.49 and the court's discretion to return the deposit).

In an action for rescission, the claimant may not also claim damages, but he may claim an indemnity in respect of any loss he has incurred as a result of some obligation under the contract (*Whittington* v. *Seale-Hayne* (1900) 82 LT 49). For example, L leases office premises to T who covenants to rebuild the office partitions. T later rescinds because of a misrepresentation by L. T can in his action for misrepresentation recover as an indemnity the loss he has incurred in complying with his contractual obligation under this covenant.

13.3.4 Standard Conditions of Sale

Rescission is available under SC 7, which applies where any plan or statement either in the contract or in the pre-contract negotiations is or was misleading or inaccurate due to an error or omission.

Standard condition 7.1.1(b) limits the right of a party to rescind the contract because of an error or omission to instances where:

(a) the error or omission is due to fraud or recklessness; or
(b) the party seeking to rescind would be obliged, to his prejudice, to transfer or accept property differing substantially from what the error or omission had led him to expect.

As a result of the Misrepresentation Act 1967, s.3, SC 7 is, of course, subject to the test of reasonableness contained in the Unfair Contract Terms Act 1977, s.11. In *Walker* v. *Boyle* [1982] 1 All ER 634, it was held that the equivalent condition in the previous National Conditions of Sale did not satisfy this test.

It should be noted that rescission is also available under SC 8.3.3.

If either party rescinds the contract, SC 7.1.2 provides that the deposit must be returned with interest unless the rescission is due to the buyer's breach of contract, and the buyer must return any documents to the seller and cancel any registration of the contract.

13.4 RECTIFICATION

13.4.1 Nature of the remedy

This is an equitable remedy whereby the effect of a document is altered to conform to the agreed or expressed intention of the parties, or of one of them. A deed may always be rectified with the concurrence of all the parties, otherwise rectification is available to either party on application to the court.

Various aspects of the remedy were considered by the Court of Appeal in *Joscelyne* v. *Nissen* [1970] 2 QB 86. It is now clear that rectification of an instrument may be granted even though there was no prior contract between the parties, provided the parties were agreed on the intended contents of the instrument. This case also commented on the standard of proof required. Traditionally, this was 'irrefragable evidence' of the prior agreement. The Court of Appeal preferred the more modern and less exacting standard of 'convincing proof'.

Rectification may be a last resort for a conveyancer who is faced with a contract not complying with the Law of Property (Miscellaneous Provisions) Act 1989, s.2.

13.4.2 Availability

Rectification is available if both parties have made the same mistake, and is also available in the following cases where only one party is mistaken:

(a) where there is only one party to the instrument, e.g. a deed poll;

(b) where the party who is not mistaken is guilty of fraud;

(c) where one party is mistaken and the other party who is not mistaken is aware of that mistake then the non-mistaken party is estopped from resisting the mistaken party's claim to rectification;

(d) where one party only is mistaken and it is possible to restore the parties to their original position, the court has jurisdiction to put the non-mistaken party to his election of accepting either rectification or rescission. Authority for this is found in *Paget* v. *Marshall* (1884) 28 ChD 255, where a lessor mistakenly included the first floor of the property in the lease and sought rectification. The lessee was put to the election of either accepting the lease as rectified to exclude the first floor, or of having the contract rescinded. This was later doubted in *May* v. *Platt* [1900] 1 Ch 616, but then approved by Denning LJ in the Court of Appeal in *Solle* v. *Butcher* [1950] 1 KB 671.

13.5 ACTION ON THE IMPLIED TITLE GUARANTEE

We have seen that the seller will give a title guarantee in the purchase deed. The effect of the doctrine of merger means that, unless there is an action based on a collateral matter, the buyer's main remedy after completion is to bring an action on the implied (or, if there is one, the express) title guarantee.

13.6 VENDOR AND PURCHASER SUMMONS

The Law of Property Act 1925, s.49, makes available to either the seller or the buyer a summary remedy for any dispute:

> in respect of any requisitions or objections, or any claim for compensation, or any other question arising out of or connected with the contract (not being a question affecting the existence or validity of the contract) ...

A vendor and purchaser summons may be used to decide the following disputes:

(a) whether the seller has shown a good title;
(b) whether the buyer has raised a valid requisition;
(c) whether either party has validly withdrawn from the contract; and
(d) whether a notice to complete served by a party is valid.

We have seen that if a seller serves a notice to complete, he may forfeit and keep the deposit; however, the Law of Property Act 1925, s.49(2) provides that:

> Where the court refuses to grant specific performance of a contract, or in any action for the return of a deposit, the court may, if it thinks fit, order the repayment of any deposit.

It was not clear in the past whether this subsection gave the court jurisdiction in a vendor and purchaser summons to order the return of the deposit on an application by the buyer in a case where the seller would have been awarded specific performance if he had claimed this instead of rescinding and forfeiting the deposit. That point arose before the Court of Appeal in *Universal Corporation* v. *Five Ways Properties Ltd* [1979] 1 All ER 552. In that case the buyer had paid a deposit of £388,500 but failed to complete, and the seller had in due course rescinded and forfeited the deposit. The buyer applied to the court for the return of the deposit and the judge struck out the claim. On appeal it was declared that the judge was wrong. Section 49(2) gave the court an unfettered discretion to award a return of a deposit where justice so required. The judge's order striking out the buyer's claim was accordingly reversed and the issue of whether the deposit ought to be returned remained to be tried.

It may be noted that the Privy Council has confirmed that the court could treat an extremely large deposit as a penalty and provide relief to the buyer. In *Workers Trust & Merchant Bank Ltd* v. *Dojap Investments Ltd* [1993] 2 All ER 370, the deposit was 25 per cent. If a deposit of more than 10 per cent is desired by the seller, this possibility must be borne in mind.

In *Aribisala* v. *St James Homes (Grosvenor Dock) Ltd* [2007] EWHC 1694 (Ch) it was held that the parties to a contract for the sale of land could not exclude the application of s.49(2). The contract term purporting to exclude s.49(2) was attempting to oust the jurisdiction of the court and was void and of no effect on the grounds of public policy.

13.7 SUMMARY

- Specific performance is available in respect of a breach of contract by either the seller or the buyer.
- If the seller fails to disclose an incumbrance over the property, damages for breach of contract may be available to the buyer where the incumbrance causes a material difference in the tenure or value of the property.
- An action for rescission may be brought following a breach of contract or on the grounds of misrepresentation, mistake, fraud, equitable fraud or any other ground on which a court of equity is prepared to set the contract aside.
- Rectification is a remedy whereby the effect of a document is altered to conform to the agreed or expressed intention of the parties, or of one of them.
- A vendor and purchaser summons provides a summary remedy for a dispute in respect of any requisitions or objections, or any claim for compensation or any other question arising out of or connected with the contract.
- After completion, it may be possible to bring a claim for breach of the implied covenants for title in the transfer deed, although this remedy is used very rarely.

CHAPTER 14

New properties

In this chapter we look at the documentation which will be supplied to a buyer's solicitor on the purchase of a new property on a building estate, and also at particular matters which need to be considered when buying a new property. A sale of a new property is a more complex transaction than the sale of an existing house or building, and some matters additional to those relevant to a sale of an existing house or building must be considered.

While this chapter deals with new properties, you should also bear the points dealt with in mind when buying a recently constructed house or flat on a subsequent sale.

14.1 BUILDING ESTATES

As the seller, usually a builder or developer, will be selling a number of plots of land on a building estate to different buyers, the documentation and procedures involved in selling each plot will be standardised. The seller's solicitor will usually send each buyer's solicitor a pack of documentation as soon as instructions have been received. The items included in this pack will all be in standard form, and amendments to the contract and purchase deed will not usually be allowed.

A typical pack supplied by a builder's solicitor will include:

(a)   draft contract in duplicate;
(b)   replies to standard enquiries before contract;
(c)   copies of planning permission and building regulations approval;
(d)   abstracts or copies of agreements and bonds under the Highways Act 1980, s.38 and the Water Industry Act 1991, s.104;
(e)   draft transfer in duplicate, or a draft lease in duplicate where a long lease is to be granted;
(f)   evidence of the builder's title;
(g)   replies to standard requisitions on title;
(h)   new home warranty and insurance scheme documentation where appropriate;
(i)   a copy of the plan of the property properly marked and coloured in accordance with Land Registry requirements, with a spare copy for search purposes;

(j)   if desired, a general information sheet for the buyer containing *inter alia* addresses of local authorities and other bodies with whom searches may need to be conducted and an explanation of the contract terms (including arrangements for deposit and completion); and

(k)   UK Finance Disclosure Form.

The evidence of title will consist of an official copy of the register and of the title plan. However, the title plan may be too large to be supplied for every sale of a plot on the estate and instead Form CI will be supplied. This form is issued by HM Land Registry and certifies that the property to which it relates is within the particular title number and which entries on the title plan affect that plot. The plot number stated on the form is then quoted by the buyer's solicitor when he carries out an official search of the register. In order to obtain a form for each plot on an estate, the builder's solicitor must lodge a copy of a plan showing the estate layout with HM Land Registry which will then approve it and issue a Form CI in respect of each plot shown on the plan. The builder's solicitor may at the same time as lodging the estate layout plan also ask HM Land Registry to approve the form of transfer which is to be used for all the plot sales.

If the builder's title is mortgaged, a release of the land being sold in Form DS3 must be obtained. If there is also a floating charge, a certificate of non-crystallisation will need to be handed over on completion.

An EPC must be provided for a new building. The builder must supply the EPC to the first buyer, who in turn, if he sells on, must supply it to a subsequent buyer. If a property is being sold before construction has been finished, the builder must provide a full EPC once the property is complete.

14.2   PLANNING PERMISSION AND BUILDING REGULATIONS APPROVAL

The erection of a new house will normally require both planning permission and building regulations approval, and copies of these will normally be supplied to the buyer's solicitor with the draft contract. The buyer's solicitor must check these and, if there are any reserved matters, must request confirmation from the builder's solicitor that these matters have been complied with. The buyer's solicitor may also request confirmation from the builder's solicitor that all conditions attached to the planning permission have been complied with; however, it is possible that the contract may include a warranty to this effect.

14.3   ROADS AND SEWERS

If the roads and sewers on the estate are not adopted and therefore not maintainable at the public expense, the builder will usually agree in the contract with each buyer to make up the estate roads and sewers. The danger for the buyer is that the builder may default on this obligation, e.g. because the builder goes into liquidation, and the local authority may then make them up and charge the buyers the cost of doing so. The buyer's solicitor should therefore ensure that the builder has entered into an agreement with the local authority under the Highways Act 1980, s.38. Under such an agreement, the builder agrees to make up the roads to the local authority's standards and the local authority agrees to adopt the roads in due course. The agreement should be supported by a bond which will provide that the buyer will be reimbursed for any costs paid to the local authority should the builder default in his obligations and the local authority make up the roads.

The buyer's solicitor should also ensure that there is a similar agreement and bond under the Water Industry Act 1991, s.104 with the water authority in relation to the making up and adoption of the drains and sewers.

Whether the roads and sewers are adopted will be revealed in replies to CON 29 and CON 29DW. These replies will also reveal whether agreements and bonds have been entered into.

If the buyer is obtaining a mortgage it will usually be a requirement of the lender that there are s.38 and s.104 agreements and bonds in place.

The buyer's solicitor must also ensure that the transfer to the buyer contains the necessary easements which the buyer will need to reach the public highway from the property, and also those required so that the drains from the property can reach the public sewer. If these easements pass over other titles, then they should be investigated in the same way.

14.4   NEW HOME WARRANTY AND INSURANCE SCHEMES

Most new residential properties will be offered with the benefit of cover under a new home warranty and insurance scheme. The most widely used is the NHBC Build-mark scheme. This scheme provides insurance protection for structural defects in the property for the first 10 years. Acceptance of Buildmark cover is managed online via the NHBC Conveyancing Portal (see **https://www.nhbc.co.uk/ homeowners/conveyancing-portal**).

Under the Buildmark scheme the builder agrees to:

(a)   build the property in a proper manner and in accordance with NHBC require-ments; and

(b)   make good any defects arising from a failure to comply with the NHBC's requirements during the first two years of the guarantee period.

NHBC agrees to:

(a)   meet any loss suffered by the buyer as a result of the builder becoming insolvent before the property has been completed, such as the cost of complet-ing the construction of the property or the refund of the deposit to the buyer, provided in either case that the financial limit (usually 10 per cent of the purchase price) is not exceeded;

(b) make good any loss suffered by the buyer as a result of the builder failing to put right any defects within the first two years; and

(c) provide an insurance-style guarantee for the remaining eight years of the cover that it will rectify damage resulting from a defect in construction, non-compliance with the building regulations or contamination that requires remediation under the Environmental Protection Act 1990, subject to a financial limit, usually the purchase price.

If the buyer is obtaining a mortgage, the lender will require that the property has NHBC cover. Under paragraph 6.7.2 of the Lenders' Handbook, the buyer's solicitor must obtain a copy of the NHBC cover note from the developer before submitting the certificate of title to the lender. The cover note must confirm that the property has received a satisfactory final inspection and that the new home warranty will be in place on or before legal completion. What will happen in practice is that NHBC will pass the cover note to the builder immediately the property has passed the final inspection. The builder or its solicitor will then pass the cover note to the buyer's solicitor. There is a similar provision in the BSA Mortgage Instructions.

If the builder is not registered with NHBC then the lender may accept a certificate by an architect confirming that the property has been properly completed. The buyer's solicitor should also insist on the builder giving warranties in the contract confirming that the property has been correctly constructed.

14.5 TERMS OF THE CONTRACT

The contract for the sale of a new house will be in the builder's standard form and incorporate the Standard Conditions of Sale. A builder will usually be unwilling to accept any amendments to the contract, as it will want every property on the development to be sold on the same terms.

Particular points to note about the contract are:

(a) If the property is in the course of development, the contract should contain provisions requiring the builder to complete the property in accordance with agreed specifications and plans and the planning permission.

(b) It may not be possible for the builder to agree a firm completion date on exchange of contracts, and if this is the case there should be a provision in the contract whereby completion will take place within a certain length of time after the property has been finished and the builder's solicitor has notified the buyer's solicitor of this. Such a provision may cause the buyer difficulties, particularly where the buyer has a dependent sale, and the buyer must be advised of this. The buyer's solicitor must also make sure that the length of time is sufficient for him to carry out the pre-completion searches and for the lender to have a final inspection of the property carried out before releasing the mortgage monies.

(c) As this is a sale of part, the contract should deal with the grant and reservation of easements, and the imposition of restrictive covenants. The easements must be checked to make sure that they are adequate, and the restrictive covenants must be checked to ensure that they are not onerous and do not impede the buyer's use of the property.

(d) The contract should also contain confirmation that the builder is registered with a new home warranty and insurance scheme, usually NHBC, and that he will provide cover under the scheme. The buyer's solicitor should check via the NHBC website that the builder is registered.

14.6 EASEMENTS AND COVENANTS

The contract will provide for the grant of easements to the buyer over the land retained by the builder and the reservation of easements by the builder over the land sold. Easements to be granted to the buyer should include:

(a) a right of way over the estate roads until they are adopted;
(b) a right to use the drains and sewers;
(c) a right to use the pipes and cables for gas, water, electricity, telephone, etc.; and
(d) rights of access to maintain these.

Easements to be reserved over the land being sold will include the right to run services (e.g. gas, water, electricity, telephone, etc.) across the land to the builder's adjoining land together with a right of access over the land in order to inspect and maintain these services.

The implied grant of easements under the rule in *Wheeldon* v. *Burrows* and the Law of Property Act 1925, s.62, will generally be excluded so that both parties rely upon the clear, express grants and reservations provided for in the contract and carried forward into the transfer.

The contract will also provide for new covenants, both restrictive and positive, to be created, e.g. to use the property as a private dwelling house and to maintain boundary fences.

14.7 TRANSFER

In practice the transfer to be used will be attached to the draft contract. This will set out the necessary easements and covenants. A charge is often made to the buyer for the plans to be attached to this transfer. In establishing the development it is good practice to have the form of the transfer and layout of the estate agreed in advance with HM Land Registry. The seller will not usually permit amendments to the transfer.

The contents of the transfer must be made clear in the contract for sale. This is usually achieved in practice by ensuring that the contract provides for the precise words of covenants and other provisions in the actual transfer. The following areas must be covered:

(a)   The description of property will almost invariably be by reference to a plan. The words incorporating the plan must make it clear whether the plan is the dominant description. Thus, 'All that land more particularly described on the plan' makes it clear the plan is paramount. The words 'All that part of the seller's land known as Moran's Field and shown for identification purposes only on the plan' makes it clear that the description in words is paramount. This can be used only if the words do accordingly describe the land to be sold.

(b)   The buyer may be required to enter into covenants as to the use of the land sold. These will be introduced in the contract as 'The buyer will enter into the following covenants' and then the actual covenants are set out. Positive and negative covenants should be separated. This is conveniently done by a schedule to the contract and then the transfer: 'the positive covenants set out in Schedule 1 Part A and the restrictive covenants set out in Schedule 1 Part B …'.

(c)   The solicitor must be able to explain to the client the different effect of positive and negative covenants and the circumstances in which they remain enforceable.

(d)   The benefit of covenants should be clearly annexed to the land retained. Words such as 'the buyer covenants for the benefit of the seller's retained land edged blue on the plan annexed and for each and every part thereof' will ensure that the benefited land is clearly identified and intended to be benefited.

(e)   The seller may require rights to be reserved over the land sold. Again, they will be set out in a schedule to the conveyance or transfer. The words used should make it clear which land is benefited and the precise nature of each right concerned. If it is a right of way, is it with all kinds of transport, and at all times?

(f)   The seller may give the buyer rights over land retained. As with reservations, they will be contained in a separate schedule or part of a schedule.

(g)   In respect of reservations and grants it will often be advisable to make it clear at what cost the drains, roads or whatever are to be maintained, and who if anybody is under an obligation to carry out the maintenance.

A declaration is commonly included that the 'buyer will have no right of light or air over the land retained'.

Where there are shared boundary features – walls, gutters, down-rights and so on – a declaration is commonly included that these are 'Party Walls and Structures'.

The rights between the parties are then governed by the Law of Property Act 1925, s.38. The Party Wall etc. Act 1996 gives important rights in respect of the construction, maintenance and repair of party walls.

14.8 UK FINANCE DISCLOSURE FORM

In order to increase transparency as to the agreed price of new homes, UK Finance requires a Disclosure Form from the builder of any new-build, converted or renovated property. The Disclosure Form requests information on all incentives and discounts offered by the builder.

Part 2 of the Lenders' Handbook requires a solicitor acting for a lender to be in receipt of a Disclosure Form before he can submit the certificate of title.

The form will be completed by the builder and supplied to the lender's solicitor by the builder's solicitor as part of the initial contract package. The lender's solicitor will then be required to report such information from the Disclosure Form as the lender requests in Part 2 of the Lenders' Handbook.

There are similar provisions in the BSA Mortgage Instructions.

14.9 CONSUMER CODE FOR HOME BUILDERS

The Consumer Code for Home Builders is a voluntary code of practice for residential builders, but its use is compulsory for builders who are registered with certain home warranty providers, including NHBC. The Code can be found at **www.consumercode.co.uk**. The Code is intended to provide additional consumer protection to individual home buyers who have made a reservation to buy a new or newly converted home.

The Code sets out what information must be provided to home buyers and requires the home builder to monitor customer satisfaction. There is an associated dispute resolution service for complaints about non-compliance with the Code arising and made within two years of completion of the purchase. Disputes are resolved using an adjudication process. Awards up to a maximum of £15,000 (inclusive of VAT) can be made, and builders who are in serious breach of the Code could be removed from the registers of the home warranty providers of which they are a member.

14.10 SUMMARY

- The builder should provide a full package of pre-contract documentation including a draft contract, replies to enquiries and a transfer deed.
- A new property will need planning permission, an EPC, and building regulations consent.

- A new home should be protected by a home warranty and insurance scheme, otherwise it may be difficult to mortgage and sell within the first 10 years of construction.
- Where the new estate roads and/or drains and sewers have not been adopted by completion, you must check that there is an agreement and bond between the developer and the relevant authority to protect the buyer should the builder become insolvent before adoption.
- As the transaction will usually be a sale of part, easements and covenants may be appropriate.
- If the property is in the course of construction, a fixed completion date cannot usually be agreed on exchange and the builder will serve a notice to complete once the property is physically complete.
- A pre-completion search at HM Land Registry is made using Form OS2 quoting the plot number on Form CI.

CHAPTER 15

The grant of a lease

Rather than selling the freehold of a property, an owner may decide to grant a lease of the property instead. The main reasons for doing this are that the owner will receive rent instead of or in addition to a capital sum, will retain an interest in the property and will be able to enforce the covenants in the lease against the tenant and his successors in title. Common examples of situations where leases are used include flats and commercial premises.

The lease will be drafted by the landlord's solicitor and then submitted to the tenant's solicitor together with a draft contract, although in certain circumstances, e.g. short leases and commercial leases, the contract will be dispensed with. The form of the draft lease is then 'negotiated' by the tenant's solicitor returning it with any amendments marked in red. If these are not agreed, the landlord's solicitor amends them in green and returns the draft to the tenant's solicitor. This process can theoretically be even further protracted and the modern practice of stating reasons why a particular clause will or will not be agreed is to be welcomed. Particularly in the case of domestic conveyancing on building estates, the form of lease is often presented to the tenant's solicitor on a 'take it or leave it' basis.

In this chapter we look at the contents of a lease and the procedure involved in its grant.

15.1 PRELIMINARY CONSIDERATIONS

Before drafting the lease, the landlord's solicitor must take full instructions from the landlord on the terms to be included in the lease, including the extent of the property to be leased, the length of the lease (otherwise known as the term), the rent and the proposed use of the property.

The landlord's title must also be investigated, and the solicitor will need to obtain the title deeds for this purpose. The purpose of this investigation is:

(a)   to find out whether there are any incumbrances affecting the property, as these may need to be made binding on the tenant; and
(b)   to ensure that the landlord has the right to grant the lease.

If the property is subject to a mortgage, then the lender should be approached for consent to the proposed lease.

15.1.1 Drafting a lease

When drafting a lease, a solicitor will usually start with a precedent. This may be one of the firm's own precedents or one taken from a precedents book such as the *Practical Lease Precedents* (Sweet & Maxwell). Great care must always be taken when using any precedent to make sure that it accords with the needs and instructions of the client. In many cases a precedent will need amending, or perhaps it may be necessary to include clauses from another precedent in order to meet your instructions.

15.1.2 HM Land Registry prescribed clauses leases

HM Land Registry has prescribed a set of clauses that have to be included at the beginning of a lease.

The clauses are compulsory in all leases granted out of registered titles, except leases that are in a form expressly required:

(a)   by an agreement entered into before 19 June 2006;
(b)   by an order of the court;
(c)   by or under an enactment; or
(d)   by a necessary consent or licence for the grant of the lease given before 19 June 2006.

Additionally, a deed varying a lease that takes effect as a surrender and re-grant of the leasehold estate does not have to be a prescribed clauses lease. This exception applies whether or not the original lease was a prescribed clauses lease.

15.1.3 Unfair terms

Part 2 of the Consumer Rights Act 2015 applies to contracts made between a 'trader' and a 'consumer'. This will include leases between a builder or professional landlord and a private individual. The requirements of the Consumer Rights Act 2015 should therefore be borne in mind when drafting the lease.

15.2 CONTENTS OF THE LEASE

15.2.1 Commencement

This will state that the document is a lease. As a lease must be granted by deed, unless it is one not exceeding three years within the provisions of the Law of Property Act 1925, s.54, it must comply with the Law of Property (Miscellaneous

Provisions) Act 1989, s.1 and make it clear on its face that it is a deed. The commencement may thus use the words 'THIS DEED OF LEASE'. Where the lease is created out of a registered title, it should have Land Registry headings at the top of its first page (e.g. county and district, landlord's title number, a brief description of the property, and its date).

15.2.2 Date

This will be completion date and must not be confused with the date of the commencement of the term of the lease. While these dates may be the one and the same, it is possible for the commencement date to be before the date of the lease or up to 21 years after the date of the lease.

15.2.3 Parties

These will be the landlord and the tenant, and they will be named in the same way as in a conveyance. The same covenants for title may be implied on the grant of a lease as on a freehold sale and so either 'with full title guarantee' or 'with limited title guarantee' will be included after the operative words.

15.2.4 Consideration

This will be the rent, a premium (i.e. a capital payment) or both. If a premium is paid then the amount of the premium must be stated and a receipt clause included. A premium will normally be paid only on the grant of a long lease, e.g. a 99-year lease of a house.

15.2.5 Operative words

These will indicate the parties' intentions, and the words used will normally be either 'demise' or 'lease'.

15.2.6 Parcels

There must be a description of the property, and usually this will include reference to a plan. If the lease is of part of the landlord's property, consideration must be given to the easements which should be included in the lease and those which should be reserved to the landlord. The rules in *Wheeldon* v. *Burrows* (1879) 12 Ch D 31 and the Law of Property Act 1925, s.62 will also apply, and it may be necessary to restrict their application.

15.2.7 Habendum

This will state the term or length of the lease and the date on which the term is to commence.

15.2.8 Reddendum

This will state the amount of the rent and when it is to be paid. The amount of the rent will vary from lease to lease, but in the case of a long lease will usually be minimal. The rent will usually be payable in advance but may sometimes be payable in arrears. The dates on which the rent is to be paid will be stated.

Quite often the rent is expressed to be paid by equal quarterly payments in advance on the usual quarter days. These are 25 December (Christmas Day), 25 March (Lady Day), 24 June (Midsummer Day) and 29 September (Michaelmas Day).

The lease may also include provisions whereby the rent can be reviewed periodically and increased.

15.2.9 Covenants

The lease will then include covenants by each party. Common covenants are covered at **15.3**.

15.2.10 Right of re-entry

A lease should contain a right for the landlord to re-enter the property, or to forfeit the lease if the tenant does not pay the rent or if there is a breach by the tenant of any other covenant in the lease. This right must be expressly included, unless the lease is conditional on the tenant observing the covenants. In the absence of such a right the landlord will be left with a perhaps valueless remedy of suing the tenant for damages for breach of covenant. The lease should also contain a right of re-entry in the case of bankruptcy of the tenant or any surety.

In the case of a long residential lease, a forfeiture clause permitting forfeiture for bankruptcy will not normally be included as it would be unacceptable to lenders.

15.3 COMMON COVENANTS

15.3.1 Covenant to pay rent

A covenant by the tenant to pay the rent will always be included even though the rent has already been reserved. The covenant will also usually include that the tenant is to pay all taxes relating to the property. There may be provision for the payment of the rent to be suspended should the property be damaged or destroyed by an insured risk.

15.3.2 Covenant to repair

The responsibility for repairing the premises will depend on the length of the term. In a long lease, the tenant will normally be responsible for all repairs.

15.3.3 Covenant by the tenant not to make any improvements or alterations

This will be included in short-term leases to make sure that the tenant hands back the property at the end of the lease in the same condition as it was in when let, and also to ensure that the landlord will not have any liability to compensate the tenant for improvements at the end of the lease. This will be less of a problem in a long-term lease.

The covenant may be either:

(a)   absolute, i.e. a total bar on the tenant making any improvements or alterations; or
(b)   qualified, that is that no improvement or alteration may be made without the landlord's consent.

If the covenant is qualified, then by virtue of the Landlord and Tenant Act 1927, s.19(2), the landlord's consent to improvements must not be unreasonably withheld. This does not, however, prevent the landlord from demanding a reasonable sum to be paid in respect of any decrease in the value of the property and to cover legal and other expenses incurred in giving the consent.

15.3.4 Covenant restricting the tenant's use of the property

This may be included in order to protect the character of the property or estate on which it is situated.

This covenant will also be either absolute or qualified. If qualified, there is no statutory provision requiring that the landlord's consent may not be unreasonably withheld and consent can be withheld or not as the landlord chooses. Section 19(3) of the Landlord and Tenant Act 1927 does provide, though, that if consent is required by the lease to a change of use then, unless a structural alteration is required, no premium or extra rent may be charged for consent. The landlord may still require reasonable payment for any legal and other expenses.

15.3.5 Covenant to insure

Where the lease is of whole, for example a house, the tenant will usually be solely responsible for insuring the property. In the case of lettings of part, for example a flat in a house or block, the landlord or management company will usually insure the whole house or block, with the cost being passed on to the tenants through the service charge or as a separate insurance rent.

In both cases, the risks insured against, the amount of cover and the application of policy monies must be checked.

15.3.6 Covenant by the tenant not to assign or sub-let

This covenant will be included to ensure that only the tenant can have an interest in the property, and it would be very unusual to find such a covenant in a long lease as it would make the lease unattractive to a prospective tenant.

The covenant may be made qualified so that the tenant may assign or sub-let with the landlord's consent. In this case the consent must not be unreasonably withheld (Landlord and Tenant Act 1927, s.19(1)(a)). The Landlord and Tenant Act 1988, s.1 provides that consent or reasons for refusal must be given within a reasonable time, and the Act also provides for damages to be paid by a landlord who refuses consent unreasonably or who delays unreasonably.

Where consent is required then, by the Law of Property Act 1925, s.144, no sum of money is to be paid for the consent except for reasonable legal and other expenses. Section 144 may be excluded by the lease and tenants must be alert to see that this is not done, as if it is the lease becomes in effect unassignable.

15.3.7 Covenant to give notice of dealings to the landlord

Where there is no restriction on the tenant's right to deal with the property there will usually be a covenant requiring that notice be given to the landlord of any dealings with the property, e.g. assignments and mortgages. A small fee is usually payable to the landlord or its solicitor on the giving of this notice.

15.3.8 Landlord's covenant for quiet enjoyment

This covenant will be implied if it is not expressly included. If such a covenant is expressly included then it can be in either a restricted or an absolute form, whereas an implied covenant will always be restricted.

If the covenant is restricted, the landlord will covenant that the tenant will not be interrupted by either himself or those claiming through or under him, whereas in an absolute covenant the landlord also covenants that the tenant's possession will not be disturbed by the landlord's predecessors in title.

15.4 DRAFTING THE CONTRACT

The contract will be prepared by the landlord's solicitor and will be in similar form to that for a freehold sale, with the following differences:

(a)   *The particulars.* These will state the estate and term which is to be vested in the tenant. Rather than the contract setting out all the terms of the draft lease, the Standard Conditions of Sale (fifth edition – 2018 revision), SC 8.2.3 provides that the draft lease is to be attached to the contract and the terms are thereby incorporated into the contract.

(b) *The conditions of sale*:

- The landlord does not have to deduce title to the freehold.
- To assist the tenant, SC 8.2.4 provides that if the term of the lease exceeds seven years the landlord must deduce a title which will enable the tenant to register the lease with absolute title. This means that the landlord must deduce the freehold title.
- If there are any covenants contained in the freehold title, then a condition should be included whereby the tenant will give an indemnity for any future breaches of these covenants.

15.5 APPROVING THE DRAFT LEASE AND DRAFT CONTRACT

Once the landlord's solicitor has drafted the lease and contract, these are sent in duplicate to the tenant's solicitor for approval. As with freehold land, the usual searches and enquiries will be carried out.

The tenant's solicitor will need to consider the terms of the draft lease and in particular will consider:

(a) whether any easements being granted are suitable and whether they will involve the tenant in any expense;

(b) whether any easements which are being reserved will prevent the tenant from using the property;

(c) whether the covenants being imposed are too restrictive or onerous bearing in mind the continuing liability of the original tenant; and

(d) whether any covenants affecting the freehold titles are also too restrictive or onerous, and whether they are enforceable.

If the tenant is obtaining a mortgage, then the lease must be acceptable to the lender. In particular, the following points must be borne in mind:

(a) If the freehold title is not being deduced, the lease will be registered with good leasehold title. Such title may not be acceptable to the lender as the right of the landlord to grant the lease is not guaranteed and there may be incumbrances, e.g. restrictive covenants, affecting the freehold title which seriously detract from the value of the lease.

(b) The insurance arrangements in the lease may not be acceptable to the lender who will want to arrange the insurance.

(c) A lender will not usually accept a lease which contains a proviso for re-entry on bankruptcy as, if the lease is forfeited by the landlord, the security for the loan will be lost.

Once the draft lease and draft contract have been approved, the procedure up to exchange is the same as for freehold land.

15.6 PREPARATION FOR COMPLETION

The steps to be taken are the same as for freehold land. However, there are two copies of the lease which need to be prepared as engrossments. Standard condition 8.2.5 provides that the landlord (seller) is to engross the lease and an identical copy of it called a counterpart lease, and is to send the counterpart to the tenant (buyer) at least five working days before the completion date. The landlord therefore executes the lease while the tenant executes the counterpart. Standard condition 8.2.6 specifically provides that the tenant (buyer) is to execute the counterpart and deliver it to the landlord (seller) on completion.

The tenant's solicitor must also carry out the usual pre-completion searches if the freehold title has been deduced.

15.7 COMPLETION

15.7.1 The tenant

On completion the tenant will:

(a) receive the lease executed by the landlord; and
(b) if the landlord's title is mortgaged, receive the lender's consent to the lease.

15.7.2 The landlord

The tenant will hand over to the landlord:

(a) the balance of the purchase price;
(b) the executed counterpart lease; and
(c) if the ground rent is payable in advance, an apportionment of this.

15.8 POST-COMPLETION STEPS

These will be the same as for freehold land, with the following differences.

15.8.1 Stamp duty land tax

SDLT may be payable both on any premium being paid and on the rent payable under the lease, and a land transaction return (SDLT1) must be submitted to HMRC in the usual way.

The amount of SDLT payable on any rent is calculated using the 'net present value' (NPV) of the total rent payable over the term of the lease. To calculate the NPV, all the rent payable under the lease is aggregated but, to reflect the fact that the rent is payable in the future, it is discounted at a rate of 3.5 per cent per annum. In practice, the NPV and the SDLT payable are calculated by using the HMRC online calculator (**www.tax.service.gov.uk/calculate-stamp-duty-land-tax**).

In relation to residential property, the SDLT payable on any premium is calculated on the same basis as for the consideration on the sale of freehold land. In relation to rent, SDLT is charged at one per cent on any element of the NPV that exceeds £125,000.

15.8.2 Registration

If the lease is for more than seven years (or is otherwise registrable) it must be registered at HM Land Registry within two months of completion if the freehold title is not registered or within the priority period of the HM Land Registry search if the freehold title is registered. If the freehold is not registered, the tenant's application is for first registration. If the freehold is registered, the tenant's application is for the registration of a dealing. Where the freehold title is registered, the lease must be noted on the reversionary title.

15.8.3 Notice

The lease may require that notice of any dealing must be given to the landlord. If the tenant has bought with a mortgage, then notice of the mortgage must be given to the landlord. The usual way of doing this is to serve written notice in duplicate on the landlord together with payment of any registration fee, and to request the landlord to return one copy of the notice duly receipted once the dealing has been registered. The receipted notice should then be placed with the deeds.

15.9 LEASES OF FLATS

Where the lease is to be of a flat there are various additional matters which need to be dealt with.

15.9.1 Parcels

The property to be included in the lease must be carefully described. A common approach is to include only the interior of a flat within the lease, and not to include the structural and exterior parts. A detailed plan must also be used so as accurately to show the extent of the leased property.

15.9.2 Easements

The easements which are being granted and reserved must be accurately described, and will need to cover such matters as access and services.

15.9.3 Ownership and management of any common parts

If there are any common parts in the building of which the flat forms part, such as stairs, lifts, entrance halls and the external structure of the building, the tenant must ensure that there are adequate provisions for their repair and maintenance. The usual way of dealing with this is to include in each lease a covenant by the tenant to pay a service charge covering the costs incurred by the landlord in repairing and maintaining the common parts. The service charge will normally be expressed to be paid by way of additional rent, so that if it is not paid the remedies for non-payment of rent will be available.

Quite often the landlord will wish to have no further dealings with the property once all the flats have been let, and so may form a management company to take control of the common parts. Such a company will be limited and will usually be controlled by the tenants who will become the members of the company. Each tenant will therefore be entitled to a share certificate in the company. The tenant's solicitor should also ensure that the company's memorandum and articles are adequate.

15.9.4 Insurance

It is important that the whole of the building is properly insured. This can be achieved either by the landlord insuring the whole of the building under a block policy and recovering the premium from the tenants, or by each tenant insuring his own flat and the landlord insuring the common parts.

If the tenant covenants to insure, the covenant may require that he uses a particular company or one selected by the landlord, and it may also provide that the tenant must produce the policy and the receipt for the premiums. It may therefore be safer and administratively simpler for the landlord to insure and to recover the premiums by way of a service charge. In any event, the lease should provide for insurance monies to be used for the reinstatement of the property.

15.9.5 Enforceability of covenants

The lease will probably include covenants restricting the use of the property. These will be enforceable by the landlord against the tenant, and may be enforceable between the tenants if there is a letting scheme which in principle is similar to a freehold building scheme.

15.9.6 Service charges

So far as service charges and other charges for repairs, maintenance or insurance are concerned, the tenant may sometimes face difficulties with possible overcharging or poor workmanship. Some protection is given by the Landlord and Tenant Act 1985, ss.20–23, which entitle the tenant to independent estimates, information as to costs and sight of accounts. Charges can be challenged on the grounds of unreasonableness (Landlord and Tenant Act 1985, s.19).

Though the quite detailed provisions do provide for costs to be reasonable and 'the provision of services or the carrying out of works . . . [to be] . . . of a reasonable standard' (Landlord and Tenant Act 1985, s.19(1)(b)), the sensible tenant will ensure before entering into the lease that the mechanism for establishing and collecting the service charge and for administering the common parts is satisfactory rather than relying on this statutory provision.

15.10 SUMMARY

- A registrable lease must contain the HM Land Registry prescribed clauses.
- A lease of part of a building must include easements so that the tenant can have access to and use all required facilities.
- The lease should make it clear who is responsible for insurance.
- A covenant may be absolute, qualified or fully qualified.
- In relation to assignment and subletting, the Landlord and Tenant Act 1927, s.19(1)(a) turns a qualified covenant into a fully qualified covenant.
- Where it would be unreasonable not to give consent to an assignment or a subletting, the landlord is also under a statutory duty to give consent within a reasonable time.
- The lease must set out who is responsible for repairs.
- When acting for a landlord, you must ensure that the lease contains a forfeiture clause.
- A long residential lease should not permit forfeiture on the insolvency of the tenant.

APPENDIX A

Standard Conditions of Sale (fifth edition – 2018 revision) including explanatory notes

CONVEYANCER'S RECORD OF EXCHANGE
Name of buyer's conveyancer:
Name of seller's conveyancer:
Law Society formula A/B/C/Personal Exchange
THE INFORMATION ABOVE DOES NOT FORM PART OF THE CONTRACT

CONTRACT

(Incorporating the Standard Conditions of Sale (Fifth Edition))

Date	:
Seller	:
Buyer	:
Property (freehold/leasehold)	:
Title number/root of title	:
Specified incumbrances	:
Title guarantee (full/limited)	:
Completion date	:
Contract rate	:
Purchase price	:
Deposit	:
Contents price (if separate)	:
Balance	:

The seller will sell and the buyer will buy the property for the purchase price.

WARNING	Signed
This is a formal document, designed to create legal rights and legal obligations. Take advice before using it.	Seller/Buyer

STANDARD CONDITIONS OF SALE (FIFTH EDITION)
(NATIONAL CONDITIONS OF SALE 25TH EDITION, LAW
SOCIETY'S CONDITIONS OF SALE 2011)

1. GENERAL

1.1 Definitions

1.1.1   In these conditions:

    (a) 'accrued interest' means:

        (i) if money has been placed on deposit or in a building society share account, the interest actually earned

        (ii) otherwise, the interest which might reasonably have been earned by depositing the money at interest on seven days' notice of withdrawal with a clearing bank

        less, in either case, any proper charges for handling the money

    (b) 'clearing bank' means a bank admitted by the Bank of England as a direct participant in its CHAPS system

    (c) 'completion date' has the meaning given in condition 6.1.1

    (d) 'contents price' means any separate amount payable for contents included in the contract

    (e) 'contract rate' means the Law Society's interest rate from time to time in force

    (f) 'conveyancer' means a solicitor, barrister, duly certified notary public, licensed conveyancer or recognised body under sections 9 or 23 of the Administration of Justice Act 1985

    (g) 'lease' includes sub-lease, tenancy and agreement for a lease or sub-lease

    (h) 'mortgage' means a mortgage or charge securing the repayment of money

    (i) 'notice to complete' means a notice requiring completion of the contract in accordance with condition 6.8

    (j) 'public requirement' means any notice, order or proposal given or made (whether before or after the date of the contract) by a body acting on statutory authority

    (k) 'requisition' includes objection

    (l) 'transfer' includes conveyance and assignment

    (m) 'working day' means any day from Monday to Friday (inclusive) which is not Christmas Day, Good Friday or a statutory Bank Holiday.

1.1.2   In these conditions the terms 'absolute title' and 'official copies' have the special meanings given to them by the Land Registration Act 2002.

1.1.3   A party is ready, able and willing to complete:

    (a) if he could be, but for the default of the other party, and

    (b) in the case of the seller, even though the property remains subject to a mortgage, if the amount to be paid on completion enables the property to be transferred freed of all mortgages (except any to which the sale is expressly subject).

1.1.4   These conditions apply except as varied or excluded by the contract.

1.2 Joint parties

If there is more than one seller or more than one buyer, the obligations which they undertake can be enforced against them all jointly or against each individually.

1.3 Notices and documents

1.3.1 A notice required or authorised by the contract must be in writing.

1.3.2 Giving a notice or delivering a document to a party's conveyancer has the same effect as giving or delivering it to that party.

1.3.3 Where delivery of the original document is not essential, a notice or document is validly given or sent if it is sent:

    (a)   by fax, or

    (b)   by e-mail to an e-mail address for the intended recipient given in the contract.

1.3.4 Subject to conditions 1.3.5 to 1.3.7, a notice is given and a document is delivered when it is received.

1.3.5 (a)   A notice or document sent through a document exchange is received when it is available for collection

    (b)   A notice or document which is received after 4.00 pm on a working day, or on a day which is not a working day, is to be treated as having been received on the next working day

    (c)   An automated response to a notice or document sent by e-mail that the intended recipient is out of the office is to be treated as proof that the notice or document was not received.

1.3.6 Condition 1.3.7 applies unless there is proof:

    (a)   that a notice or document has not been received, or

    (b)   of when it was received.

1.3.7 A notice or document sent by the following means is treated as having been received as follows:

    (a)   by first-class post: before 4.00 pm on the second working day after posting

    (b)   by second-class post: before 4.00 pm on the third working day after posting

    (c)   through a document exchange: before 4.00 pm on the first working day after the day on which it would normally be available for collection by the addressee

    (d)   by fax: one hour after despatch

    (e)   by e-mail: before 4.00 pm on the first working day after despatch.

1.4 VAT

1.4.1 The purchase price and the contents price are inclusive of any value added tax.

1.4.2 All other sums made payable by the contract are exclusive of any value added tax and where a supply is made which is chargeable to value added tax, the recipient of the supply is to pay the supplier (in addition to any other amounts payable under the contract) a sum equal to the value added tax chargeable on that supply.

1.5 Assignment and sub-sales

1.5.1 The buyer is not entitled to transfer the benefit of the contract.

1.5.2 The seller cannot be required to transfer the property in parts or to any person other than the buyer.

1.6 Third party rights

Unless otherwise expressly stated nothing in this contract will create rights pursuant to the Contracts (Rights of Third Parties) Act 1999 in favour of anyone other than the parties to the contract.

2. FORMATION

2.1 Date

2.1.1 If the parties intend to make a contract by exchanging duplicate copies by post or through a document exchange, the contract is made when the last copy is posted or deposited at the document exchange.

2.1.2 If the parties' conveyancers agree to treat exchange as taking place before duplicate copies are actually exchanged, the contract is made as so agreed.

2.2 Deposit

2.2.1 The buyer is to pay or send a deposit of 10 per cent of the purchase price no later than the date of the contract.

2.2.2 If a cheque tendered in payment of all or part of the deposit is dishonoured when first presented, the seller may, within seven working days of being notified that the cheque has been dishonoured, give notice to the buyer that the contract is discharged by the buyer's breach.

2.2.3 Conditions 2.2.4 to 2.2.6 do not apply on a sale by auction.

2.2.4 The deposit is to be paid:

(a) by electronic means from an account held in the name of a conveyancer at a clearing bank to an account in the name of the seller's conveyancer or (in a case where condition 2.2.5 applies) a conveyancer nominated by him and maintained at a clearing bank, or

(b) to the seller's conveyancer or (in a case where condition 2.2.5 applies) a conveyancer nominated by him by cheque drawn on a solicitor's or licensed conveyancer's client account.

2.2.5 If before completion date the seller agrees to buy another property in England and Wales for his residence, he may use all or any part of the deposit as a deposit in that transaction to be held on terms to the same effect as this condition and condition 2.2.6.

2.2.6 Any deposit or part of a deposit not being used in accordance with condition 2.2.5 is to be held by the seller's conveyancer as stakeholder on terms that on completion it is paid to the seller with accrued interest.

2.3 Auctions

2.3.1 On a sale by auction the following conditions apply to the property and, if it is sold in lots, to each lot.

2.3.2 The sale is subject to a reserve price.

2.3.3 The seller, or a person on his behalf, may bid up to the reserve price.

2.3.4 The auctioneer may refuse any bid.

2.3.5 If there is a dispute about a bid, the auctioneer may resolve the dispute or restart the auction at the last undisputed bid.

2.3.6 The deposit is to be paid to the auctioneer as agent for the seller.

3. MATTERS AFFECTING THE PROPERTY

3.1 Freedom from incumbrances

3.1.1 The seller is selling the property free from incumbrances, other than those mentioned in condition 3.1.2.

3.1.2 The incumbrances subject to which the property is sold are:

    (a)   those specified in the contract
    (b)   those discoverable by inspection of the property before the date of the contract
    (c)   those the seller does not and could not reasonably know about
    (d)   those, other than mortgages, which the buyer knows about
    (e)   entries made before the date of the contract in any public register except those maintained by the Land Registry or its Land Charges Department or by Companies House
    (f)   public requirements.

3.1.3   After the contract is made, the seller is to give the buyer written details without delay of any new public requirement and of anything in writing which he learns about concerning a matter covered by condition 3.1.2.

3.1.4   The buyer is to bear the cost of complying with any outstanding public requirement and is to indemnify the seller against any liability resulting from a public requirement.

3.2 Physical state

3.2.1   The buyer accepts the property in the physical state it is in at the date of the contract unless the seller is building or converting it.

3.2.2   A leasehold property is sold subject to any subsisting breach of a condition or tenant's obligation relating to the physical state of the property which renders the lease liable to forfeiture.

3.2.3   A sub-lease is granted subject to any subsisting breach of a condition or tenant's obligation relating to the physical state of the property which renders the seller's own lease liable to forfeiture.

3.3 Leases affecting the property

3.3.1   The following provisions apply if any part of the property is sold subject to a lease.

3.3.2 (a)   The seller having provided the buyer with full details of each lease or copies of the documents embodying the lease terms, the buyer is treated as entering into the contract knowing and fully accepting those terms.

    (b)   The seller is to inform the buyer without delay if the lease ends or if the seller learns of any application by the tenant in connection with the lease; the seller is then to act as the buyer reasonably directs, and the buyer is to indemnify him against all consequent loss and expense.

    (c)   Except with the buyer's consent, the seller is not to agree to any proposal to change the lease terms nor to take any step to end the lease.

    (d)   The seller is to inform the buyer without delay of any change to the lease terms which may be proposed or agreed.

    (e)   The buyer is to indemnify the seller against all claims arising from the lease after actual completion; this includes claims which are unenforceable against a buyer for want of registration.

    (f)   The seller takes no responsibility for what rent is lawfully recoverable, nor for whether or how any legislation affects the lease.

    (g)   If the let land is not wholly within the property, the seller may apportion the rent.

4. TITLE AND TRANSFER

4.1 Proof of title

4.1.1   Without cost to the buyer, the seller is to provide the buyer with proof of the title to the property and of his ability to transfer it, or to procure its transfer.

4.1.2   Where the property has a registered title the proof is to include official copies of the items referred to in rules 134(1)(a) and (b) and 135(1)(a) of the Land Registration Rules 2003, so far as they are not to be discharged or overridden at or before completion.

4.1.3   Where the property has an unregistered title, the proof is to include:

(a)   an abstract of title or an epitome of title with photocopies of the documents, and

(b)   production of every document or an abstract, epitome or copy of it with an original marking by a conveyancer either against the original or an examined abstract or an examined copy.

4.2   Requisitions

4.2.1   The buyer may not raise requisitions:

(a)   on any title shown by the seller before the contract was made

(b)   in relation to the matters covered by condition 3.1.2.

4.2.2   Notwithstanding condition 4.2.1, the buyer may, within six working days of a matter coming to his attention after the contract was made, raise written requisitions on that matter. In that event, steps 3 and 4 in condition 4.3.1 apply.

4.2.3   On the expiry of the relevant time limit under condition 4.2.2 or condition 4.3.1, the buyer loses his right to raise requisitions or to make observations.

4.3   Timetable

4.3.1   Subject to condition 4.2 and to the extent that the seller did not take the steps described in condition 4.1.1 before the contract was made, the following are the steps for deducing and investigating the title to the property to be taken within the following time limits:

Step		Time limit
1.	The seller is to comply with condition 4.1.1	Immediately after making the contract
2.	The buyer may raise written requisitions	Six working days after either the date of the contract or the date of delivery of the seller's evidence of title on which the requisitions are raised whichever is the later
3.	The seller is to reply in writing to any requisitions raised	Four working days after receiving the requisitions
4.	The buyer may make written observations on the seller's replies	Three working days after receiving the replies

The time limit on the buyer's right to raise requisitions applies even where the seller supplies incomplete evidence of his title, but the buyer may, within six working days from delivery of any further evidence, raise further requisitions resulting from that evidence.

4.3.2   The parties are to take the following steps to prepare and agree the transfer of the property within the following time limits:

Step		Time limit
A.	The buyer is to send the seller a draft transfer	At least twelve working days before completion date
B.	The seller is to approve or revise that draft and either return it or retain it for use as the actual transfer	Four working days after delivery of the draft transfer
C.	If the draft is returned the buyer is to send an engrossment to the seller	At least five working days before completion date

4.3.3 Periods of time under conditions 4.3.1 and 4.3.2 may run concurrently.

4.3.4 If the period between the date of the contract and completion date is less than 15 working days, the time limits in conditions 4.2.2, 4.3.1 and 4.3.2 are to be reduced by the same proportion as that period bears to the period of 15 working days. Fractions of a working day are to be rounded down except that the time limit to perform any step is not to be less than one working day.

4.4 Defining the property

The seller need not:

   (a) prove the exact boundaries of the property

   (b) prove who owns fences, ditches, hedges or walls

   (c) separately identify parts of the property with different titles further than he may be able to do from information in his possession.

4.5 Rents and rentcharges

The fact that a rent or rentcharge, whether payable or receivable by the owner of the property, has been, or will on completion be, informally apportioned is not to be regarded as a defect in title.

4.6 Transfer

4.6.1 The buyer does not prejudice his right to raise requisitions, or to require replies to any raised, by taking any steps in relation to preparing or agreeing the transfer.

4.6.2 Subject to condition 4.6.3, the seller is to transfer the property with full title guarantee.

4.6.3 The transfer is to have effect as if the disposition is expressly made subject to all matters covered by condition 3.1.2 and, if the property is leasehold, is to contain a statement that the covenants set out in section 4 of the Law of Property (Miscellaneous Provisions) Act 1994 will not extend to any breach of the tenant's covenants in the lease relating to the physical state of the property.

4.6.4 If after completion the seller will remain bound by any obligation affecting the property which was disclosed to the buyer before the contract was made, but the law does not imply any covenant by the buyer to indemnify the seller against liability for future breaches of it:

   (a) the buyer is to covenant in the transfer to indemnify the seller against liability for any future breach of the obligation and to perform it from then on, and

   (b) if required by the seller, the buyer is to execute and deliver to the seller on completion a duplicate transfer prepared by the buyer.

4.6.5 The seller is to arrange at his expense that, in relation to every document of title which the buyer does not receive on completion, the buyer is to have the benefit of:

  (a)   a written acknowledgement of his right to its production, and
  (b)   a written undertaking for its safe custody (except while it is held by a mortgagee or by someone in a fiduciary capacity).

4.7 Membership of company

Where the seller is, or is required to be, a member of a company that has an interest in the property or has management responsibilities for the property or the surrounding areas, the seller is, without cost to the buyer, to provide such documents on completion as will enable the buyer to become a member of that company.

5. RISK, INSURANCE AND OCCUPATION PENDING COMPLETION

5.1.1 The property is at the risk of the buyer from the date of the contract.
5.1.2 The seller is under no obligation to the buyer to insure the property unless:

  (a)   the contract provides that a policy effected by or for the seller and insuring the property or any part of it against liability for loss or damage is to continue in force, or
  (b)   the property or any part of it is let on terms under which the seller (whether as landlord or as tenant) is obliged to insure against loss or damage.

5.1.3 If the seller is obliged to insure the property under condition 5.1.2, the seller is to:

  (a)   do everything necessary to maintain the policy
  (b)   permit the buyer to inspect the policy or evidence of its terms
  (c)   if before completion the property suffers loss or damage:

    (i)   pay to the buyer on completion the amount of the policy monies which the seller has received, so far as not applied in repairing or reinstating the property, and
    (ii) if no final payment has then been received, assign to the buyer, at the buyer's expense, all rights to claim under the policy in such form as the buyer reasonably requires and pending execution of the assignment hold any policy monies received in trust for the buyer

  (d)   cancel the policy on completion.

5.1.4 Where the property is leasehold and the property, or any building containing it, is insured by a reversioner or other third party, the seller is to use reasonable efforts to ensure that the insurance is maintained until completion and if, before completion, the property or building suffers loss or damage the seller is to assign to the buyer on completion, at the buyer's expense, such rights as the seller may have in the policy monies, in such form as the buyer reasonably requires.
5.1.5 If payment under a policy effected by or for the buyer is reduced, because the property is covered against loss or damage by an insurance policy effected by or on behalf of the seller, then, unless the seller is obliged to insure the property under condition 5.1.2, the purchase price is to be abated by the amount of that reduction.
5.1.6 Section 47 of the Law of Property Act 1925 does not apply.

5.2 Occupation by buyer

5.2.1 If the buyer is not already lawfully in the property, and the seller agrees to let him into occupation, the buyer occupies on the following terms.

5.2.2 The buyer is a licensee and not a tenant. The terms of the licence are that the buyer:

   (a) cannot transfer it
   (b) may permit members of his household to occupy the property
   (c) is to pay or indemnify the seller against all outgoings and other expenses in respect of the property
   (d) is to pay the seller a fee calculated at the contract rate on a sum equal to the purchase price (less any deposit paid) for the period of the licence
   (e) is entitled to any rents and profits from any part of the property which he does not occupy
   (f) is to keep the property in as good a state of repair as it was in when he went into occupation (except for fair wear and tear) and is not to alter it
   (g) if the property is leasehold, is not to do anything which puts the seller in breach of his obligations in the lease, and
   (h) is to quit the property when the licence ends.

5.2.3 The buyer is not in occupation for the purposes of this condition if he merely exercises rights of access given solely to do work agreed by the seller.

5.2.4 The buyer's licence ends on the earliest of: completion date, rescission of the contract or when five working days' notice given by one party to the other takes effect.

5.2.5 If the buyer is in occupation of the property after his licence has come to an end and the contract is subsequently completed he is to pay the seller compensation for his continued occupation calculated at the same rate as the fee mentioned in condition 5.2.2(d).

5.2.6 The buyer's right to raise requisitions is unaffected.

6. COMPLETION

6.1 Date

6.1.1 Completion date is twenty working days after the date of the contract but time is not of the essence of the contract unless a notice to complete has been served.

6.1.2 If the money due on completion is received after 2.00 pm, completion is to be treated, for the purposes only of conditions 6.3 and 7.2, as taking place on the next working day as a result of the buyer's default.

6.1.3 Condition 6.1.2 does not apply and the seller is treated as in default if:

   (a) the sale is with vacant possession of the property or any part of it, and
   (b) the buyer is ready, able and willing to complete but does not pay the money due on completion until after 2.00 pm because the seller has not vacated the property or that part by that time.

6.2 Arrangements and place

6.2.1 The buyer's conveyancer and the seller's conveyancer are to co-operate in agreeing arrangements for completing the contract.

6.2.2 Completion is to take place in England and Wales, either at the seller's conveyancer's office or at some other place which the seller reasonably specifies.

6.3 Apportionments

6.3.1 On evidence of proper payment being made, income and outgoings of the property are to be apportioned between the parties so far as the change of ownership on completion will affect entitlement to receive or liability to pay them.

6.3.2 If the whole property is sold with vacant possession or the seller exercises his option in condition 7.2.4, apportionment is to be made with effect from the date of actual completion; otherwise, it is to be made from completion date.

6.3.3 In apportioning any sum, it is to be assumed that the seller owns the property until the end of the day from which apportionment is made and that the sum accrues from day to day at the rate at which it is payable on that day.

6.3.4 For the purpose of apportioning income and outgoings, it is to be assumed that they accrue at an equal daily rate throughout the year.

6.3.5 When a sum to be apportioned is not known or easily ascertainable at completion, a provisional apportionment is to be made according to the best estimate available. As soon as the amount is known, a final apportionment is to be made and notified to the other party. Any resulting balance is to be paid no more than ten working days later, and if not then paid the balance is to bear interest at the contract rate from then until payment.

6.3.6 Compensation payable under condition 5.2.5 is not to be apportioned.

6.4 Amount payable

The amount payable by the buyer on completion is the purchase price and the contents price (less any deposit already paid to the seller or his agent) adjusted to take account of:

(a) apportionments made under condition 6.3
(b) any compensation to be paid or allowed under condition 7.2
(c) any sum payable under condition 5.1.3.

6.5 Title deeds

6.5.1 As soon as the buyer has complied with all his obligations under this contract on completion the seller must hand over the documents of title.

6.5.2 Condition 6.5.1 does not apply to any documents of title relating to land being retained by the seller after completion.

6.6 Rent receipts

The buyer is to assume that whoever gave any receipt for a payment of rent or service charge which the seller produces was the person or the agent of the person then entitled to that rent or service charge.

6.7 Means of payment

The buyer is to pay the money due on completion by a direct transfer of cleared funds from an account held in the name of a conveyancer at a clearing bank and, if appropriate, an unconditional release of a deposit held by a stakeholder.

6.8 Notice to complete

6.8.1 At any time after the time applicable under condition 6.1.2 on completion date, a party who is ready, able and willing to complete may give the other a notice to complete.

6.8.2 The parties are to complete the contract within ten working days of giving a notice to complete, excluding the day on which the notice is given. For this purpose, time is of the essence of the contract.

6.8.3 On receipt of a notice to complete:

(a) if the buyer paid no deposit, he is forthwith to pay a deposit of 10 per cent

(b) if the buyer paid a deposit of less than 10 per cent, he is forthwith to pay a further deposit equal to the balance of that 10 per cent.

7. REMEDIES

7.1 Errors and omissions

7.1.1 If any plan or statement in the contract, or in the negotiations leading to it, is or was misleading or inaccurate due to an error or omission by the seller, the remedies available to the buyer are as follows.

(a) When there is a material difference between the description or value of the property, or of any of the contents included in the contract, as represented and as it is, the buyer is entitled to damages.

(b) An error or omission only entitles the buyer to rescind the contract:

(i) where it results from fraud or recklessness, or

(ii) where he would be obliged, to his prejudice, to accept property differing substantially (in quantity, quality or tenure) from what the error or omission had led him to expect.

7.1.2 If either party rescinds the contract:

(a) unless the rescission is a result of the buyer's breach of contract the deposit is to be repaid to the buyer with accrued interest

(b) the buyer is to return any documents he received from the seller and is to cancel any registration of the contract.

7.2 Late completion

7.2.1 If there is default by either or both of the parties in performing their obligations under the contract and completion is delayed, the party whose total period of default is the greater is to pay compensation to the other party.

7.2.2 Compensation is calculated at the contract rate on an amount equal to the purchase price, less (where the buyer is the paying party) any deposit paid, for the period by which the paying party's default exceeds that of the receiving party, or, if shorter, the period between completion date and actual completion.

7.2.3 Any claim for loss resulting from delayed completion is to be reduced by any compensation paid under this contract.

7.2.4 Where the buyer holds the property as tenant of the seller and completion is delayed, the seller may give notice to the buyer, before the date of actual completion, that he intends to take the net income from the property until completion. If he does so, he cannot claim compensation under condition 7.2.1 as well.

7.3 After completion

Completion does not cancel liability to perform any outstanding obligation under this contract.

7.4 Buyer's failure to comply with notice to complete

7.4.1 If the buyer fails to complete in accordance with a notice to complete, the following terms apply.

7.4.2 The seller may rescind the contract, and if he does so:

(a) he may

(i) forfeit and keep any deposit and accrued interest
(ii) resell the property and any contents included in the contract
(iii) claim damages

(b) the buyer is to return any documents he received from the seller and is to cancel any registration of the contract.

7.4.3 The seller retains his other rights and remedies.

7.5 Seller's failure to comply with notice to complete

7.5.1 If the seller fails to complete in accordance with a notice to complete, the following terms apply.

7.5.2 The buyer may rescind the contract, and if he does so:

(a) the deposit is to be repaid to the buyer with accrued interest
(b) the buyer is to return any documents he received from the seller and is, at the seller's expense, to cancel any registration of the contract.

7.5.3 The buyer retains his other rights and remedies.

8. LEASEHOLD PROPERTY

8.1 Existing leases

8.1.1 The following provisions apply to a sale of leasehold land.

8.1.2 The seller having provided the buyer with copies of the documents embodying the lease terms, the buyer is treated as entering into the contract knowing and fully accepting those terms.

8.2 New leases

8.2.1 The following provisions apply to a contract to grant a new lease.

8.2.2 The conditions apply so that:
'seller' means the proposed landlord
'buyer' means the proposed tenant
'purchase price' means the premium to be paid on the grant of a lease.

8.2.3 The lease is to be in the form of the draft attached to the contract.

8.2.4 If the term of the new lease will exceed seven years, the seller is to deduce a title which will enable the buyer to register the lease at the Land Registry with an absolute title.

8.2.5 The seller is to engross the lease and a counterpart of it and is to send the counterpart to the buyer at least five working days before completion date.

8.2.6 The buyer is to execute the counterpart and deliver it to the seller on completion.

8.3 Consent

8.3.1 (a) The following provisions apply if a consent to let, assign or sub-let is required to complete the contract.

(b)   In this condition 'consent' means consent in the form which satisfies the requirement to obtain it.

8.3.2 (a)   The seller is to apply for the consent at his expense, and to use all reasonable efforts to obtain it.

(b)   The buyer is to provide all information and references reasonably required.

8.3.3   Unless he is in breach of his obligation under condition 8.3.2, either party may rescind the contract by notice to the other party if three working days before completion date (or before a later date on which the parties have agreed to complete the contract):

(a)   the consent has not been given, or

(b)   the consent has been given subject to a condition to which a party reasonably objects. In that case, neither party is to be treated as in breach of contract and condition 7.1.2 applies.

9. CONTENTS

9.1   The following provisions apply to any contents which are included in the contract, whether or not a separate price is to be paid for them.

9.2   The contract takes effect as a contract for sale of goods.

9.3   The buyer takes the contents in the physical state they are in at the date of the contract.

9.4   Ownership of the contents passes to the buyer on actual completion.

SPECIAL CONDITIONS

1   (a)   This contract incorporates the Standard Conditions of Sale (Fifth Edition).

(b)   The terms used in this contract have the same meaning when used in the Conditions.

2   Subject to the terms of this contract and to the Standard Conditions of Sale, the seller is to transfer the property with either full title guarantee or limited title guarantee, as specified on the front page.

3   (a)   The sale includes those contents which are indicated on the attached list as included in the sale and the buyer is to pay the contents price for them.

(b)   The sale excludes those fixtures which are at the property and are indicated on the attached list as excluded from the sale.

4   The property is sold with vacant possession.

(or)

4   The property is sold subject to the following leases or tenancies:

5   Conditions 6.1.2 and 6.1.3 shall take effect as if the time specified in them were […] rather than 2.00 pm.

6 Representations

Neither party can rely on any representation made by the other, unless made in writing by the other or his conveyancer, but this does not exclude liability for fraud or recklessness.

7 Occupier's consent

Each occupier identified below agrees with the seller and the buyer, in consideration of their entering into this contract, that the occupier concurs in the sale of the property on the terms of this contract, undertakes to vacate the property on or before the completion date and releases the property and any included fixtures and contents from any right or interest that the occupier may have.

Note: this condition does not apply to occupiers under leases or tenancies subject to which the property is sold

Name(s) and signature(s) of the occupier(s) (if any):

Name

Signature

Notices may be sent to:

Seller's conveyancer's name:

E-mail address:*

Buyer's conveyancer's name:

E-mail address:*

*Adding an e-mail address authorises service by e-mail: see condition 1.3.3(b).

EXPLANATORY NOTES ON THE STANDARD CONDITIONS OF SALE (FIFTH EDITION)

(April 2011)

General

The fifth edition of the Standard Conditions of Sale (the 'SCS') takes effect on 1 April 2011 and supersedes the fourth edition of the SCS issued in October 2003.

The revisions to the fourth edition have been made to bring the SCS in line with current law and practice with the aim of reducing the need for special conditions. The changes are intended to achieve a balance between the interests of the buyer and seller.

The main change is that, reflecting the position under the general law, the buyer is now to assume the risk from the date of exchange. Nonetheless, as explained below, there are certain cases in which the seller is obliged to insure.

The SCS are intended primarily for use in residential sales. Although they may be suitable for the sale of small business premises, conveyancers are likely to find that, for most commercial transactions, the Standard Commercial Property Conditions (the 'SCPC') are better suited to their needs.

The revisions maintain the policy of using plain English rather than legal terminology where possible.

The fifth edition of the SCS represents the 25th edition of the National Conditions of Sale and the Law Society's Conditions of Sale 2011.

Definitions

'contents price'

Condition 1.1.1(d) now refers to 'contents' rather than 'chattels'.

'direct credit'

The previous definition of 'direct credit' (meaning a 'direct transfer of cleared funds to an account nominated by the seller's conveyancer and maintained by a clearing bank') has been deleted, since this concept is now used only in condition 6.7. See also the explanation of the changes to condition 2.2.4.

'mortgage'

A new definition of 'mortgage' has been added, which clarifies the meaning of the term in condition 1.1.3(b) and is used in the new paragraph (d) of condition 3.1.2.

VAT

Condition 1.4.1 has been amended to make it clear that the agreed purchase price and contents price for a property are inclusive of VAT. This reflects the fact that the SCS are intended primarily to be used for residential transactions, which are usually exempt for VAT purposes.

If the sale does constitute a chargeable supply for VAT purposes, a special condition should be inserted if the seller requires the buyer to pay a sum equal to the VAT. In commercial or mixed use transactions, it is likely to be more appropriate to use the SCPC.

By virtue of condition 1.4.2, any other sums payable under the contract (i.e. sums other than the purchase price and contents price) will continue to be exclusive of VAT. In these circumstances, the recipient of a taxable supply will be liable to pay to the supplier a sum equal to the VAT chargeable on that supply.

Assignment and sub-sales

A new condition 1.5.2 provides that the seller cannot be required to transfer the property, or any part of it, to any person other than the buyer. The amendment is intended to protect the seller from becoming involved in a transaction with an unknown third party. This change clarifies the position and ensures consistency with the SCPC.

Third party rights

Condition 1.6 has been added to exclude the operation of the Contracts (Rights of Third Parties) Act 1999. This ensures that a third party will not have any rights under the contract by virtue of that Act.

Deposit

Condition 2.2.1 has been amended so that the 10% deposit is calculated by reference only to the purchase price and not, as before, the total of the purchase price and any separate contents price. This has been changed in order to provide certainty at an early stage as to the amount of the deposit that will be required. The buyer will not be required to pay 10% of the contents price, which can still be the subject of negotiation up until the point at which contracts are exchanged. If the deposit is also to take account of the contents price, this should be provided for by special condition. This change largely reflects practice.

As noted above, the definition of 'direct credit' has been deleted from the SCS. In condition 2.2.4, reference to 'direct credit' has been replaced by a reference to the deposit being paid by 'electronic means'. This has the effect that, unlike payments due on completion, the deposit does not have to be paid in cleared funds. Additional wording has been inserted so that the money transfer must now be made from an account held in the name of a conveyancer at a clearing bank to an account maintained at a clearing bank held in the name of either the seller's conveyancer or, where condition 2.2.5 applies, a conveyancer higher up the chain. It is hoped that limiting payments to those from a conveyancer's account will assist the seller's conveyancer in complying with anti-money laundering obligations. Express provision by way of special condition will be required for any alternative arrangements. Condition 2.2.4(b) continues to make provision for the payment of the deposit by cheque but, where condition 2.2.5 applies, now permits the cheque to be made payable to a conveyancer higher up the chain.

Matters affecting the property

Condition 3.1.2(d) has been added to provide that the property is sold subject to any incumbrances (other than mortgages) which the buyer knows about. It is not considered fair for a buyer to be able to take action against a seller in respect of a matter which he knew about, but which was not expressly a matter subject to which the property was sold.

Retained land

Condition 3.4 in the fourth edition of the SCS has been deleted. It sought to deal with the situation where land is retained by the seller. Issues relating to retained land, such as rights and covenants, should be dealt with by way of special condition and by annexing an agreed form of transfer.

Requisitions

The wording of condition 4.2.1(a) has been slightly amended to make it clear that the buyer cannot raise requisitions on any title shown by the seller before the contract was made. This is consistent with practice where title is deduced in full before exchange.

Defining the property

Condition 4.4.2 of the fourth edition has been deleted so that the buyer can no longer require the seller to provide a statutory declaration about facts relevant to matters such as boundaries, hedges, ditches and walls. It is not considered to be reasonable to expect the seller to provide a statutory declaration after exchange of contracts when investigation of title has taken place prior to exchange.

If necessary, this issue should be dealt with by special condition.

Transfer

The wording in condition 4.6.3 has been amended. In the case of a transfer of leasehold property, the contract requires the transfer to contain an express statement modifying the title guarantee by excluding the operation of section 4 of the Law of Property (Miscellaneous Provisions) Act 1994 in respect of any breach of the tenant's covenants in the lease relating to the physical state of the property. This has been inserted because similar provisions are widely used in practice and it is consistent with condition 3.2.2.

Membership of company

Condition 4.7 has been inserted to enable the buyer to become a member of a management company or any other relevant company that has an interest in the property. This addition will reduce the need for a special condition to deal with this point. The condition stipulates that all relevant documents (which may include membership or share certificates and/or a duly signed stock transfer form) are to be provided to the buyer on completion. The condition has been drafted to apply not only to those companies with responsibilities in relation to leasehold property but also to those which have management obligations in relation to freehold property.

Risk, insurance and occupation pending completion

Significant changes have been made to the conditions relating to risk and insurance. The principal effect is that the risk position is reversed (from that in the fourth edition of the SCS) and the buyer bears the risk from exchange. Previous editions of the SCS left the risk with the seller until completion and, in practice, special conditions were frequently included to make the buyer bear the risk from exchange. This change brings the SCS broadly into line with the SCPC.

Even though the buyer takes the risk from exchange (meaning he still has to complete if the property is destroyed between exchange and completion), the seller may still have an obligation to insure the property between exchange and completion by virtue of condition 5.1.2. Under this condition, the seller is obliged to insure if the contract so provides or if the property is leasehold and the seller (whether as landlord or as tenant) is obliged to insure under the terms of the lease.

Condition 5.1.3 sets out the seller's obligations where he is required to insure.

Under condition 5.1.4, where the property is leasehold and insurance is effected by a landlord or other third party, the seller is to use reasonable efforts to ensure that the insurance is maintained until completion and if, before completion, the building suffers any loss or damage, the seller is to assign to the buyer any rights that the seller may have in the policy monies.

Condition 5.1.5 has been added in an attempt to clarify the position as regards 'double insurance'. This is where both the seller and buyer insure the property between exchange and completion. The new condition provides that where a payment under the buyer's insurance is reduced because the property is covered under an insurance policy taken out by or on behalf of the seller, then, provided the seller is not obliged to insure the property under condition 5.1.2, the purchase price is to be abated by the amount of that reduction. The position in this respect is now similar to that under the SCPC.

Occupation by buyer

Condition 5.2.2(d) has been amended in line with condition 2.2.1 so that the licence fee is to be calculated by reference to the purchase price only.

Condition 5.2.2(g) of the fourth edition of the SCS, which dealt with the buyer's duty to insure the property, has been deleted because the risk will have passed to the buyer under the amended condition 5.1. The new condition 5.2.2(g) stipulates that, if the property is leasehold, the buyer is not to do anything which puts the seller in breach of his obligations in the lease.

Apportionments

Condition 6.3.1 has been amended to require the party requesting apportionment to provide evidence of payment in relation to the relevant income and outgoings of the property.

Title deeds

The wording in condition 6.5.1 has been slightly amended so that the reference to the buyer's obligations is expressly limited to those under the SCS.

Means of payment

The wording in condition 6.7 has been amended and now refers to a 'direct transfer' of cleared funds on completion. The previous edition used the defined term 'direct credit' which, as noted above, has been deleted in these conditions. This new wording makes it clear that the completion monies should come from and be paid to an account held in the name of a conveyancer. As with conditions 1.5.2 and 2.2.4, this change was made with the aim of combating fraud and assisting compliance with anti-money laundering measures.

Notice to complete

Condition 6.8.1 has been amended so that notice to complete cannot be given before 2 pm on the day of completion. This change is intended to prevent the seller from serving a notice to complete on the morning of completion date.

Late completion

Under condition 7.2.2, and in line with other relevant provisions in the SCS, compensation for late completion is calculated by reference to the purchase price only and not the purchase price and the contents price.

Commonhold land

Condition 9 of the fourth edition of the SCS has been deleted. Commonhold is not widely used as a form of tenure. Where relevant, provision for commonhold land should be made by special condition.

Contents

As previously noted, all references to 'chattels' in the SCS have been changed to 'contents'.

Front and back pages

The general layout of the front page has been changed to allow conveyancers to record on the contract cover sheet details of the exchange of contracts including the names of the respective solicitors acting for the parties, the time of exchange and the relevant formula used.

Special conditions

Contents and fixtures

A revised special condition 3 makes clear which contents are included in the sale and which fixtures are excluded.

Completion

Special condition 5 allows the parties to vary condition 6.1.2 by specifying a time other than 2.00 pm in order to identify the day on which completion is to be treated as taking place for the purposes of condition 6.3 (apportionments) and 7.2 (compensation for late completion). This time will also become the earliest time for giving a notice to complete under condition 6.8.1. It is a special condition so that the parties will need to make a conscious decision if they wish to depart from the fallback provision in condition 6.1.2. It may be particularly useful where there is a chain of transactions. For example, the seller under the first contract in a chain might require payment of the purchase price by 1.30 pm to allow sufficient time to receive those funds and transmit them on his own purchase by 2.00 pm.

Representations

The limitation on liability for representations in special condition 6 aims to exclude liability for oral statements made by or on behalf of the parties. It does not exclude liability for fraud or recklessness. The exclusion is mutual but it is most likely in practice to be relied upon by the seller. Terms similar in effect to special condition 6 are commonly found in contracts. It has been included as a special condition (rather than one of the general conditions) in the light of judicial comments in *Morgan* v. *Pooley* [2010] EWHC 2447 (QB) that the clause in that case should be given effect because it was a special condition printed in large type and easily readable.

Occupier's consent

Special condition 7 is frequently required and has been inserted for ease of use and reference.

E-mail service of notice

The general position under the conditions is that service by e-mail is not authorised. If the parties wish to authorise service by e-mail they will need to add an e-mail address in the space indicated at the end of the special conditions.

APPENDIX B

Law Society Conveyancing Protocol[1]

This protocol is known as the Law Society Conveyancing Protocol ('the Protocol').

The Protocol has been designed as the framework for the sale and purchase of a home for an owner occupier. It is assumed that both seller and buyer have lenders and that where a lender is involved it is also a client of the solicitor. It sets out a series of procedures that may be adapted for use in other types of land and property transfers. This Protocol is not intended for use in the purchase of new build homes.

The steps in the Protocol are not exhaustive and should not be regarded as a conveyancing 'checklist'. The transaction may not proceed in a fixed order, and many of the processes can take place simultaneously or be undertaken in a changed order. The use of the Protocol is intended to ensure that all clients are treated fairly and are protected when dealing with high value assets and liabilities. Processes that are open and transparent help make the experience more efficient and reduce wasted time and costs.

PROTOCOL: GENERAL SOLICITOR OBLIGATIONS IN A CONVEYANCING TRANSACTION

The key to reducing stress in a transaction is to manage the client's expectations; to do this you should be taking instructions on matters that could affect the chain (e.g. are parties separating, are they first time buyers, are their circumstances likely to change soon?). It is important to engage proactively with the client when getting your initial instructions. Clients may have been given unrealistic expectations by an estate agent or others about the conveyancing process or the timeframes and they may be unaware of the competing interests; you should engage with those expectations upfront and, where necessary, reset them.

There are many uncertainties in any conveyancing transaction and you cannot be definitive at the beginning of the process. You need to manage your client's expectations at the start and throughout the transaction.

Solicitors are bound by professional obligations to their clients throughout the transaction. A solicitor is required to act in the best interests of each client and those obligations will take precedence over this Protocol.

The following obligations form part of the broader set of obligations of a solicitor and should be undertaken as a matter of course:

(a) To ensure that the transaction can proceed smoothly, you should ensure that all information is shared, subject to any confidentiality obligations that have not been waived.

(b) Ensure that you have managed and covered timing and other expectations and linked transactions such as chains appropriately.

(c) Consider any potential conflicts of interest during the whole transaction. These can arise when you are acting for more than one party: sellers, buyers and lenders.

(d) Ensure that you comply with duties to lenders.

---

[1] © The Law Society 2019.

(e) Act with courtesy and co-operate with third parties.

(f) Respond promptly particularly in relation to despatch and receipt of money, exchange of contracts and completion.

(g) Agree at an early stage how you will communicate with all others involved and respond promptly to communications.

(h) Ensure you always comply with regulatory and statutory requirements and SRA warnings.

(i) Ensure proper internal and external arrangements for file management have been communicated to your client in relation to holiday and sickness absence.

(j) Where you are acting for a lender as well as for either the buyer or the seller, the duties owed to the lender client are professional obligations and are subject to the lender client's specific instructions.

(k) Maintain high standards of courtesy and deal with others in a fair and honest manner.

(l) Use the most up-to-date version of the Code for Completion by Post, contract, forms and formulae and accompanying guidance published by the Law Society or such approved equivalent publications as may be notified by the Society through periodic updates made on its website at **www.lawsociety.org.uk**. Care should be taken to check the website regularly.

(m) Ensure you comply with the Money Laundering, Terrorist Financing and Transfer of Funds (Information on the Payer) Regulations 2017 and client identification requirements.

(n) Ensure that your publicity and costs information (including any website) meets the requirements of the SRA rules and codes of conduct and, to ensure transparency of costs and expenses, ensure you give an accurate estimate to your clients at the time of engagement and adjustments thereafter if relevant.

(o) Make a record of the advice given to seller, buyer and lender clients at all stages.

(p) Have regard to the risk management requirements of your professional indemnity insurer.

(q) Have a continuing awareness of potential cyber security issues.

INTERPRETATION

This section helps with interpretation of the general obligations.

1. Timetable for exchange and completion

Every transaction is different, and the time it may take for each stage in the transaction will be different. Moreover, the timetable that will be expected by the parties at the outset may change and the order in which processes are undertaken may alter. There is no 'normal' transaction and you should communicate this to your clients who need to be made aware that timetables are often set by third parties and the original timetable is no more than a general indication.

2. Transparency

Recognise the value of making the process as transparent as possible. This is likely to assist your clients and help them to be better informed about the process.

3. Lenders

A lender may choose to instruct the conveyancer acting for the seller or the buyer to act on its behalf. Where the lender is a member of UK Finance, the provisions of the UK Finance

Mortgage Lenders' Handbook ('Lenders' Handbook') will apply and should be followed (see **www.cml.org.uk/lenders-handbook**). Where a lender is a member of the Building Societies Association (BSA) it may choose to use the BSA Mortgage Instructions. In addition, lenders may have further and additional requirements that alter from time to time.

Lenders who are not members of UK Finance will have their own instructions and requirements which may differ from those in the Lenders' Handbook. Where you are instructed to act for those lenders or to transact through their separate representatives, you should consider the possible impact on timing. You should let those affected know.

If acting solely for the lender, the lender's conveyancer is expected to:

- follow such parts of the Protocol as apply to that retainer; and
- take all action as is necessary to enable both the buyer's conveyancer and the seller's conveyancer to comply with the timescales.

4. Practice points

Solicitors and all their conveyancing staff are expected to:

- consider and stay up to date with all relevant Law Society practice notes (see **www.lawsociety.org.uk**);
- attend regular training to ensure that they remain up to date with law, regulation and best practice.

5. Preferred practice

Use of this Protocol is considered preferred practice. It is only fully effective if both the seller's conveyancer and the buyer's conveyancer adopt it. However, if one party does not agree to adopt it, that does not prevent the use of the procedures by the other party.

PROTOCOL FRAMEWORK

The Protocol sets out a framework for some of the work undertaken.

The seller of a property may be the buyer of another property and likewise the buyer may be the seller of another property. This chain of transactions may be extended by linked transactions. It may be necessary for exchange of contracts to take place simultaneously across the chain. The subsequent completions will usually need to coincide.

Where this occurs, there will be steps that are ascribed in the Protocol to the seller or buyer that the conveyancer will need to be taking at the same time in the mirror transaction in the chain that is linked. Those collateral steps are not set out in the Protocol but need to be considered and applied by conveyancers to ensure that the chain progresses smoothly.

Conveyancers may be instructed at different points in the buying and selling process and therefore the timings in this Protocol can only be indicative. Parties will enter the chain at different times and a chain can only progress as fast or as slow as the slowest member in it and/or the last person to join it.

Where a conveyancer is instructed solely on behalf of the lender and not jointly for both the lender and the borrower then the lender's conveyancer is expected to follow such parts of the Protocol as apply to the retainer and take all action as is necessary to enable both the buyer's conveyancer and the seller's conveyancer to comply with agreed timescales.

Every party will be progressing with their own agenda, which means that agreeing a realistic timetable and reaching final agreement on critical time limits and dates can be challenging. It is important to remember that moving dates or completion dates can only be set credibly and realistically when certain stages have been reached and certain initial requirements fulfilled.

Stage	Steps
A: Instructions	1–9
B: Pre-exchange – submitting a contract	10–19
C: Prior to exchange of contracts	20–21
D: Exchange of contracts	22–27
E: Completion	28–32
F: Post-completion	33–35

STAGE A: INSTRUCTIONS

	Contact	Acting for the seller	Acting for the buyer	Contact
1	*Seller*	**Client instruction**	**Client instruction**	*Buyer*
	Agent	Obtain and confirm all instructions and establish the nature of the transaction.	Obtain and confirm all instructions and establish the nature of the transaction.	*Agent*
		Obtain the agent's commission terms.		
		Send to the seller the Property Information Form (TA6) and Fittings and Contents Form (TA10) (see paragraph (l) of general obligations for further guidance on the use of forms).		
		Linked transactions/chain of transactions	**Linked transactions/chain of transactions**	
		Check whether the seller has property to buy and whether an offer has been accepted and whether there is any linked transaction or chain of transactions. Remember that when you are acting for a seller, you may also be acting for that seller in his capacity as a buyer.	Check whether the buyer has property to sell and whether an offer has been accepted and whether there is any linked transaction or chain of transactions. Remember that when you are acting for a buyer, you may also be acting for that buyer in their capacity as a seller.	

Contact	Acting for the seller	Acting for the buyer	Contact
	Occupiers	**Searches**	
	Ascertain the identity of all people aged 17 or over living in the property and consider whether their consent to the sale is required and whether they require independent advice. This may be relevant where they or anyone else may have made any financial contribution towards purchase of the property, mortgage payments, other outgoings or improvements.	Advise the buyer about obtaining searches. Consider which searches would be appropriate to obtain. If so instructed, instigate the searches. If there are two or more buyers, advise on the ways in which property can be owned.	
2 *Seller*	**Regulatory requirements**	**Regulatory requirements**	*Buyer*
	Comply with all regulatory requirements (including Transparency Rules): (1) Provide an estimate of fees and disbursements. (2) Provide client care/ retainer information and other information required by regulators. (3) Provide your terms and conditions. (4) Make clients aware of fraud risks and the methods for avoiding them. (5) Consider whether other tax advice may be relevant.	Comply with all regulatory requirements (including Transparency Rules): (1) Provide an estimate of fees and disbursements. (2) Quantify and explain non-optional disbursements: (a) HM Land Registry fees; (b) stamp duty land tax (SDLT), land transaction tax (LTT) including higher rate SDLT/LTT and multiple dwellings relief.	

Contact	Acting for the seller	Acting for the buyer	Contact
		If you cannot do so, refer the client to your tax department, a tax solicitor or accountant and/or advise your client to take specialist tax advice.	
		(3) Explain other disbursements and give estimates, e.g. environmental report.	
		(4) Provide client care/ retainer information and other information required by regulators.	
		(5) Provide your terms and conditions.	
		(6) Make clients aware of fraud risks and the methods for avoiding them.	
		(7) Consider whether other tax advice may be relevant.	
3	**Client identity and verification** Take steps to satisfy yourself and to satisfy any third-party obligation as to the identity of your clients and continue to keep this under review.	**Client identity and verification** Take steps to satisfy yourself and to satisfy any third-party obligation as to the identity of your clients and continue to keep this under review.	

Contact	Acting for the seller	Acting for the buyer	Contact
	You should be aware that the buyer's conveyancer will expect you to comply with the undertakings in the Law Society Code for Completion by Post and if you are not able or willing to comply this should be communicated to the buyer's conveyancer at the earliest stage possible.	Satisfy yourself that the seller's conveyancer will give the undertakings for completion in the Law Society Code for Completion by Post which means you do not need to raise further questions at this stage unless there are fraud indicators.	
	Authority to instruct	**Power of attorney**	
	Consider which, if any, documents may need to be signed by an attorney and check whether powers of attorney are available.	Consider which, if any, documents may need to be signed by an attorney and check whether powers of attorney are available.	
	If your client is acting as trustee/executor consider what documents might need to be signed.	Prepare or encourage the buyer to instruct someone to prepare any power that may be necessary.	
	Take steps to satisfy yourself as to the identity of any signatory to contract or transfer so as to be able to satisfy HM Land Registry requirements upon registration.		

Contact	Acting for the seller	Acting for the buyer	Contact
	Obtain instructions for dealing with remittance of gross/net sale proceeds and details provided by the seller of UK bank account for remittance of proceeds. Obtain evidence that the bank account is properly constituted as an account conducted by the seller for a period of at least 12 months. Confirm that remittance will be made to that account only.		
4 *Seller* *Agent* *Lender/* *Broker*	**Mortgage redemption** Ask the seller how many mortgage accounts need to be redeemed and the approximate amounts outstanding on each account and monthly payment date. Obtain redemption figures and advise as to costs of obtaining redemption statements and any later updates and redemption charges. Check the mortgage or other loans and consider obtaining a statement of account to ascertain redemption penalties or negative equity. If it is apparent that there is negative equity, or for some other reason the seller will not be able to discharge the registered charges from the proceeds of sale, discuss what actions need to be taken.	**Mortgage requirements** Check whether the buyer requires a mortgage offer in connection with any related purchase and, if so, whether: (a) a decision in principle has been obtained; (b) an application has been made; and (c) a mortgage offer has been issued. If a mortgage offer has been made, check that the special conditions can be satisfied. Suggest the buyer consults an independent surveyor for advice on different types of survey and home buyer reports.	*Buyer* *Agent* *Lender/* *Broker*

Contact	Acting for the seller	Acting for the buyer	Contact
	Advise the seller about continuing to make mortgage payments, ground rent and service charge payments that are due up to and including the completion date.		
	Restrictions		
	Consider how to deal with any restrictions appearing on the register.		
	Lender representation	**Lender representation**	
	Tell the buyer's conveyancer whether you act for the seller's lender and if not, advise the buyer's conveyancer as to the identity of any solicitor who may be acting for the seller's lender.	If you are not to be instructed by the prospective lender, find out who is and check their identity.	
	Mortgage documentation	Suggest the buyer obtains quotations for buildings insurance and advise that the terms of any policy taken out must be compliant with the lender's requirements (where applicable).	
	If you are not formally instructed by the seller's lender and you are not aware of any conveyancer who has been instructed to act for it, obtain relevant written authority from the seller to deal with the seller's existing lender.		
	Obtain the title deeds, if any and/or ask the seller.		

Contact		Acting for the seller	Acting for the buyer	Contact
		In respect of any existing charges entered into by the seller, consider what evidence of discharge or undertakings for discharge are likely to be required by the conveyancers for the buyer's lender and the buyer.		
5	*Seller*	**Written confirmation requirements**	**Written confirmation requirements**	*Buyer*
		Ensure the seller has written confirmation of:	Ensure the buyer has written confirmation of:	
		(a) the name and status of the person who will carry out the work;	(a) the name and status of the person who will carry out the work;	
		(b) the name of the regulated individual supervising the work;	(b) the name of the regulated individual supervising the work;	
		(c) the complaints procedure; and	(c) the complaints procedure; and	
		(d) cancellation notice where applicable (referring to a cancellation notice if the client decided not to instruct the solicitor).	(d) cancellation notice where applicable (referring to a cancellation notice if the client decided not to instruct the solicitor).	
6	*Seller*	**Costs, checks and payments on account**	**Costs, checks and payments on account**	*Buyer*
		Agree costs estimated and terms for abortive charges.	Agree costs estimated and terms for abortive charges.	
		Carry out and record:	Carry out and record:	
		(a) assessment of transaction risks;	(a) assessment of transaction risk;	
		(b) potential conflicts;	(b) potential conflicts;	
		(c) capacity of client;	(c) capacity of client;	

Contact	Acting for the seller	Acting for the buyer	Contact
	(d) scope of authority to act, where there is more than one seller (issues of conflict between them are outside scope – affects remittance of proceeds of sale).	(d) scope of authority to act, where there is more than one buyer (issues of conflict between them are outside scope – affects remittance of proceeds of sale).	
	This obligation continues throughout the transaction.	**This obligation continues throughout the transaction.**	
7	**Title**	**Material information**	*Agent*
	If the title is registered, obtain:	Review the Memorandum of Sale and/or Property Particulars together with valid energy performance certificate.	*Lender*
	• up-to-date official copies of the register and title plan;		
	• official copies of all filed documents;	Explain the likely timescale of the transaction and discuss any factors that may affect it. Keep this under review throughout the transaction.	
	• an official copy of any registered lease; and		
	• those documents on which the buyer can reasonably be expected to rely in order to deduce title (e.g. a certified copy of a grant of probate, a power of attorney).	Establish the funding requirements.	
	If the title is unregistered, obtain:	**Potential lender requirements**	
	• a land charges search against the seller and any other appropriate names;	When you know who the lender is, check the Lenders' Handbook, Part 2 for information about the lender's requirements.	
	• an official search of the index map;		

Contact	Acting for the seller	Acting for the buyer	Contact
	• an epitome of title; • those documents on which the buyer can reasonably be expected to rely in order to deduce title (e.g. a certified copy of a grant of probate, a power of attorney).	As required by the Lenders' Handbook, if you need to report a matter to the lender you must do so as soon as you become aware of it. You should tell the lender what the issue is, identify the relevant provision and provide a summary of the legal risks and your recommendations.	
	Note: check all plans on copied documents are complete and coloured accurately. **Defect in title** Consider and advise in relation to any apparent defect in title or missing items in title documents, e.g. missing lease or discrepancies in names or addresses. In some cases, indemnity insurance might be appropriate.		
8 *Seller* *Landlord* *Managing agent*	**Leasehold properties** (1) Obtain the lease or official copy of the lease and any deeds of variation.	**Leasehold properties** Ensure that the client is aware of the difference between freehold and leasehold ownership.	*Buyer* *Managing agent* *Landlord* *Lender*

Contact	Acting for the seller	Acting for the buyer	Contact
	(2) Send to the seller a Leasehold Information Form (TA7) in addition to the Property Information Form (TA6) (see paragraph (I) of general obligations for further guidance on the use of forms) and obtain any documents that will be required, including a receipt for ground rent, service charge accounts and insurance details.	Check any lender requirements and report to lender as necessary. Each lender is different and has its own requirements in relation to leasehold properties. Consider the lease and advise the buyer as necessary as soon as you have the information concerning:	
	(3) Obtain from the seller the contact details for the landlord and/or managing agent and obtain the cost of replies to enquiries in form LPE1 and obtain funds from the seller if required.	(a) the residual lease term; (b) the amount of ground rent payable; (c) the method and timing of increases in the ground rent; (d) the amount of service charge payable.	
	(4) Consider the lease and advise as necessary concerning the residual lease term.	When you have the information provided by the managing agents in response to LPE1, particularly any potential or proposed works to the property which could lead to a substantial increase in the amount of service charge payable, report this to the buyer.	
	(5) Consider timing of submission of LPE1 questions to the landlord/managing agent.		
	(6) Consider whether any third parties will need to consent to the sale (e.g. landlord or management company).		

Contact	Acting for the seller	Acting for the buyer	Contact
9	**Continuing obligations**	**Continuing obligations**	
	Review the costs estimate and revise if necessary, updating information regarding fees or disbursements including managing agent's fees.	Review the costs estimate and revise if necessary, updating information regarding fees or disbursements.	
		Consider the timeframe. If the property is leasehold, ensure that the buyer is aware that any enquiries may need to be answered by a third party and adjust the timeframe accordingly.	
	Chain of transactions	**Chain of transactions**	
	Consider and advise in relation to any dependent purchase or sale. Advise the seller in relation to their potential tax liability or advise the seller to obtain tax advice as to the order of transactions, where related transactions may not be simultaneous, for SDLT or LTT impact.	Consider and advise in relation to any dependent purchase or sale. Advise the buyer in relation to their potential tax liability or advise the buyer to obtain tax advice as to the order of transactions, where related transactions may not be simultaneous, for SDLT or LTT impact.	

STAGE B: PRE-EXCHANGE – SUBMITTING A CONTRACT

The seller's conveyancer should generally carry out these steps within five days of confirmation of instructions and submit the draft contract upon receiving confirmation from the buyer's conveyancer that they are instructed.

If there is any delay, explain to the seller, the buyer's conveyancer and the estate agents.

Following acceptance of an offer:

	Contact	Acting for the seller	Acting for the buyer	Contact
10	*Seller*	**Clients' instructions**	**Clients' instructions**	*Buyer*
		Confirm the seller's instructions including checking whether any preliminary deposit or other direct payments have been offered or received. Advise seller not to accept any payment from the buyer.	Confirm the buyer's instructions including checking whether any preliminary deposit or other direct payments have been offered or received. Advise buyer not to accept any payment from the seller or make any payments direct to the seller.	*Lender* *Surveyor*
		Confirm and update, where necessary, replies to enquiries if completed more than two months earlier.	Advise on liability for SDLT or LTT if you have not already done so. Explain the potential liability for higher rate SDLT/LTT and the circumstances in which this can be reclaimed or advise the buyer.	
			Check availability of deposit.	
			You should advise the buyer that there may be defects in the property which are not revealed by the valuation. You should also advise the borrower to obtain their own survey about the condition of the property.	
			Advise the buyer to investigate the proposed buildings insurance.	
			Where there are two or more people buying a property together, discuss the different types of co-ownership and whether a Declaration of Trust is required.	

Contact	Acting for the seller	Acting for the buyer	Contact
	Chain	**Chain**	
	The estate agent should ensure, so far as is possible, that the fullest information is made available as to the status of other transactions in the chain if not provided with the memorandum of sale.	Ensure, so far as is possible, that the fullest information is made available as to the status of other transactions in the chain.	
11	**Conveyancer identification** Check the identity of the buyer's conveyancer. Follow the latest SRA and Law Society guidance.	**Conveyancer identification** Check the identity of the seller's conveyancer. Follow the latest SRA and Law Society guidance.	
12	**Confirmation of instructions** Provide the name of the seller, price and other terms agreed. State whether there is any related purchase(s) and extent of chain or any remortgage(s). Inform if seller requires mortgage or any other funding. Inform promptly of any changes.	**Confirmation of instructions** Provide the name of the buyer, price and other terms agreed. State whether there is any related sale(s) and extent of chain or any remortgage(s). Inform if buyer requires mortgage or any other funding. Inform promptly of any changes.	
	Confirm use of the Protocol and Law Society Code for Completion by Post and expected time required to prepare and submit pre-contract pack of documents.	Confirm use of the Protocol and Law Society Code for Completion by Post. Check details of client bank account.	
	Provide the seller with the information received from the buyer's conveyancer about any related sale by the buyer and any other transactions in the chain and details of the buyer's funding arrangements and mortgage if not previously supplied.	Provide the buyer with the information received from the seller's conveyancer about any related purchase by the seller and any other transactions in the chain.	

239

Contact	Acting for the seller	Acting for the buyer	Contact
13	**Communication**		
	If you intend to email the contract bundle, please tell the buyer's conveyancer that you intend to do so.		
	Delivery of contract bundle by email is acceptable but each document should be a separately identifiable attachment or uploaded individually.		
	Contract bundle		
	If there is likely to be a delay in submitting a contract bundle, inform the seller, the buyer's conveyancer and the estate agents. So far as possible send the whole package at once.		
	Prepare and submit to the buyer's conveyancer a contract bundle, which includes:		
	(1) The draft contract:		
	(a) incorporating the latest edition of the Standard Conditions of Sale; and		
	(b) only with such additional clauses as are absolutely necessary for the purposes of the transaction; and		
	(c) if appropriate FME1 in relation to service or maintenance charges with accompanying documentation.		

Contact	Acting for the seller	Acting for the buyer	Contact
	(2) If the title is registered:		
	(a) up-to-date official copies of the register and title plan;		
	(b) official copies of all filed documents; and		
	(c) those documents on which the buyer can reasonably be expected to rely in order to deduce title (e.g. a certified copy of a grant of probate, a power of attorney, etc.).		
	At the time of submitting the contract bundle, entries in the register of title should be less than six months old. If any information needs to be updated (change of name, death of proprietor) the register should be updated.		
	(3) If the title is unregistered:		
	(a) a land charges search against the seller and any other appropriate names;		
	(b) an official search of the index map;		
	(c) an epitome of title;		

Contact	Acting for the seller	Acting for the buyer	Contact
	(d) those documents on which the buyer can reasonably be expected to rely in order to deduce title (e.g. a certified copy of a grant of probate, a power of attorney, etc.).		
	Note: check all plans on copied documents are accurately coloured.		
	(4) Property Information Form (TA6) with supporting documentation. **Note:** copies of competent person certificates are not always required if the existence of the certificate is clear as mentioned in the result of enquiries and noted on the relevant website (such as FENSA).		
	(5) Fittings and Contents Form (TA10).		
	(6) Required consents (e.g. under restrictive covenants or restrictions).		
	(7) In relation to leasehold property:		
	(a) Leasehold Information Form (TA7);		
	(b) LPE1 in relation to service charge and ground rent with accompanying documentation;		

Contact	Acting for the seller	Acting for the buyer	Contact
	(c) official copies of the freehold and intermediate titles;		
	(d) a copy of the seller's share certificate for any landlord/ management company where appropriate;		
	(e) draft of any required deed of covenant.		
	Confirm you will complete using the Law Society Code for Completion by Post if you have not already done so. (See paragraph (I) of general obligations for further guidance on the use of forms.)		
	Consider including a draft transfer.		
	Inform the estate agent and the seller when the contract bundle has been submitted.		
	If any document is unavailable or awaited, submit the contract bundle with an explanation as to when it is likely to be supplied.		
14		**Receipt of contract bundle**	*Buyer*
		Notify the buyer that the contract bundle has been received.	

Contact	Acting for the seller	Acting for the buyer	Contact
		Notify the seller's conveyancer if expecting to be instructed by the lender or communicate the identity of any other conveyancer instructed by the lender when known.	
		Search requirements	
		If you are not going to make such searches as are required on receipt of the draft contract, notify the seller's conveyancer and provide an indication as to why there may be a delay in submitting searches and when it is likely that they will be submitted.	

	Contact	Acting for the seller	Acting for the buyer	Contact
15	*Agent*	**Additional enquiries**	**Additional enquiries**	
	Seller	Obtain the seller's responses to additional enquiries. Explain that if inappropriate enquiries have been raised, answers need not be given.	**Raise only specific additional enquiries** required to clarify issues arising out of the documents submitted, or which are relevant to the title, existing or planned use, nature or location of the property or which the buyer has expressly requested.	
		Respond to the additional enquiries from the buyer's conveyancer. You do not have to answer inappropriate enquiries.	**Do not raise any additional enquiries** about the state and condition of the building unless arising out of your conveyancing search results, your buyer's own enquiries, inspection or their surveyor's report.	
		The seller should not be required to supply more information than is available in the documents.	**Indiscriminate use of 'standard' additional enquiries may constitute a breach of this Protocol. If such enquiries are submitted, they are not required to be dealt with by the seller/seller's conveyancer.**	
		Inform the seller and the estate agent of any matters likely to delay exchange of contracts.	The seller's conveyancer does not need to obtain the seller's answers to any enquiry seeking opinion rather than fact.	
16	*Seller*	**Fittings and contents**	**Fittings and contents**	*Buyer*
		Take instructions and agree any apportionment of the purchase price in respect of fittings and contents.	Take instructions and agree any apportionment of the purchase price in respect of fittings and contents.	

245

Contact	Acting for the seller	Acting for the buyer	Contact
		Advise the buyer as to the impact of an apportionment of the purchase price for fittings and contents on any mortgage offer and SDLT/LTT.	
17		**Report to buyer**	
		Report to the buyer on the documentation received and the results of investigations made.	
		Check title against lender's requirements.	
		Draft SDLT/LTT form and signature of documentation.	
		Prepare (from tax advice received if necessary) a draft online SDLT or LTT return. Consider timing and arrange for signature of any transfer, mortgage deed and SDLT or LTT return. Can be carried out later – see the Lenders' Handbook or the BSA Mortgage Instructions.	
18		**Mortgage instructions**	*Buyer*
		Consider the mortgage instructions from the lender or the lender's conveyancer.	*Lender*
		Check the mortgage offer conditions with the buyer and if all approved obtain the buyer's signature to the mortgage deed.	

Contact	Acting for the seller	Acting for the buyer	Contact
		Consider the instructions from lenders in the Lenders' Handbook or the BSA Mortgage Instructions.	
		If you have reported an issue to the lender, check you have the lender's further written instructions before exchange of contracts because the lender may withdraw or change the mortgage offer.	
19 *Seller*	**Contract** Deal with any amendments to the contract after taking instructions if necessary. Reply to the Completion Information and Undertakings form (TA13) (see paragraph (l) of general obligations for further guidance on the use of forms). **Beware how you submit your bank details. It is good practice not to submit bank details by email.**	**Contract** Approve and return to the seller's conveyancer the draft contract (including the buyer's full name and address) and any necessary amendments. Submit a draft transfer deed and Completion Information and Undertakings form (TA13) (see paragraph (l) of general obligations for further guidance on the use of forms).	*Buyer*

STAGE C: PRIOR TO EXCHANGE OF CONTRACTS

	Contact	Acting for the seller	Acting for the buyer	Contact
20	*Seller*	**Signing of contracts/ transfer**	**Signing of contracts/ transfer**	*Buyer*
		Report to the seller with the contract for signature (including occupier if relevant) and arrange for the contract to be signed.	Report to the buyer on the purchase documentation and send the contract for signature. Arrange for the contract to be signed and for the buyer to transfer the deposit, preferably electronically.	
		Propose and agree deposit requirements, taking account of any deposit already paid.	Take instructions on the deposit. Agree arrangements for the amount and holding of the deposit where it is to be sent by or held by a third party.	
		Agree the completion date. Ensure the seller is aware of the obligation to give vacant possession by the latest time in the contract (especially if the property is occupied or tenanted).	Take account of any deposit paid under any reservation or pre-contract agreement.	
		Ask the buyer's conveyancer to check the date with others in the buyer's chain to see if it is agreed.	Agree the completion date and time. Ensure that the buyer is aware of the binding nature of the commitment.	
			Check the proposed date with the buyer and the buyer's chain to see if it is agreed. Tell the seller's conveyancer.	
			Consider the terms on which the deposit is to be held and by whom. Advise the buyer of potential consequences of default if, for example, the deposit is held to order, is less than 10%, or is not held as stakeholder.	

	Contact	Acting for the seller	Acting for the buyer	Contact
21	*Seller*	**Apportionments**	**Apportionments**	*Buyer*
	Managing agent/ *Freeholder*	Advise the seller about any apportionments that may be requested in addition to completion monies. Obtain the relevant receipts.	Remind the buyer about the availability of balance of completion monies. Advise as to the date cleared monies are required for completion and any relevant apportionments.	
			Check that the buyer has investigated the availability and cost of buildings insurance, so it is ready to be put in place on exchange or as required by the contract.	

STAGE D: EXCHANGE OF CONTRACTS

	Contact	Acting for the seller	Acting for the buyer	Contact
22	*Seller*	**Exchange of contracts**	**Exchange of contracts**	*Buyer*
		Use the appropriate Law Society formula for exchange of contracts.	Use the appropriate Law Society formula for exchange of contracts.	
		Notify seller and seller's agent that exchange has taken place immediately after exchange of contracts.	Notify buyer that exchange has taken place immediately after exchange of contracts.	
23		**Completion information and undertakings**	**Completion information and undertakings**	
		Complete TA13 if not already supplied (see paragraph (l) of general obligations for further guidance on the use of forms).	Check replies to TA13 (see paragraph (l) of general obligations for further guidance on the use of forms).	

Contact	Acting for the seller	Acting for the buyer	Contact
24	**Transfer**	**Transfer**	
	Provide the buyer's conveyancer with a copy of the transfer executed by the seller, to be delivered on completion.	Check execution of the copy transfer supplied. Consider whether the transfer requires execution by the buyer and whether a duplicate should be signed by the buyer in advance of completion.	
25		**Pre-completion searches**	
		Submit pre-completion searches.	
26 *Lender*	**Redemption figures**		
	Obtain up-to-date redemption figures.		
27		**Certificate of title**	*Lender*
		Send the certificate of title and/or requisition for funds to the lender (or the lender's conveyancer, if separately represented) promptly.	

STAGE E: COMPLETION

Contact	Acting for the seller	Acting for the buyer	Contact
28 *Seller*	**Completion procedure**	**Completion procedure**	*Buyer*
Agent	To manage expectations, explain to clients that there are two parts to completion:	To manage expectations, explain to clients that there are two parts to completion:	*Lender*
	(a) legal completion: involving the transfer of funds and receipt by the seller's conveyancer; and	(a) legal completion: involving the transfer of funds and receipt by the seller's conveyancer; and	

Contact	Acting for the seller	Acting for the buyer	Contact
	(b) practical completion: checking the property has vacant possession and is empty, and arrangements for collection of keys by the buyer.	(b) practical completion: checking the property has vacant possession and is empty, and arrangements for collection of keys by the buyer.	
	Explain that these rarely happen simultaneously and that you will let them, or the estate agent, know when the keys can be handed over. This should be no later than the time stated in the contract.	Explain that these rarely happen simultaneously and that you will let them know when completion monies are transferred, and they will need to liaise with the estate agent or the seller as regards the release of keys.	
	On the day before completion, or as early as reasonably possible on the day of completion, consider whether there is likely to be any delay. If there is, notify the buyer's conveyancer and thereafter agree how communication will be handled during the day until completion has taken place.	On the day before completion, or as early as reasonably possible on the day of completion, consider whether there is likely to be any delay. If there is, notify the seller's conveyancer and thereafter agree how communication will be handled during the day until completion has taken place.	
29	**Completion by post**	**Completion by post**	
	Comply with the Law Society Code for Completion by Post without variation unless there has been prior agreement to vary. General exclusions of liability for obligations within the code will be viewed as a breach of this Protocol in addition to any other consequences.	Comply with the Law Society Code for Completion by Post without variation unless there has been prior agreement to vary. General exclusions of liability for obligations within the code will be viewed as a breach of this Protocol in addition to any other consequences.	

	Contact	Acting for the seller	Acting for the buyer	Contact
30	*Seller* *Agent*	**Completion monies and method of completion** On receipt of completion monies, complete the transaction in accordance with the Law Society Code for Completion by Post. This must take place by the latest time stated in the contract. Inform the buyer's conveyancer immediately if this is not possible. Report completion to the seller and proceed with any related purchase. On completion notify the estate agent and/or any other key holder and authorise release of the keys. Date the transfer deed. Send the transfer and any title deeds to the buyer's conveyancer. Send sufficient monies to any lender in accordance with any undertakings.	**Completion monies and method of completion** Inform the seller's conveyancer of the commitment of funds to the banking system or instructions given to the bank in accordance with the code. Report completion of the purchase and the mortgage to the buyer. Date and complete the mortgage deed.	*Buyer* *Agent*
31	*Agent* *Seller*	**Payment of estate agent fees** Pay the estate agent's or property seller's commission, if so authorised.		

	Contact	Acting for the seller	Acting for the buyer	Contact
32	*Seller*	**Outstanding balance of sale proceeds** Account to the seller for any balance of the sale proceeds. Check funds are only being sent to the account details supplied at the beginning of the transaction.		

STAGE F: POST-COMPLETION

	Contact	Acting for the seller	Acting for the buyer	Contact
33	*Lender*	**Discharge of undertaking** Provide the buyer with sealed Form DS1 (and ID forms where applicable) as soon as it is received and obtain related discharge of undertaking or confirmation as to lodging of END1 by lender if so notified.	**Application to HM Land Registry** Lodge the appropriate SDLT or LTT form with HMRC or the Welsh Revenue Authority as applicable and pay any SDLT/LTT due. Upon receipt of the transfer, lodge your application for registration at HM Land Registry within the priority period of the official search. To reduce the incidence of requisitions being raised by HM Land Registry, check the contents of the application very carefully: ensure that all necessary documents are dated, properly executed and attached and that any name discrepancies between deeds and the register are resolved or explained. Lodge Form DS1 when received (if applicable).	*Lender* *HMRC or Welsh Revenue Authority* *HM Land Registry*

Contact	Acting for the seller	Acting for the buyer	Contact
34		**Registration**	*Lender*
		When registration (whether subject to 'early completion' or not) has been effected:	*Buyer*
		(1) Check the title information document carefully, including the address for service.	
		(2) Supply a copy of the title information document to the buyer and remind the buyer to keep the address for service up to date. Advise the client of the existence of the HM Land Registry Property Alert service.	
		(3) Ask the buyer to check the contents of the title information document.	
		(4) Advise the buyer (and any lender) of completion of registration.	
		(5) Deal with any other documents, e.g. mortgage loan agreements, planning permissions, indemnity policies, etc. in accordance with the lender's instructions.	

	Contact	Acting for the seller	Acting for the buyer	Contact
35	*Seller*	**File closure**	**File closure**	*Buyer*
		Close file after checking and confirm custody of sale contract and sale documents.	Check accounts balance, that addresses are updated, and ledger archived.	
		Return to the client any original documents save for documents which it has been agreed should be retained.	Return to the client any original documents save for documents which it has been agreed should be retained.	

* Please provide any feedback in relation to the Protocol to **property@lawsociety.org.uk**

Index

257